The Supreme Court on Trial

The Supreme Court on Trial

Charles S. Hyneman

Routledge
Taylor & Francis Group
LONDON AND NEW YORK

First published 2009 by Transaction Publishers

2 Park Square, Milton Park, Abingdon, Oxfordshire OX14 4RN
711 Third Avenue, New York, NY 10017

Routledge is an imprint of the Taylor & Francis Group, an informa business

First issued in hardback 2017

Library of Congress Catalog Number: 2007022241

Library of Congress Cataloging-in-Publication Data

Hyneman, Charles S., 1900-1985
The Supreme Court on Trial / Charles S. Hyneman.
p. cm.
Originally published: New York : Atherton Press, 1963.
Includes bibliographical references and index.
ISBN 978-0-202-30992-7 (alk. paper)
1. United States. Supreme Court. 2. Judicial review—United States.
I. Title.

KF8748.H95 2007
347.73'26—dc22 2007022241

ISBN 13: 978-0-202-30992-7 (pbk)
ISBN 13: 978-1-138-53899-3 (hbk)

In memory of
Frank G. Bates
He stood at the gate

PREFACE

Our time is a time of national self-criticism. The American people are engaged in a severe examination of their basic commitments, their way of life, the direction they appear to be going. Our contemporary literature—over the air, in newspaper editorials and columns, in books and articles—is heavy with protest, admonition, and exhortation. The American citizen as common man is exalted by writing which cites his claims to dignity and pleads for a securing of his civil rights. He is—perhaps in equal measure—deposed from a seat of honor by writing which deplores his cultural provincialism, his fear of intellectual endeavor, his espousal of conformity.

The Supreme Court is a contributor to this national self-survey. But it is also the object of critical examination, for the self-study which is under way includes a re-evaluation of our political institutions. We have created Hoover commissions to study the national administrative system; the Electoral College has been the subject of persistent scrutiny since World War II. At the moment there is a surging demand for reconstitution of our state lawmaking bodies. Perhaps the two emphases in this comprehensive reassessment are most obviously combined in the deep concern we now display for the character and quality of our public school curriculum and for the administrative structure which maintains and manages our schools.

I hope that this book will contribute to the national self-survey. My purpose is to examine critically the place of the Supreme Court in our political system. I wish to improve the public understanding of what the Supreme Court does, how its acts have been received, and how its way of influencing public policy is related to other methods of making public policy.

Several years ago, I wrote a book—*Bureaucracy in a Democracy* (New York: Harper & Bros., 1950)—which attempted to place our great administrative organizations in relation to the elected officials of the national government. In that book I was very liberal about saying what I liked and did not like. I decided to keep my personal preferences out of the present book to the extent that one can. I have tried to confine myself to statements of what exists and what has occurred and to that kind of search for relationships which is called analysis. Necessarily, my ideas about what constitutes the good life and my convictions about how man brings himself under order have greatly affected what I believe to be the realities of the social situations with which I deal, what I believe to be feasible and inevitable relationships, and what I believe possible in reconstituting institutions. I think it not worth the reader's attention for me to try to tell him what my preferences, my predilections, my social bent may be. I have learned that, when I stand up to be counted, my position is sometimes embarrassingly different from what my easy talk had led me and my friends to suppose it would be.

I do not know how many people contributed to my collection of beliefs or helped me discipline them for a book. The list of main contributors might begin with the man to whom the book is dedicated. He was, for me, a truly great teacher; he widened and sharpened my vision without impeaching the basic values that I carried from the farm. Professor Henry Wolf Biklé, of the University of Pennsylvania Law School, gave me an insightful and discriminating course in American constitutional law. (I do not have a law degree, and I do not have the special competence of a lawyer.) I talked with many people about the book as I wrote it, but to these more than others: Byrum E. Carter, Warner O. Chapman, and Albert L. Kohlmeier, of the faculty of Indiana University; my graduate students, George W. Carey, Kenneth F. Janda, and Thomas M. Watts (now teaching, respectively, at Georgetown University, Northwestern University, and Indiana University); and George T. Schilling, lawyer of LaFayette, Indiana, and his father, George A. Schilling, also trained in law, of Rowayton, Connecticut. All but two of these read parts of my manuscript.

During two weeks at the State University of Iowa, where I delivered eight lectures on the relation of judicial review to democratic government, I received warm encouragement and sharp criticism from all of the political science faculty. I am especially grateful to Professors Vernon Van Dyke and James N. Murray and to three graduate students—Joel B. Grossman, Jack Walker, and Richard Wells—one or another of whom assaulted every presumption and conviction I brought with me to the Iowa campus.

Finally, acknowledgement is due five men who read every page of the manuscript at one stage or another—Charles E. Gilbert, of Swarthmore College; Lawrence J. R. Herson, of Ohio State University; John Honnold, of the University of Pennsylvania law faculty; Karl O'Lessker, of Wabash College; and Cornelius P. Cotter, a staff member of the United States Commission on Civil Rights and an advisory editor for Atherton Press. It is little short of humiliating to contemplate how much imprecision they pointed out, how much underdeveloped territory they found, how much irrelevance they commanded me to excise. I excised, I restated, and I added to such an extent that any reader who likes the book may render thanks to each of them. But I am a stubborn man, and did not comply with many of their suggestions. There is enough variance from their advice that any of the five who does not like the final product can rightly say that he is in no way responsible for its essential character.

Charles S. Hyneman

February 1963

CONTENTS

I • A COURT ON TRIAL

This book opens with a brief account of the Segregation decisions of 1954 and 1955—what the Supreme Court said and did and the relation of its words and acts to a changing interpretation of the equal-protection clause of the Constitution. This is followed, in Chapter II, by a résumé of the attack on the Supreme Court which came in the wake of the Segregation cases. Chapters III and IV reach back into history to show that contemporary defiance of our highest tribunal has had many precedents. And Chapter V offers some explanation of why the nation has not lived comfortably under dramatic demonstrations of judicial power.

CHAPTER ONE

An End to Segregation

1. "SEPARATE BUT EQUAL" HAS NO PLACE
2. A BIT OF LEGAL HISTORY
3. GROWTH OF A PRINCIPLE

On May 17, 1954, the United States Supreme Court announced that racial segregation in public schools is forbidden by the Constitution. A year later, the same court issued orders telling federal and state judges how they should proceed in bringing segregation to an end. These decisions are known as "the Segregation cases."

The Segregation cases combined five separate law suits, four of them relating to the schools of four states and one relating to the District of Columbia. The decisions which disposed of the first four suits were reported as *Brown* v. *Board of Education of Topeka* (347 U.S. 484). The decision applying to the District of Columbia appears in the reports as *Bolling* v. *Sharpe* (347 U.S. 497).

1. "SEPARATE BUT EQUAL" HAS NO PLACE

Both the Brown and Bolling cases ruled that Negroes and whites may no longer be required to attend separate schools. In the Brown case, the Court asserted that enforced separation denies to Negroes the equal protection of the laws which the Fourteenth Amendment requires each state to extend to all persons within its jurisdiction. The Constitution does not specify that Congress, in making laws for the nation or for its territories, shall provide equal protection of the laws, but it does say, in the Fifth Amendment, that the national government shall not deprive any person of life, liberty, or property without due process of law. The Court ruled in the Bolling case that racial segregation in the public schools of the District of Columbia deprives Negro children of liberty without due process of law and is therefore forbidden by the Constitution.

Both decisions were reached unanimously. Both opinions were written by Chief Justice Earl B. Warren. The opinions were brief, to the point, and in language readily comprehensible to the layman.

> We come then [said the Chief Justice in the Brown case], to the question presented: Does segregation of children in public schools solely on the basis of race, even though the physical facilities and other "tangible" factors may be equal, deprive the children of the minority group of equal educational opportunities? We believe that it does. . . . To separate them [grade and high school children] from others of similar age and qualifications solely because of their race generates a feeling of inferiority as to their status in their community that may affect their hearts and minds in a way unlikely ever to be undone. . . . We conclude that in the field of public education the doctrine of "separate but equal" has no place. Separate educational facilities are inherently unequal. Therefore, we hold that the plaintiffs and others similarly situated for whom the actions have been brought are, by reason of the segregation complained of, deprived of the equal protection of the laws guaranteed by the Fourteenth Amendment. (Pp. 493, 495.)

The Chief Justice also quoted with approval part of the opinion written for one of the cases in a lower court.

> Segregation of white and colored children in public schools has a detrimental effect upon the colored children. The impact is greater when it has the sanction of the law; for the policy of separating the races is usually interpreted as denoting the inferiority of the Negro group. A sense of inferiority affects the motivation of a child to learn. Segregation with the sanction of law, therefore, has a tendency to retard the educational and mental development of Negro children and to deprive them of some of the benefits they would receive in a racially integrated school system. (P. 494.)

The Bolling case throws no further light on the reasons for bringing segregation in the education of children to an end. The special significance of that case lies in the fact that the Court construed the due-process requirement to restrict national policy exactly as the equal-protection clause restricts the policy of state and local governments. In his opinion on the Bolling case, Warren said:

> Although the Court has not assumed to define "liberty" with any great precision, that term is not confined to mere freedom from

> bodily restraint. Liberty under law extends to the full range of conduct which the individual is free to pursue, and it cannot be restricted except for a proper governmental objective. Segregation in public education is not reasonably related to any proper governmental objective, and thus it imposes on Negro children of the District of Columbia a burden that constitutes an arbitrary deprivation of their liberty in violation of the Due Process Clause. (Pp. 499–500.)
>
> In view of our decision that the Constitution prohibits the states from maintaining racially segregated public schools, it would be unthinkable that the same Constitution would impose a lesser duty on the Federal Government. We hold that racial segregation in the public schools of the District of Columbia is a denial of the due process of law guaranteed by the Fifth Amendment of the Constitution. (P. 500.)

The decisions in the Brown and Bolling cases were announced and the two opinions of the Chief Justice read on May 17, 1954. On that day, the Court announced that it would delay the issuance of decrees until attorneys had presented further argument as to how the new interpretation should be made effective. A year later (on May 31, 1955), having heard argument, the Supreme Court remanded the five cases to the lower courts which originally heard them and instructed these courts "to take such proceedings and enter such orders and decrees consistent with this opinion as are necessary and proper to admit to public schools on a racially nondiscriminatory basis with all deliberate speed the parties to these cases" (*Brown* v. *Board of Education of Topeka,* 349 U.S. 294).

2. A BIT OF LEGAL HISTORY

If "equal protection of the laws" means identical application of the law to all persons or requires treatment which is absolutely the same in every respect, it is self-evident that legal separation of the races in schools is not equal protection of the laws. In that case, it would be irrelevant whether the separate schools were equal or unequal in tangible respects; it would be superfluous for a judge to point out that segregation generates a feeling of inferiority or has any other detrimental effect. If equal protection means treatment which is absolutely the same for all in every respect, would it not be unlawful to give the blind man state aid that is denied to the man with good eyesight? Unlawful to give the bright boy a scholarship at the state university but make the plodder pay tuition? Unlawful even to admit the six-year-old child to public school but make his younger brothers and sisters wait until they reach the prescribed age?

The fact is, of course, that U. S. judges have never contended that equal protection of the laws means identical application of the law to all persons. It is also a fact that they have not supplied us with language which makes clear just what equal protection does require. It has been said that "equal protection of the laws" is a catch phrase or slogan which only suggests a standard of conduct for government to live up to. This statement underestimates the guiding and restraining quality of the concept. But it must also be admitted that the most frequently quoted reformulations of the requirement leave wide range for speculation as to how the general rule is to be applied in specific situations. Consider these, changed slightly in phrasing because they are lifted out of the context of the judicial opinion in which they were uttered.

> Equal protection of the laws merely requires that all persons subjected to a law shall be treated alike, under like circumstances and conditions, both in the privileges conferred and in the liabilities imposed. (*Hayes* v. *Missouri,* 120 U.S. 68, 71–72.)
>
> Reasonable classification is permitted, but such classification must be based on some real and substantial distinction, bearing a reasonable and just relation to the things in respect to which such classification is imposed. (*Southern Ry. Co.* v. *Greene,* 216 U.S. 400, 417.)

The lawmakers of a state may classify the citizens of a state as helpless or not helpless, make clear what persons (for example, those without eyes or arms or legs) are to be viewed as helpless, and provide that the helpless shall receive assistance from the state which no one else may receive. The state may even give aid to blind men but deny it to men so badly crippled that they can do no work. Such classifications, the judges hold, bear a reasonable and just relation to a public policy of aiding the needy. They differentiate people according to the circumstances of their existence and fix the same privileges and liabilities for all persons who fall into the same group.

The Negro can be differentiated from the white, a fact amply proven by long-standing social practices throughout the United States. But are there circumstances which vary with color of sufficient significance to justify variance in the privileges conferred and the liabilities imposed on the two racial groups? Does a classification on the basis of color bear a reasonable and just relation to any legitimate objective of governmental action?

For a period of well over a hundred years and running at

least until the Segregation cases which we have just examined, it was a rule of U. S. law that differential treatment of white men and those of other races was proper for a wide range of purposes. The landmark decision in which the Supreme Court acknowledged the legitimacy of racial segregation was *Plessy* v. *Ferguson,* decided in 1896 (163 U.S. 537). The issue before the Court was the validity of a Louisiana statute which required railway companies carrying passengers within the state to provide "equal but separate accommodations for the white and colored races" and forbade persons of either race to occupy any seats other than those assigned to that race. Seven of the eight judges who participated in the decision thought this classification of persons and differentiation of the treatment accorded to them reasonable and not a denial of equal protection of the laws. One justice dissented.

The majority opinion in *Plessy* v. *Ferguson* rested the validity of segregation on two main grounds: (1) there was abundant precedent for separation of the races in long-standing usage, and (2) separation of the races was a response to social conditions which law cannot eradicate and to which law must yield. On the first point, the opinion stated:

> So far, then, as a conflict with the Fourteenth Amendment is concerned, the case reduces itself to the question whether the statute of Louisiana is a reasonable regulation, and with respect to this there must necessarily be a large discretion on the part of the legislature. In determining the question of reasonableness it is at liberty to act with reference to the established usages, customs, and traditions of the people, and with a view to the promotion of their comfort, and the preservation of the public peace and good order. Gauged by this standard, we cannot say that a law which authorizes or even requires the separation of the two races in public conveyances is unreasonable or more obnoxious to the Fourteenth Amendment than the acts of Congress requiring separate schools for colored children in the District of Columbia, the constitutionality of which does not seem to have been questioned, or the corresponding acts of state legislatures. (Pp. 550–551.)

On the second point on which the Plessy decision was based, the reasoning was as follows:

> The object of the amendment was undoubtedly to enforce the absolute equality of the two races before the law, but in the nature of things it could not have been intended to abolish distinctions based upon color, or to enforce social, as distinguished from political, equality, or a commingling of the two races upon terms unsatisfactory to either. . . . We consider the underlying fallacy of the

> plaintiff's argument to consist in the assumption that the enforced separation of the two races stamps the colored race with a badge of inferiority. . . . The argument also assumes that social prejudices may be overcome by legislation, and that equal rights cannot be secured to the negro except by an enforced commingling of the two races. We cannot accept this proposition. If the two races are to meet upon terms of social equality, it must be the result of natural affinities, a mutual appreciation of each other's merits and a voluntary consent of individuals. . . . Legislation is powerless to eradicate racial instincts or to abolish distinctions based upon physical differences, and the attempt to do so can only result in accentuating the difficulties of the present situation. If the civil and political rights of both races be equal, one cannot be inferior to the other civilly or politically. If one race be inferior to the other socially, the Constitution of the United States cannot put them upon the same plane. (Pp. 544, 551–552.)

The ruling in *Plessy* v. *Ferguson* was subsequently treated as good law, and its effect was extended far beyond the issue which was immediately before the Court in that case, racial segregation in railway cars. During the years from 1896 to 1954, many forms of racial segregation required by state law and local ordinance in the Southern states, in states outside the South, and in the District of Columbia were challenged in state and lower federal courts and were given judicial approval on the authority of *Plessy* v. *Ferguson*. In 1927, when the United States Supreme Court for the first time stated expressly that separate-but-equal educational facilities do not conflict with the requirement of equal protection of the laws, Chief Justice William Howard Taft was able to cite decisions of ten state supreme courts and three of lower federal courts to the same effect (*Gong Lum* v. *Rice,* 275 U.S. 78).

It will be clear from what has been said that, up to the 1954 decision of *Brown* v. *Board of Education,* the constitutional law of the country permitted discriminatory treatment on the basis of race or color as long as a decent showing was made that the treatment accorded one race was equal to that accorded the other. Separate schools were lawful as long as the education provided in the colored school was equal to that provided in the school for whites. Separate drinking fountains in the city hall were lawful if they were hooked to the same water supply, were placed in equally convenient locations, were kept equally clean. Assignment to separate parts of a bus was lawful if front and back seats were upholstered alike and front and back end of the bus traveled the same streets and stopped at the same corners.

This is how it was until 1954, when the Supreme Court

terminated the separate-but-equal doctrine for public education and in so doing shook any legal rationale which might still be offered for separation of the races in other matters. The 1954 decision cannot have come wholly as a surprise to observant lawyers, for the successful assault had been presaged by two persistent attacks on the separate-but-equal doctrine.

First, there had been, during the six decades since *Plessy* v. *Ferguson,* a growing public conviction and an increasingly angry complaint that separate facilities, at least in most places in the Deep South, were not in fact anywhere near equal for the two races and that what was legally justified as separate-but-equal treatment was in intent and practical effect rank anti-Negro discrimination. The justices of the Supreme Court knew about this spreading conviction and stiffening antagonism simply because they read the newspapers, talked to people, and were alive. But they had it formally called to their attention in four cases that came to the highest tribunal for settlement in 1938, 1948, and 1950. In each of these cases, Negroes sought admission to study in the graduate or professional schools of a state university. In each case, admission had been denied on the ground that the state had provided separate-but-equal opportunities for Negroes in a special university for Negroes only or by meeting his costs of education in nonsegregated universities outside the state. In each case, the protesting Negro argued that the opportunities afforded him were in fact not equal to the opportunities enjoyed by whites in their attendance at the state university. In each case, the Supreme Court inquired into the comparative advantages and disadvantages involved in the provisions for higher education, found that the provisions were in fact not nearly equal, ruled that the state had denied Negroes the equal protection of the laws, and ordered admission of the complaining Negroes to the university which the state made available to its white citizens.[1]

In none of these four cases did the Supreme Court express itself on the question whether separate schools could ever be made equal. In refusing to speak to this point, it withstood for the time being a *second* persistent line of attack on the separate-but-equal doctrine. Ever since the Fourteenth Amendment was adopted, it had been argued in and out of court that the amendment was in-

[1] The four cases are *Missouri ex rel. Gaines* v. *Canada* (305 U.S. 337, 1938); *Sipuel* v. *Board of Regents of University of Oklahoma* (332 U.S. 631, 1948); *Sweatt* v. *Painter* (339 U.S. 629, 1950); and *McLaurin* v. *Oklahoma State Regents* (339 U.S. 637, 1950). There were other cases involving discrimination in other areas of living.

tended to outlaw all discrimination based solely on race, to outlaw differential treatment even though it be equal treatment. Precedent in pre-Civil War custom and legislation is irrelevant, it was argued; the objective in adopting the Fourteenth Amendment was to terminate custom, to forbid absolutely and forever any and all action by state governments which make race, color, or previous condition of servitude a ground for difference in status or treatment.

This inclusive bar to racial discrimination was urged on the Supreme Court in the four cases involving admission of Negroes to graduate and professional schools, but the Court chose to rest its decisions on the narrower ground that opportunities for education were in fact not equal for the two races. In the Segregation cases, the Court went only about half the distance between the narrowest basis on which it could have decided the issue and the broadest basis which opponents of racial discrimination would have preferred the Court adopt. If the Court had preferred a narrow basis, it could have announced a conclusion only as to whether the schools provided for Negroes in the five jurisdictions involved in the Segregation cases were in fact approximately as good as those provided for whites in the same five jurisdictions. The broadest basis which the Court could reasonably have adopted would have resulted in comprehensive assertions as to whether the Fourteenth Amendment allows any legal recognition of racial difference whatever and, if it does, in what areas of governmental policy recognition of racial differences is proper.

3. GROWTH OF A PRINCIPLE

It is clear that Warren's opinions in the Segregation cases were not suitable to either of the two extremes in judicial position. But we cannot be sure just where the Supreme Court judges wished to draw the line between lawful and unlawful differentiation in governmental treatment of the races, and subsequent events have enlarged, rather than narrowed, the areas of uncertainty. We do not know yet whether the new constitutional protections apply only to Negroes or equally to other races, including the American Indian. We do not know whether the new constitutional regime relates only to separation of races in places where they would otherwise mix or whether other kinds of discriminatory policy, heretofore tolerated, are now forbidden. And we do not know whether the new protection against discrimination on racial grounds is available to religious groups and other nonracial minorities who may be the victims of discriminatory policies.

In his two opinions justifying the Segregation decisions, Warren adopted language which focused attention exclusively on public education. There was no assertion, no dropping of hints, that separation of the races in other governmentally owned or operated facilities should also be viewed as inherently unequal and *ipso facto* forbidden by the Constitution. But, exactly one week after the opinions of 1954 were read, the Supreme Court projected the Brown case into a noneducation field of public policy. In Louisville, Negroes had asked a federal district court for an order throwing open to Negroes the recreational facilities of public parks which the city had reserved for whites. The district court found that in some respects the public park facilities of Louisville were not equal for the two races, but held that, insofar as facilities were equal, segregation in the use of the parks was not unlawful. On appeal, the federal circuit court upheld the district court's judgment and asserted that it was not a denial of equal protection to deny Negroes admission to the only theater in a park inasmuch as the theater was leased to a privately owned enterprise and the city did not participate either directly or indirectly in the theater's operation.

The Supreme Court accepted the Louisville case for review and, on the Monday following announcement of the Brown and Bolling decisions, vacated the circuit court's judgment and remanded the case "for consideration in the light of the *Segregation Cases* . . . and conditions that now prevail" (*Muir* v. *Louisville Park Theatrical Association,* 347 U.S. 971). The circuit judges, taking the Segregation cases into account, reversed their former position and ruled separation of the races in the public parks of Louisville unlawful. Asked to review this new decision, the Supreme Court refused to grant a hearing. The new constitutional regime was thus extended from public schools to public parks and playgrounds without any explanation by the Supreme Court as to why this was a proper or a necessary application of the Constitution's language.

Subsequent to this action by inaction at the top of the judicial structure, there has been a great noise of falling statutes, city ordinances, and other governmental regulations which the white man designed to keep the Negro from rubbing his shoulders in a wide range of facilities and social services. The thunder reverberates most loudly in the South, of course, but more than one discriminatory policy has crashed in the North as well. Judges in state and lower federal courts have acted on the presumption that *Plessy* v. *Ferguson* and its doctrine of separate-but-equal facilities is now inapplicable in any area of life where forced separation is applied, and this view has thus far been approved above. On such crucial issues as segregation in transportation the Supreme Court has affirmed lower court decisions terminating segregation; on other issues, presumably thought less crucial, the Supreme Court has put a blessing on the decision below by refusing to bring it to review above. In no instance, no matter how apparent the need for explanation, has the Supreme Court yet provided the nation with an opinion which relates the equal-protection and due-process clauses to any of these facilities and services as the Segregation opinions related them to public education.

CHAPTER TWO

A Court on Trial

The Supreme Court of the United States is commonly said to be the nation's highest tribunal. It is the court of last resort on many issues of great social importance. But the Supreme Court cannot decide finally all questions on which it speaks with great show of authority. One question it cannot finally determine is: What are the limits to the Supreme Court's own power?

The Constitution ordained a Supreme Court, but left its establishment to the lawmaking body. The Court came into existence through a statute voted by a majority of each house of Congress and approved by the president in 1789. This statute and later enactments by Congress and the president specify how many judges the Court shall comprise, fix the salaries of the judges, and in large measure determine what kinds of questions may be presented to the Court for settlement. Individual judges become members of the Court on appointment by the president with approval by a majority of the Senate. The two houses of Congress are empowered to remove judges by impeachment.

These are means by which the Court is in some measure subject to the will of the other two branches of the government. One must be careful, however, not to read too much into these provisions for control. Statutes altering the appellate jurisdiction have been enacted, but these are few in number. Presidents and senators are careful as to whom they put on the Court, but they do not pledge the appointee to enthrone particular views or policies. On one occasion, a judgeship was added to the Court with the apparent intention of influencing its orders, but many more efforts to pack or unpack the Court have failed. Salaries are never reduced to punish judges for their decisions; the Constitution forbids this. And only once has a serious effort been made to remove a justice of the Supreme Court by impeachment, that time without success.

There is a broader sense in which the power of the Supreme Court is fixed by others. Supreme Court justices recognize that they are part of a government set up by the American people. They recognize that this system of government is one of self-government—that we have a government of the people, by the people, and for the people. Recognition of this fact implies some degree of sensitivity to public criticism, some concern to exercise judicial power in accordance with a national vision as to how judicial power ought to be exercised. Certainly, at many times, and possibly at all times, some people think the judges are intolerably hard of hearing. But even a brief glance at experience reveals that the Court can be shaken by a storm of public disapproval.

A major issue in a case often involves the jurisdiction of the tribunal. Viewed strictly as a legal question, the Supreme Court is final as to its jurisdiction and the extent of its power under the laws of the time. There is, in law, no court which can overrule the Supreme Court. But, when actions of the Court excite widespread disapproval, a higher tribunal, figuratively speaking, comes into existence. The Supreme Court itself goes on trial. The evidence is heard, and the case is argued on radio and in the newspapers, in law reviews and meetings of the bar, in legislative chambers and the many other forums of political controversy. One knows how the case was decided when he observes the subsequent behavior of the Supreme Court.

The Supreme Court is clearly on trial now.

Denunciation of the Supreme Court hit the newspapers promptly after the first decisions in the Segregation cases were announced. Not every complaint of a malcontent is entitled to an answer, of course. But, within a year after the federal district judges were instructed to proceed in all deliberate speed with desegregation of the schools, men who speak for great sectors of the population had charged the Supreme Court with abuse of power. We shall first note the adverse reaction of certain people in the South to the demand for a new policy in education of Negroes. This protest and resistance have had many evidences to date, three of which deserve attention here: (1) the "Declaration of Constitutional Principles" by Southern congressmen, (2) resolutions of interposition by Southern state legislatures, and (3) refusal by state and local officials in the South to proceed with integration. Displeasure growing out of the Segregation cases was reinforced by unhappiness over other decisions of the Court, especially several relating to the authority of national and state lawmakers to deal with Communists. This broader discontent led to two more assaults on the Supreme Court worthy of attention here: (4) a resolution of state supreme court justices and (5) effort in Congress to alter the statutes fixing the jurisdiction of the Supreme Court.

1. DEFIANCE IN THE SOUTH

The Declaration of Constitutional Principles, popularly called "the Southern Manifesto," was entered in *The Congressional Record* on March 12, 1956.[1] It was not a resolution submitted to Congress for approval. It was a statement of personal conviction signed by nineteen senators and seventy-seven members of the House of Representatives. The congressmen charged the Supreme Court with having substituted "naked power" for power regulated by law.

> We regard the decision of the Supreme Court in the school cases as a clear abuse of judicial power. It climaxes a trend in the Federal Judiciary undertaking to legislate, in derogation of the authority of Congress, and to encroach upon the reserved rights of the States and the people. . . .
>
> Though there has been no constitutional amendment or act of Congress changing this established legal principle [the separate-but-equal rule of *Plessy* v. *Ferguson*] almost a century old, the Supreme Court of the United States, with no legal basis for such action, undertook to exercise their naked judicial power and substituted their personal political and social ideas for the established law of the land. . . .
>
> We decry the Supreme Court's encroachments on rights reserved to the States and to the people, contrary to established law, and to the Constitution.

This indictment cannot be dismissed as the petulant complaint of petty men. In the group are men of considerable renown in the study and practice of law. It is unlikely that they spoke with tongue in cheek, wishing only to please fanatics at home, for the

[1] Vol. 102, pp. 4460 and 4515–4516.

signers included men credited with great courage by their Northern colleagues in Congress, men who had sponsored and fought for legislation generally viewed as basic to present public policy, men who (except for questions of race relations) are considered stalwart defenders of liberal causes. Surely the following men, to cite well-known senators only, rise above suspicions of bigotry or spinelessness in the face of current hysteria: Lister Hill and John Sparkman of Alabama, James W. Fulbright and John McClellan of Arkansas, Walter George and Richard Russell of Georgia. These were among the signers of the declaration.

Before the ninety-six congressmen had made public their declaration, several Southern legislatures had adopted or were preparing resolutions of interposition.[2] The Virginia Senate and House of Delegates spoke first, in a resolution dated February 1, 1956. The federal government, said the resolution, possesses only the powers granted to it in the Constitution of the United States, and these grants were voluntary delegations by the states of powers previously held by the states which entered the Union. Only by amendment of the Constitution could the national government acquire any power not included in the original delegation by the states. In ratifying the Fourteenth Admendment, Virginia and the other ratifying states did not agree that this addition to the Constitution forbade the states to maintain separate schools for different races. With no exception, both federal and state courts approved this understanding, and for eighty years after the Fourteenth Amendment was adopted certain of the states maintained separate schools.

The 1954 decision in which the Supreme Court announced that racially separate public schools are forbidden by the Constitution, the Virginia resolution asserted, "constitutes a deliberate, palpable, and dangerous attempt by the court itself to usurp the amendatory power that lies solely with not fewer than three-fourths of the States." Whenever the federal government attempts such unauthorized exercise of power, the resolution continued, "the States who are parties to the compact have the right, and are in duty bound, to interpose for arresting the progress of the evil, and for preserving the authorities, rights and liberties appertaining to them." Virginia therefore appealed to other states to join in an effort to adopt an amendment to the Constitution which will settle this issue of contested power, and, pending this ultimate settlement of

[2] Citations for the several resolutions are supplied in Bibliographic Note 2.

the issue, Virginia pledges itself (and urges other states to pledge themselves) "to take all appropriate measures honorably, legally and constitutionally available to us, to resist this illegal encroachment upon our sovereign powers, and . . . to check this and further encroachment by the Supreme Court, through judicial legislation, upon the reserved powers of the states."

Eight of the eleven states that once seceded from the Union adopted protests, commonly known as "interpositions." Alabama, Florida, Georgia, Louisiana, Mississippi, South Carolina, and Virginia spoke in resolutions by the legislature. Arkansas spoke in two declarations adopted by state-wide popular vote. The Virginia protest, quoted in part above, is one of the most restrained. The Alabama and Georgia legislatures declared the Segregation decisions of 1954 and 1955 "null, void, and of no effect"; the Mississippi legislature declared those decisions "a usurpation of power reserved to the several states . . . in violation of the Constitutions of the United States and the State of Mississippi, and therefore . . . unconstitutional, invalid and of no lawful effect within the confines of the State of Mississippi." The Arkansas electorate in one vote adopted a petition asserting that the state had never given up its right to maintain separate schools for different races, pledging the state to resist federal encroachments on the powers reserved to the separate states, and suggesting language for an amendment to the United States Constitution which would affirm the right of the states to maintain "racially separate but substantially equal public schools." In a second vote, the Arkansas electorate approved an amendment to the state constitution requiring the state legislature to oppose the Segregation decisions "in every Constitutional manner" and to employ the full power of the state for nullification of these decisions and all other deliberate, palpable, and dangerous invasions of the state's powers by any office or branch of the United States government or any international organization.

The third manifestation of defiance directed against the Segregation decisions is the drastic, stubborn, and persistent resistance to integration of public schools in the South. The general character of these recent events is too familiar to require recital here. Organization of White Citizens' Councils, public picketing of school buildings, intimidation and physical maltreatment of Negro pupils, closing of schools by statute and order of public officials and confirmation of this by popular vote, adoption of statutes and constitutional amendments designed to deploy the whole legal structure of the state in contravention of the Supreme Court orders—

all these devices and maneuvers have been incorporated into the strategy of anti-integration politics. Each of these devices and maneuvers has been formulated, sold to the public, and put into operation with conscious animus toward the United States Supreme Court, with determination to rebuke that high tribunal, and in the hope of forcing it to admit error and acknowledge defeat.

2. REBUKE BY JUDGES AND ATTACK IN CONGRESS

During the rise of protest against and resistance to the Segregation cases, other decisions of the Supreme Court brought it under attack from influential persons who may have thought the Segregation decisions wholly proper. It is not practicable to discuss those other cases here, for they are too many in number and too varied in character. It seems fair to say that the most persistent and most vigorous critics of the Supreme Court see two tendencies in its recent policy, both of which they think highly objectionable: (1) a tendency to restrict unduly the authority of national and state legislative, executive, and administrative bodies; (2) a tendency to restrict unduly the discretion of state judges or, it may be, to restrict unduly the discretion of all state and federal judges except the Supreme Court itself.

The most sensational rebuke to the Supreme Court other than the Southern defiance already noted came in the summer of 1958 at the hands of the Conference of State Chief Justices, an association of the presiding judges in the highest courts of the states and territories.[3] The rebuke was expressed in a series of resolutions adopted by the conference and in a committee report which the conference approved. Forty-three chief state judges joined in the voting; judges of three states (Arkansas, Connecticut, and Indiana) were not in attendance, and those of two states (Nevada and North Dakota) abstained from voting. Seven voted against the report and resolutions. They presided over the highest courts of California, New Jersey, Pennsylvania, Rhode Island, Utah, Vermont, and West Virginia. The chief judges of the remaining thirty-six states voted for the report and resolutions. These thirty-six states contained 66 per cent of the combined population of the forty-eight states then in the Union. It appears that two territorial courts had membership in the conference. Of these, the chief judge of Puerto Rico was not present, and the chief judge of Hawaii voted against the report.

[3] Citation supplied in Bibliographic Note 2.

The six resolutions adopted by the Conference of State Chief Justices make no assault on the Supreme Court; if they condemn, they do so by implication and insinuation. They declare attachment to the federal system which divides authority between a national government and the governments of the states; assert that issues of division of authority between nation and states should be tested solely by provisions of the Constitution and its amendments; and urge the Supreme Court, in deciding issues of division of authority, to exercise self-restraint and act in keeping with what the Constitution says rather than with what a majority of the Supreme Court judges may think desirable.

The resolutions were accompanied by a committee report which the first resolution declared approved. The committee report is in remarkably restrained language, but it makes clear that great impatience stirred in the judges who wrote and approved it.

> We believe that, in the fields with which we are concerned and as to which we feel entitled to speak, the Supreme Court too often has tended to adopt the role of policy maker without proper judicial restraint. We feel this is particularly the case in both of the great fields we have discussed—namely, the extent and extension of the federal power, and the supervision of State action by the Supreme Court by virtue of the Fourteenth Amendment. In the light of the immense power of the Supreme Court and its practical nonreviewability in most instances, no more important obligation rests upon it, in our view, than that of careful moderation in the exercise of its policy-making role. We are not alone in our view that the Court, in many cases arising under the Fourteenth Amendment, has assumed what seem to us primarily legislative powers. See Judge Learned Hand on the Bill of Rights.
>
> We do not believe that either the framers of the original Constitution or the possibly somewhat less gifted draftsmen of the Fourteenth Amendment ever contemplated that the Supreme Court would, or should, have the almost unlimited policy-making powers which it now exercises. . . .
>
> It has long been an American boast that we have a government of laws and not of men. We believe that any study of recent decisions of the Supreme Court will raise at least considerable doubt as to the validity of that boast. . . .
>
> It is our earnest hope, which we respectfully express, that that great Court exercise to the full its power of judicial self-restraint by adhering firmly to its tremendous, strictly judicial powers and by eschewing, so far as possible, the exercise of essentially legislative powers when it is called upon to decide questions involving the validity of State action, whether it deems such action wise or unwise. The value of our system of federalism, and of local self-government in local matters which it embodies, should be kept

firmly in mind, as we believe it was by those who framed our Constitution.

We do not know how deep was the concern or how strong the emotional tension behind this even-tempered language. A few words can go a long way, and mild words can cut deeply when men of high professional status speak of one another. One can start a small war in a medical association by reporting that one distinguished surgeon says another distinguished surgeon is "casual" in postoperative care. We are entitled to believe that only great displeasure and a firm conviction of the rightness of their position would induce thirty-six chief state judges to formally adopt and publicly issue the statements quoted. It is reasonable to suppose that some judges who shared that displeasure and that conviction were among the seven who voted against the issuance of a formal protest. It is reasonable to suppose, also, that the declarations which were formally voted by the thirty-six chief judges represented the views of many other judges who sit as members of the highest state courts.

A thoughtful observer who is sensitive to the dignity of judges and the protocol which regulates their communications might contend that the mild words of the state judges carried more sting for the nine Supreme Court justices than did the charge of "clear abuse of judicial power" and assumption of "naked judicial power" by the ninety-six congressmen who signed the Declaration of Constitutional Principles. At the least, it must be admitted that the document approved by the state judges put a stamp of respectability on language more violent than the judges themselves used and made credible for many people derogatory statements that otherwise would have been dismissed as uninformed or as a self-serving assault on a noble institution.

Since World War II, a number of the Supreme Court justices have used forceful language in support of positions commonly labeled "liberal," and defenders of the Court frequently assert that, regardless of the grounds offered, attack on the Court is a protest of conservatives against liberal doctrine. It is possible that the specific grounds for complaint underlying the action of the chief state judges are compatible with this conclusion. It is a certainty that the effort in Congress to restrict the jurisdiction of the Supreme Court rested almost wholly on aversion to decisions which supporters of the legislation called "liberal."

This legislative proposal was laid before the Senate by Sen.

William E. Jenner (R., Ind.) on July 26, 1957.[4] The bill had a single purpose: to terminate jurisdiction of the United States Supreme Court to hear on appeal or to review in any manner the decision of any lower federal court, state court, or territorial court which involved or drew into question the validity of certain specified acts of national, state, or local government authorities. If, in any of the specified categories of litigation, an issue of validity of governmental action should be raised, no part or aspect of the ruling below could be reviewed by the Supreme Court.

The categories of litigation which the Jenner bill would have removed from consideration by the Supreme Court—summarized and therefore not stated with complete accuracy here—were those relating to: (1) actions and orders of committees and subcommittees of Congress and to proceedings against witnesses charged with contempt of Congress; (2) policies and acts of the executive-administrative branch of the national government designed to eliminate security risks from federal employment; (3) state laws and regulations designed to curb subversive activities; (4) regulations adopted by school boards and educational officials to cope with subversive action by teachers; and (5) state laws, regulations, actions, or proceedings pertaining to admission to the practice of law.

It will be observed that every one of these intended withdrawals of jurisdiction was directly connected with governmental effort to deal with subversive activities, though the first and last were more inclusive. Senator Jenner allowed no doubt that his purpose was to render the Supreme Court powerless to impede the efforts of the rest of the nation to outwit and outlaw Communists. Justifying his bill on the floor of the Senate, he asserted that recent decisions of the Supreme Court . . .

> have gone infinitely [*sic*] in undermining efforts of the people's representatives at both the national and State levels to meet and master the Communist plot against the security and freedom of this Nation. . . .
>
> The Supreme Court has dealt a succession of blows at key points of the legislative structure erected by the Congress for the protection of the internal security of the United States against the world Communist conspiracy.
>
> Time after time, Congress has acted to shore up these legislative bulwarks; and time after time, the Supreme Court has knocked the props out from under the structure which Congress has built.

4 Citations to the bill, hearing, committee report, and debate are supplied in Bibliographic Note 2.

To accomplish the obstructive purposes which he attributed to it, the Supreme Court had, according to Jenner, read out of the Constitution whatever it did not like and read into that document whatever it thought ought to be there. In introducing his bill, Jenner said:

> There was a time when the Supreme Court conceived its function to be the interpretation of the law. For some time now, the Supreme Court has been making law—substituting its judgment for the judgment of the legislative branch. . . .
>
> By a process of attrition and accession, the extreme liberal wing of the Court has become a majority; and we witness today the spectacle of a Court constantly changing the law, and even changing the meaning of the Constitution, in an apparent determination to make the law of the land what the Court thinks it should be.

Jenner found considerable support in the Senate for his views that the Supreme Court had been unduly tender toward Communists and fellow-travelers and had pulled the Constitution out of shape in order to thrust some of its provisions between the Communist and the public officials who sought to thwart or punish him. But it turned out that he stood almost alone in his choice of a remedy. Four of his five categories of litigation were stricken from the bill in committee; as reported by the committee, the bill would have removed from the Supreme Court's review only cases relating to admission to the practice of law. Rather than strip the Supreme Court of appellate power in a wide range of litigation, the committee thought it better to enact positive legislation which, by more precise language or by language less offensive to the Court, would win the Court's approval in later litigation.

In this greatly altered form, Jenner's bill was recommended for passage by a majority of the committee. A minority opposed the bill as poorly drafted, unwise, and possibly unconstitutional. On the floor, the Senate divided almost evenly, the amended bill being defeated by a vote of forty-one to forty. Hearings, debate, correspondence, and editorial comment on the bill in its original and amended forms made two facts abundantly clear. First, the dislike of the Supreme Court's decisions which led to introduction of the bill was shared by a substantial portion of the American people. Second, people trained in law—in practice, in law schools, and in Congress—were opposed to limitation of the Supreme Court's power to review the decisions of lower courts; those who spoke were in agreement by overwhelming majority, and their opposition to this remedy for the supposed abuse of judicial power was deeply rooted and vigorously expressed.

There can be no doubt that this part of the recent campaign against the Supreme Court failed in its main objective. There is no likelihood that legislation will significantly alter the Court's power to review decisions on appeal. But Jenner and those who supported him may reasonably contend that their repulse fell short of total defeat. Legislation has since been adopted to evade some of the consequences of the Court's decisions relating to loyalty and subversion. And these supporters, with the new rebels of the South and all others who believe that the Supreme Court has been too willing to bend the Constitution to suit its policies, may see a fragment of victory in a question which a Senate subcommittee has recently put to persons nominated for judgeships. Since the spring of 1958, it appears, many of the president's appointees to federal judgeships have, before recommendation for confirmation by the Senate, been asked this question:

> Do you, ______________________, in contemplation of the necessity of taking an oath to support and defend the Constitution of the United States, understand that such oath will demand that you support and defend the provisions of Article I, section 1, of the Constitution, that "all legislative powers herein granted shall be vested in a Congress of the United States, which shall consist of a Senate and House of Representatives" and that therefore you will be bound by such oath not to participate knowingly in any decision designed to alter the meaning of the Constitution itself or of any law as passed by the Congress and adopted under the Constitution.[5]

[5] Supplied in a letter from the clerk of the Senate Committee on the Judiciary.

CHAPTER THREE
A Question of Sovereignty

The suggestion that the Supreme Court can be put on trial is offensive to many people. It is said that, if anyone is on trial now, they are those individuals or sectors of the population who do not like what the highest tribunal has decreed, who do not want to live under our Constitution as it is interpreted by the Supreme Court. This is surely the case; no doubt everyone in the United States is on trial. The prisoner is not the only person on trial in the criminal proceeding in the courthouse. The judge and the jury are on trial, too, and the attorneys, and all others who share responsibility for a system of law and adjudication that has justice as its goal. Granting that those who practice racial discrimination in America stand as the prisoners at bar today, we may nonetheless inquire whether the tribunal that condemns their behavior, the Supreme Court, is adequate for the cause and can be trusted to give justice in the case.

1. DUE PROCESS OF POLITICS

If the Supreme Court is on trial, it is a trial by due process of politics rather than due process of law. The events recited in the preceding chapter show that the charges against the Court are imprecise, the testimony undisciplined, the arguments extravagant, the whole proceeding tempestuous. In the view of many thoughtful persons, it is a proceeding unworthy of a democratic nation. Writing to a member of the subcommittee which reported on Senator Jenner's bill to restrict the Supreme Court's appellate jurisdiction, the dean of a leading law school recommended that the measure be rejected in its entirety. Speaking with main reference to that bill as amended by the subcommittee, he said:

> The committee would do much better to devote its attention to means of making the rule of law in this country operate even-handedly without regard to race, creed, or color than to attack the highest court in the land because of disagreement with some of its decisions. It is alien to the genius of American political thought and subversive of the American constitutional system to attack the institution and processes of one or another of the three coordinate branches of the National Government because you disagree with some of its decisions.[1]

If the dean, as his words indicate, seeks immunity from extravagant and ill-mannered criticism for all three branches of the government, it is unlikely that many thoughtful people would agree with him. Most thoughtful people would surely argue that discontent at the failure of Congress to enact a law is good reason for denouncing the power of senators to filibuster, that unhappiness with an act of military or civil administrative authorities (for example, in removing persons of Japanese ancestry from the West Coast during World War II) is good reason for attacking the institutions and processes that brought the displeasing act to fruition.

There is, however, a strong conviction—one shared by many informed and thoughtful observers of politics—that it is wrong to subject a judicial body to the kind of criticism that is wholly proper for the political branches of government. But the conclusion that such attack is "alien to the genius of American political thought and subversive of the American constitutional system" surely implies a special meaning for the words "alien" and "subversive"; otherwise one is obliged to conclude, also, that American political thought has been violated and the constitutional system subverted repeatedly since the Supreme Court came into existence.

There is nothing new in the attack on the Supreme Court which followed its recent unpopular decisions. For every denunciation, for every act of resistance, for every move to reduce the Court's

[1] Dean Jefferson B. Fordham to Sen. Thomas C. Hennings, Jr. (D., Mo.), April 17, 1958, printed in Senate Report No. 1586, 85th Congress, 2nd Session, p. 55.

effectiveness, there is ample precedent in previous attacks on that tribunal. And in all cases the attack was precipitated by disgust or dismay or anger at certain decisions of the Court.

Southern political leaders in speeches and Southern newspapermen in editorials have made some caustic and bruising remarks about Chief Justice Warren and his colleagues since they announced the Segregation decisions. I doubt that they have equalled—I do not see how they could have outdone—the worst of the denunciation piled on the Supreme Court at a half-dozen times when its decisions turned the course of public policy at high cost to a substantial sector of the population. Immediately following the Court's decision in the Dred Scott case in 1857, a newspaperman in Washington wrote: "If epithets and denunciation could sink a judicial body, the Supreme Court of the United States would never be heard of again." Undoubtedly, this decision relating to the status of slaves at a moment when the nation was making up its mind to go to war over slavery aroused the most bitter denunciation the Supreme Court has encountered in its history. But it is only one of many decisions that have infuriated great numbers of American people. Summaries and verbatim reports of efforts to destroy the Supreme Court with words constitute no small part of the contents of Charles Warren's highly regarded *The Supreme Court in United States History*.[2]

Epithets and denunciation unsupported by other acts do not destroy courts or overthrow other firmly rooted institutions. But words reveal states of mind, alter states of mind, and stimulate men to action. There is every reason to believe that verbal attack more than once chastened members of the Supreme Court, causing them to hesitate, to reconsider, and, one suspects, to change in some degree a course of action on which they were bent. Just as surely, attack on the Court—whether in the form of epithet and denunciation or closely reasoned argument—on several occasions shattered confidence and lowered the esteem in which the Court was held by important segments of the population.

Little would be gained by summarizing the flow of words or reciting even the most biting invective. It will be profitable, however, to observe the main lines of action which men have pursued in their efforts to alter the Court's decisions or curb its power. We start that account in this chapter, examining a contention that the fundamental character of the Union has been altered—that Congress,

[2] Cf. Bibliographic Note 4.

the president, and the Supreme Court have ignored or deliberately violated a basic intention of the Constitution by enlarging the powers of the national government and reducing the state governments to impotence.

2. INTERPOSITION AND NULLIFICATION

The most drastic of the recent interposition resolutions of the Southern states declare the Segregation decisions null and void within a state and announce a determination to render them ineffective within that state. Interposition has been widely and resoundingly condemned as a revival of nullification, a doctrine of ignoble origin long since discredited and discarded. Nullification may have been discredited, but its origin was noble enough, and it has had a hardy existence.

Throughout their deliberations, the possibility of state defiance of national law was prominent in the minds of the men who drew up the Constitution. The record of their decisions and what we know about their talk indicate a constant concern to provide for this eventuality, but also great variance in judgment as to what ought to and could be done about it. Those who favored the greatest concentration of authority in the national government proposed that the new national government—acting either through its lawmaking body or through one or another of two or three proposed arrangements utilizing the president, senators, and Supreme Court justices—be empowered to veto state laws, either through automatic review of every state law by the national government or through a provision that whatever vetoing agent was established could order laid before it for review any state law which the agent felt needed reviewing. The possible grounds for thus vetoing a state law were that it violated the United States Constitution, that it conflicted with national policy, or that, in the judgment of the vetoing agent, it was not a wise or proper law.

This means for dealing with state defiance of national action was at least twice rejected in the Constitutional Convention, and we may reasonably suppose it was rejected because more than a few of the delegates thought any national government they were likely to create might occasionally exceed its intended authority and need to be set back on its heels by a defiant state government. There is some support for this supposition in the language that was finally chosen to establish national supremacy (Article VI of the Constitution). As finally adopted, the words are:

> This Constitution and the laws of the United States which shall be made in pursuance thereof and all treaties made, or which shall be made, under the authority of the United States, shall be the supreme law of the land, and the judges in every State shall be bound thereby, anything in the Constitution or laws of any State to the contrary notwithstanding.

Futhermore:

> The Senators and Representatives before mentioned, and the members of the several State Legislatures, and all executive and judicial officers, both of the United States and of the several States, shall be bound by oath or affirmation to support this Constitution. . . .

At first reading, this language may seem to leave no important question of authority or obligation unsettled. All responsible officials of the states pledge themselves to support the Constitution, and judges are required to enforce the Constitution and the laws and treaties of the national government no matter what the constitution or laws of a state may say to the contrary. But a careful reading of these two sentences suggests that a significant differentiation of obligation may have been intended. The lawmakers and the executive officials of the state are not required by this language to take an oath to support the laws and treaties of the national government. Only the judges of a state are explicitly declared bound by national law subsidiary to the Constitution.

The meager report of debate in the Convention does not remove the uncertainty that is created by the language written into the document. On July 25, the Convention, voting seven states against three, rejected the proposal that state laws come before the national government for review. Immediately, Luther Martin of Maryland moved as an alternative that the legislative acts and treaties of the national government be the supreme law of the respective states and binding on state *judges* no matter what the state's own enactments might say to the contrary. This motion was adopted unanimously. Subsequent amendment and rephrasing brought the provision to its final form, and at no time, so far as available evidence reveals, did anyone propose that the lawmaking and executive officials of the states be required, like state judges, to treat statutes and treaties of the national government as superior to state enactments.

Martin later asserted that, at the time he introduced his proposal, he supposed that all litigation would first be tried in state courts and get into a national or federal court only on appeal. When it was decided that a system of federal trial courts could or should be established by legislation, he said, it became "worse than useless" to make the treaties and laws of the national government superior to the state constitutions. If the proposed new constitution containing this national-supremacy clause is ratified and put into operation, he declared, "it will amount to a total and unconditional surrender to that [national] government by the citizens of this state, of every right and privilege secured to them by our [state] constitution, and an express compact and stipulation with the general government that it may, at its discretion, make laws in direct violation of those rights."

Oliver Ellsworth, a delegate to the Convention from Connecticut and a bitter opponent of Luther Martin during the ratification stage, used language that can be read two ways. It is necessary, Ellsworth told the Connecticut ratifying convention, to establish a coercive power in order to make the new federal government a success. "The only question is, Shall it be a coercion of law, or a coercion of arms? . . . I am for coercion of law—that coercion which acts only upon delinquent individuals." Was this declaration sufficient to mark Ellsworth as wholly in favor of a national supremacy which subjects the states to national legislation and treaties in the actual conduct of government? He continued his address: "This Constitution does not attempt to coerce sovereign bodies, states, in their political capacity. No coercion is applicable to such bodies, but that of armed force."

I do not contend that the evidence cited above forces a conclusion that the framers of the Constitution wished to allow for state nullification of national law. Ellsworth may have intended all his sentences to be read as argument against such a conclusion. Historians have expressed doubt that Martin after the Convention was an accurate reporter of the state of mind of Martin in the Convention. A predominant proportion of the delegates who stuck it out to the end and signed the proposed new constitution had for a time supported a thorough subjection of the state governments to a new national government—by giving the national government a veto over state legislation, by allowing the national government to appoint the state governors who in turn would hold such a veto power, or by writing into the new constitution a provision that the national government could call forth its full resources to enforce its will on recalcitrant states. Still, it must be remembered that these men did not get all they asked for in the Convention and that they repeatedly reminded one another that they ought not ask for more than the popular mind in the several states might be willing to concede.

What I do contend is this: that the Constitution as finally phrased and adopted does not clearly, definitively, incontrovertibly state what the citizen may do—by individual action or in concert through his state government—when convinced that his national government has exceeded the authority conferred on it by the Constitution. There is no language in the Constitution which clearly specifies the final recourse in orderly protest before angry citizens assert their naturally endowed capacity to rebel against a government they are no longer willing to put up with.

This lack of finality in the wording of the document helps one to understand why James Madison could so closely skirt a doctrine of nullification ten years after the Constitution was ratified. He wrote the famous Virginia Resolutions of 1798 and justified them in a carefully reasoned address. In both documents he lent his authority to the contention that the Union was a compact among member-states, that the powers of the national government were limited to what the Constitution conferred, and that, "in case of a deliberate, palpable, and dangerous exercise of other powers, not granted by the said compact," the member states have a right and a duty to "interpose for arresting the progress of the evil, and for maintaining within their respective limits, the authorities, rights and liberties appertaining to them."

This is not the language of a man who intends to assert forthrightly that any state or combination of states has authority under the Constitution to void any act of the national government which state legislators and officials believe contrary to the Constitution. But Madison knew, when he drafted and endorsed the Virginia Resolutions, that he was bound to be identified with other men who were talking the language of outright nullification.

How far some of Madison's associates were willing to go and the logic of their position was revealed in the second round of protest, the Kentucky Resolutions of 1799. Contentions that the national government is the exclusive judge of the extent of its powers "stop not short of despotism," said the Kentucky legislature. If those who administer the national government be permitted to transgress the limits fixed for them by the Constitution, the several states, "being sovereign and independent, have the unquestionable right to judge of the infraction." When the judgment is that the national government has exceeded the authority given it, "a Nullification of those sovereignties, of all acts done under color of that instrument is the rightful remedy."

Very likely this language was too strong for Madison, great leader and teacher of his colleagues in the formation of the Constitution. Just as likely, it was said exactly right for his close friend and political associate, Thomas Jefferson.

We need not detail the further history of state challenge to national power. The classic statement of the constitutional right of the states to suspend or nullify national legislation was developed by John C. Calhoun and delivered to the nation by the people of South Carolina about forty years after the Constitution was adopted. The cause for complaint was an act of Congress fixing duties on imported goods. Southerners generally viewed the rates as discriminatory against the South and contended that some of them were designed to achieve purposes not within the authority of the national government. Calhoun, then vice-president of the United States and soon to be re-elected to that office, was commissioned to draw up a protest. His "Exposition" went beyond protest to formulate a carefully reasoned statement of how disputes about placement of authority under the Constitution should be settled. He asserted that the people of any state are under no obligation to comply with national legislation lacking constitutional authorization; he asserted that the proper way for the people of any state to decide the issue of authority and adopt a course of corrective action is by a convention of delegates chosen by the voters of the state to determine those specific matters; and he concluded that such a convention could only suspend enforcement within its borders of the acts it found invalid, the suspension being effective only until action on a proposed amendment to the Constitution should finally determine where authority lay in the points at dispute. The South Carolina legislature formally approved the "Exposition" in 1828 and laid it before the American people.

Congress and the president responded to the rumbling in South Carolina by enacting tariff legislation in 1832 which further antagonized the South. This time, South Carolina responded, at least partially, in the manner prescribed in the "Exposition." A convention was elected specifically to consider the objectionable legislation. The result was the adoption of the famous Nullification Ordinance of 1832. The ordinance specified certain acts and parts of acts of the national government which, it declared, "are unauthorized by the Constitution of the United States, and violate the true meaning and intent thereof, and are null, void, and no law, nor binding upon this State, its officers or citizens." To make this declaration effective, the ordinance pronounced void within the state any court orders, state or federal, which might attempt to enforce the objectionable tariff legislation and forbade state and federal officials to attempt to collect the duties imposed by the acts. The ordinance called on other states "to prevent the enforcement and arrest the operation" of the condemned legislation. But it did not specify that nullification should be temporary, awaiting a national decision to be made by adopting or rejecting a constitutional amendment.

South Carolina's plea for other states to prevent the enforcement and arrest the operation of the tariff legislation failed to rally any other state to the cause of nullification. The response, in the main, was not that nullification was too strong a remedy for the current offense; rather, the response revealed lack of confidence that nullification was a proper remedy for any offense.

Virginia, Kentucky, and South Carolina were not the only states to espouse the view that member states of the Union, acting alone or in concert, might rightfully identify excess of power by the national government and rightfully impede its execution. Obstruction of federal authority, declarations of right to nullify national law, and threats of secession brewed in New England for ten angry years until the termination of the War of 1812 brought relief from strain within the nation. Resistance to national legislation on the return of runaway slaves began in a number of Northern states about 1830 and continued until the acts of secession and outbreak of the Civil War. More than one state lawmaking body in the North specifically declared that provisions of the national statutes were not supreme law within the states, and judges in more than one Northern state followed the state enactment rather than Article VI of the Constitution on this point.

It has been my purpose in these pages to show that there has been a substantial precedent for the interposition statements issued by Southern states since announcement of the Segregation decisions in 1954 and 1955. What I have said and the quotations I have offered must not be thought to present both sides of the constitutional question involved. Everything Luther Martin said, and he said much more than I quoted, about national law not being superior to state law was countered by equally emphatic and far more numerous statements by other delegates who upheld national supremacy. Every subsequent effort of a state to nullify a national policy aroused vigorous outcry that the Constitution was thereby subverted and the Union endangered. Daniel Webster formulated and delivered the classic counterargument in 1830, debating in the Senate with Robert Hayne of South Carolina. Andrew Jackson, president when the Nullification Ordinance was issued, struck at the doctrine in a sentence remarkable for its completeness and its vigor: "I consider, then, the power to annul a law of the United States, assumed by one State, incompatible with the existence of the Union, contradicted expressly by the letter of the Constitution, unauthorized by its spirit, inconsistent with every principle on which it was founded, and destructive of the great object for which it was formed."

A contention that one state, or a concert of states, has a right to nullify national law does not necessarily imply a right to secede from the Union. But secession may be viewed as a grand attempt at nullification. It is easy, therefore, to see why so many students of American politics conclude that the Civil War and concurrent preservation of the Union forever settled the great issue about where authority to interpret the Constitution lies and forever outlawed state efforts to void the acts of the national government. It may indeed be the case that all thoughtful men, in moments of emotional tranquility, will insist that the recent interposition statements of Southern states are themselves void for want of authority under the Constitution. But it should be noted that the three amendments to the Constitution adopted at the close of the Civil War contained no language designed to settle the question as to where authority to fix the meaning of the Constitution lies and added nothing to make it clear that the elective branches of state government, like the judges, are required to recognize the laws of the national government as supreme and subordinate their own policies and actions to them.

3. COURTS AGAINST COURT

The doctrine of nullification presented a thesis about the placement of authority to interpret the Constitution and constructed a remedy for trespass on state power by any branch or office of the national government. The discontent and resistance were directed mainly at policies enacted into statutes by Congress and the president. In the controversies cited, nullification struck at the Supreme Court, in the main, only as court orders attempted to make the objectionable legislation effective.

But the Supreme Court has itself been the central object of attack many times in our history—attacked for issuing orders it allegedly had no authority to issue because of wrong views about the authority given it by the Constitution. The most bitterly fought of these contests were waged between the Supreme Court and the courts of one or more of the states, frequently with state legislature and governor coming to the aid of the local judges.

State judges are told by the Constitution (Article VI, Paragraph 2) that there are three bodies of law which they shall recognize as supreme over any state law, including the state constitution. They are the Constitution of the United States, laws of the the United States made in pursuance of that Constitution, and treaties made under the authority of the United States. Orders of the Supreme Court are not included in the list. And state judges are not told which of the three is to be regarded as the "supremest" law of the land in case of conflict between Constitution, national laws, and treaties.

Article VI of the Constitution must be read in connection with Article III, which says that there shall be a Supreme Court and such inferior courts as the national lawmaking body may establish. It says that the power of these courts shall extend to "all cases in law and equity arising under this Constitution, the laws of the United States, and treaties made, or which shall be made, under their authority" and, in addition to cases arising in these ways, to cases and controversies involving several classes of litigants specified in this article. Additional language in Article III differentiates the original and the appellate jurisdiction of the Supreme Court (a matter to be considered later), defines the crime of treason, and fixes certain procedures for trial of treason and other crimes.

Having read articles III and VI together in this way, one cannot avoid the conclusion that an essential instruction was overlooked in the framing of the Constitution. When there is difference of opinion as to whether state law is in conflict with national law, whose judgment is final? If the highest court of the state says that the Constitution, acts of Congress, or treaties do not forbid the state to do what it has done, but the Supreme Court of the United States says that the state's act is forbidden, which court's decision is to stand? Complicate the issue a bit. The state court may find that the state law is in conflict with an act of Congress but also be convinced that the act of Congress is a violation of the Constitution. This may result in a decision that the state law is valid and should be enforced. Presume that the Supreme Court subsequently rules that the act of Congress is not in conflict with the Constitution and is good law. Must the state court now recognize that the state law is invalid, or may it stand by its own judgment that the national statute is void and continue to enforce the state statute?

The language of the Constitution provides no clear instruction on these questions. If one finds a rule of action on these matters, he puts it into the Constitution by inference. State judges and members of the Supreme Court made different inferences, and bitter conflict between the Supreme Court and state courts resulted.

Before the Supreme Court had been in existence ten years, the highest courts of North Carolina and Pennsylvania had refused to obey its orders. If national court and state court disagree as to where the Constitution places authority, said the chief justice of Pennsylvania in 1798, "there is no common umpire but the people who should adjust the affair by making amendments in the constitutional way, or suffer from the defect. . . . There is no provision in the Constitution that in such a case the judges of the Supreme Court of the United States shall control and be conclusive." Within another decade, state troops were called out in Pennsylvania to keep a federal marshal from enforcing an order of the Supreme Court making a disposition of property contrary to what the Pennsylvania court had previously ordered.

The Supreme Court won its battle with Pennsylvania. Its orders controlled the distribution of the three properties which were in litigation. A federal court convicted and sentenced the general and other officers who led the Pennsylvania troops, President Madison promptly remitting the sentence. And other state legislatures refused to join Pennsylvania in a call for a constitutional amendment which would establish "an impartial tribunal" to settle disputes between the national and state governments. The Virginia legislature replied that the Supreme Court of the United States, with which Pennsylvania was at odds, was better qualified to decide such disputes in an enlightened and impartial manner than any new court which could be created.

The judges of the highest court of Virginia might have recommended a different reply if they had been consulted by the Virginia legislature, for the Virginia court was having its troubles with the Supreme Court at the time. This was the litigation that later produced the famous opinion of Justice Joseph Story in *Martin* v. *Hunter's Lessee* (1 Wheaton 304, decided in 1816), a document heavily relied on in teaching constitutional law in this country. The Virginia Court of Appeals (the highest tribunal of the state) ruled that the act of Congress which authorized the Supreme Court to entertain appeals from the courts of a state "is not in pursuance of the Constitution of the United States," that the Supreme Court therefore had no authority to act in the case, and that the mandate of the Supreme Court would not be obeyed by the Virginia Court of Appeals.

The Supreme Court won this battle, also. The opinion of Justice Story was accompanied by an order of the Supreme Court addressed directly to the lower court of Virginia which heard the suit in the first instance. The order appears to have been executed.

In the long run, the Supreme Court was indisputably triumphant in all its battles with state judges. Today, the judiciary of each state is firmly integrated in a nation-wide judicial structure of state and federal courts, and the Supreme Court of the United States is final for all these courts, state and federal alike, on significant issues of interpretation of the federal Constitution and the laws and treaties of the United States. It was not a total rout of the state judges and the elected officials who supported them, for the Supreme Court made some concessions. Nor was the general victory quickly and easily won. Charles Warren writes that, prior to the Civil War, the highest courts of seven states denied that the Constitution permitted the Supreme Court to entertain appeals from state courts on writ of error. Still other state tribunals, including the highest courts of North Carolina and Pennsylvania in the instances mentioned above, resisted orders of the Supreme Court attempting to remove cases in trial from state to federal judiciary. Warren lists eight states whose legislatures adopted resolutions or statutes backing up the state courts in their resistance.

The last rattle of arms, at least as of the time I write, in this long war between judges occurred in Wisconsin during the years 1854 to 1859. A newspaper editor, abolitionist, and citizen of Wisconsin (Sherman M. Booth) was arrested by a federal marshal (Stephen V. R. Ableman) for aiding a slave to escape in violation of an act of Congress, the Fugitive Slave Law. The Wisconsin Supreme Court ordered Booth released, ruling the Fugitive Slave Law unconstitutional. Ableman obtained a writ of error from the United States Supreme Court, and the clerk of the Wisconsin Supreme Court sent up the record in compliance. About the same time, Booth was indicted by a federal grand jury, placed under arrest again by the federal marshal Ableman, tried in federal district court, found guilty, and sentenced. Again, the Wisconsin Supreme Court ordered Booth released, and Ableman complied. Once more the Supreme Court of the United States, this time on motion of the attorney general of the United States, issued a writ of error ordering the clerk of the Wisconsin court to send up the record of the state court's action. This time, the Wisconsin judges were alert and, in Warren's words, ordered their clerk "to make no return and to enter no order concerning the same on his journal or records."

The clerk retained the record just as he was told to do by the Wisconsin judges. Unfortunately for them, however, the clerk had some time before given a copy of the record to the federal district attorney, and the national Supreme Court obtained this and acted on it. Chief Justice Roger B. Taney, speaking for the Supreme Court, defended its jurisdiction in firm language, contending, as Story, the great Chief Justice John Marshall, and other judges before him had done, that the subjection of state courts to a national supreme court is essential to the maintenance of a federal system. The Wisconsin court, it appears, never did revoke its orders releasing Booth, and the latter seems never to have served the sentence pronounced on him in the federal district court. The behavior of the Wisconsin judges is doubtless accounted for in part by the strong abolitionist sentiment that prevailed in the state at the time. The Wisconsin Legislature supported the judges in a resolution that reached back to Kentucky and 1799 for doctrine and phraseology. The proposition that the national government is the exclusive judge of the powers delegated to it, said the Legislature, "stops nothing short of despotism, since the *discretion* of those who administer the government and not the *constitution* would be the measure of their powers." The member states of the Union, "being sovereign and independent," have an unquestionable right to judge whether the Constitution is being complied with, and, if they find that unauthorized acts are being done or attempted, "positive defiance" by the state governments is the rightful remedy.

This particular skirmish may be viewed as at least a draw if not as a small victory for the right of the states to share in deciding how the Constitution divides authority between the national and state governments. Whatever one's judgment on the point, it seems necessary to conclude that the long-drawn-out contest for supremacy was won by the Supreme Court. Even today, state judges frequently manage to do a good deal less than the Supreme Court tells them to. But the absence, since the Civil War, of any contest with the Supreme Court comparable to that of Pennsylvania about 1810 and that of Wisconsin fifty years later suggests that the finality of the Supreme Court in constitutional interpretation is now accepted by all the nation's judges. The fact that no Southern state court has declared a Constitution-given right to ignore the orders of federal courts in school integration cases seems to confirm this. In view of the robust combat waged a century and more ago, the rebuke of the Supreme Court issued by the chief state judges in 1958 seems notably restrained and diplomatic.[3]

[3] The principal court decisions involved in this episode are *United States* v. *Booth* (18 Howard 476, 1855); *Ableman* v. *Booth* (21 Howard 506, 1858); and *Ableman* v. *Booth* (11 Wisconsin 517, 1859). The Wisconsin declaration of nullification is in *Wisconsin Laws, 1859,* pp. 248–249.

CHAPTER FOUR

The Judges before Their Peers

The Constitution states that the two houses of Congress may jointly remove judges from office, the House impeaching and pressing the charges and the Senate hearing and deciding whether removal is justified. Only one member of the Supreme Court has been impeached; he was not removed, and the trial is now long past—Justice Samuel Chase, tried in 1805. There has been too little threat of impeachment since to believe that it has had any significant effect on the attitudes or behavior of Supreme Court judges.

Two avenues of approach to the Supreme Court—two leverages which president and Congress may apply if they wish to move the Supreme Court from its position on constitutional issues—merit brief examination here. They are evidenced (1) in the selection of men to serve on the Court and (2) in efforts to curb the Supreme Court by legislation or constitutional amendment.

1. SELECTING THE JUDGES

On May 7, 1930, the Senate voted not to give consent to the appointment of John J. Parker, then a federal circuit judge, to the Supreme Court. The motion to give consent failed by a vote of thirty-nine to forty-one. The nomination of Judge Parker was the 107th appointment to the Supreme Court sent to the Senate since that tribunal was established in 1789.

This was the ninth case of the Senate's refusing consent to a Supreme Court appointment on formal vote. The first instance occurred in 1795, when the Senate refused to approve Pres. George Washington's nomination of John Rutledge as chief justice; the rejection of Parker is the latest. In addition to the nine positive rejections, the president on ten occasions either withdrew his nomination or did not submit it again after the Senate allowed the session to expire without voting. It appears that, in each of these ten cases, the president believed that his insistence on a vote would either result in denial of consent or arouse a bigger fight than he or his candidate wished to engage in. In one additional case, a nomination was made obsolete in 1866, when Congress, overriding Pres. Andrew Johnson's veto, hastily enacted a statute reducing the number of places on the Supreme Court from ten to nine. In many other instances, the nominee was vigorously opposed in debate and consent given by divided vote.

These many controversies centering on selection of judges for the Supreme Court defy satisfactory interpretation. Nineteen cases may be viewed as rejections by the Senate—nine adverse votes and ten retreats by the president. Four of these nominations went to the Senate between the election in November and the following March 4, when a new president would take office. Perhaps a half-dozen of the rejections are best explained as casualties of party warfare. It was a time of party realignment, and the candidate was punished because of the alliances he had made and broken. Or a majority of the Senate was not of the president's party, and the nomination came up in election year. Or the senators from the nominee's state were politically opposed to him, and it was a time when senatorial courtesy was extended to all appointments requiring Senate approval.

Allowing for the impact of partisan considerations and the convictions of senators, evident in a few cases, that the nominee had not achieved distinction in the law, it may still be said that the nominee's position on political issues of great importance has always been a major concern of the president and senators in filling positions on the Supreme Court. This is proven by correspondence, memoirs, Senate debates, and other records relating to the filling of vacancies on the Court both before and after the rejection of Parker in 1930.

Alexander Wolcott, rejected in 1811, had vigorously enforced the federal embargo laws which New England federalists held to be in excess of national power and which excited them to threats of nullification. Action on the appointment of Roger B. Taney as associate justice was indefinitely postponed in the spring of 1835. A year later, the Senate approved his appointment as chief justice, succeeding John Marshall. Both times, Taney's appointment was stubbornly opposed because of his support of President Jackson in financial policy and because of his views about the allocation of power between national and state governments. Speaking of the possibility of Taney's becoming chief justice, Sen. Daniel Webster wrote: "Judge [Joseph] Story . . . thinks the Supreme Court is *gone* and I think so too." [1]

Pres. James K. Polk said in his diary: "I resolved to appoint no man who was not an original Democrat and a strict constructionist, and who would be less likely to relapse into the broad Federal doctrine of Judge Marshall or Judge Story." [2]

The most bitter contest in the present century was waged over the confirmation of Louis D. Brandeis, confirmed on June 1, 1916. A wide range of reasons for doubting Brandeis' fitness to be a judge were given, and among his opponents were numbered many eminent lawyers. But Joseph Harris, who recently wrote an entire book on the role of the Senate in appointments, concluded that: "The opposition to Brandeis was chiefly due to the fact that his opponents regarded him as a dangerous radical and a crusader and hence unfit to sit on the Supreme Court, which they regarded as the bulwark of conservatism." The political convictions which prevailed when Brandeis was finally approved were mainly responsible for the rejection of Parker in 1930. Parker was believed to be averse to organized labor and possibly to the political advancement of the Negro. "When we are passing on a judge," said Sen. George W. Norris (R., Neb.), "we not only ought to know whether he is a good lawyer, not only whether he is honest—and I admit that this nominee [Parker] possesses both of those qualifications—but we ought to know how he approaches these great questions of human rights."

These illustrative cases could be extended for several pages. Probably no one appreciated the influence of Supreme Court judges in the political realm more fully than William Howard Taft, president for four years and later chief justice for nine years. Sizing up

1 Quoted in Warren, *Supreme Court,* Vol. 2, p. 10 (cf. Bibliographic Note 4).

2 Quoted in Harris, *Advice and Consent of the Senate,* p. 439 (cf. Bibliographic Note 5). The quotations in the next paragraph relating to the confirmation of Justice Brandeis and Judge Parker are from Harris, pp. 113, 130.

Pres. Herbert Hoover as "a Progressive" and expecting him to appoint men of that persuasion to the Court, Chief Justice Taft wrote: "Although I am older and slower and less acute and more confused, . . . as long as things continue as they are and I am able to answer in my place, I must stay on in the Court in order to keep the Bolsheviki from getting control." [3]

The minimum conclusion forced on us by the many contests aroused in replacing judges is that presidents and senators have recognized from its earliest period that the Supreme Court has enormous power to determine the character of public policy. Even very little probing into a few of these incidents reveals widely differing views of the consequences of judicial power and of where the bounds of judicial power ought to be drawn. Rarely, if ever, has a genuine contest been waged solely over the fitness of the president's nominee for a position of high responsibility. Mixed with questions about personal qualities are issues of how the man proposed for the Court would use his power as a judge, whether the Constitution sanctions what the Supreme Court judges have been doing, and whether the good life would not be more certainly assured if judicial power were curtailed.

The center of attention in these cases, however, has been the individual under consideration for the Court and not the group of judges already on the Court. The fullest airing of views about the nation's tribunal takes place when legislation or constitutional amendments are introduced to alter the structure, procedure, or jurisdiction of the Supreme Court.

2. CURBING THE COURT

Five principal strategies have been adopted for restricting the Supreme Court's power by enactment of statutes or adoption of constitutional amendments.

Senator Jenner's effort to limit the cases which can come to the Supreme Court for review represents the *first* strategy. This restriction of the Court's attempted power was a moderate measure when compared with some others which we are to note.

At least ten proposals to restrict the Supreme Court's appellate jurisdiction were considered in Congress during the six decades, 1821 to 1882. Most of them were designed to terminate

[3] Quoted in Henry F. Pringle, *The Life and Times of William Howard Taft* (2 vols.; New York: Farrar and Rinehart, 1939), Vol. 2, p. 967.

review of decisions by state courts only, not to keep the Supreme Court from taking certain types of questions on appeal from lower federal courts, as Jenner wished to do. The one measure that became law, however, was of the latter type. In 1867, overriding a veto by President Johnson, Congress repealed that part of an earlier statute which authorized the Supreme Court to review the decision of any lower federal court granting or refusing to grant a writ of habeas corpus. In a case instantly famous (*Ex Parte McCardle,* 7 Wallace 506, decided in 1868), the Supreme Court acknowledged the right of Congress to so restrict its jurisdiction, and it made the new legislation applicable even to litigation which was in process when the statute was passed.

The jurisdiction taken from the Supreme Court in 1868 was restored by a statute of 1885. Not until Jenner introduced his bill in 1957 did either house of Congress again seriously consider a proposal to thwart the Supreme Court judges by denying them access to particular categories of litigation. Legislation was passed during this ninety-year period which redefined the Supreme Court's appellate power, but the purpose was to ease the burden of the Court and enlarge its effectiveness, and the more important features of these acts were enacted with the approval of the judges, if not at their request.

This particular type of legislative measure, removing specific issues from the appellate power, fell into disuse, it seems, because it was generally believed an inappropriate means for dealing with the Court. Certainly other means of reducing the Court's power or controlling its exercise of power continued to be pushed with vigor.

A *second* strategy for curbing the Court attempts to take away its power to render statutes—acts of Congress, of state legislatures, or of both—invalid because of conflict with the United States Constitution. Such a result, achieved by constitutional amendment, would make the lawmaking authority final as to what the Constitution permits, forbids, and requires. We shall see in a later chapter how the Supreme Court rose to its pre-eminent position in respect to interpretation of the Constitution. The earliest bid of the judges for this power was challenged in Congress. As early as 1805, amendments to the Constitution which would make all statutes binding on the Supreme Court were laid before Congress. They have been laid there off and on ever since, for example during the Progressive movements headed by Theodore Roosevelt (around 1912) and by Robert M. La Follette (around 1920) and during the New Deal period (1934 to 1937). None of these projects received enough support to give friends of the Supreme Court a scare.

Given the apparent impossibility of putting over an amendment that wholly strips the Court of power to declare laws invalid, a promising alternative is to require that an extraordinary majority of judges concur in the judgment. This is the *third* of the strategies to be noted.

In the first forty years of its existence, the Supreme Court invalidated one or more state statutes in decisions approved by less than a majority of the Court's full membership, because of some judges' not sitting on the case. About 1834, the judges adopted a rule requiring agreement of a majority of all members in order to invalidate a statute, whether an act of Congress or of a state legislature. This change in practice undoubtedly took the edge off one line of attack on the Supreme Court, but it did not put an end to it. The rule of invalidation by a bare majority of all judges has repeatedly encountered opposition. The judgment of the lawmakers supported by four Supreme Court judges is a more trustworthy guide to the intent of the Constitution than any contrary view concurred in by five Supreme Court judges—this contention always gets a sympathetic ear from a big audience. The weight of respectable opinion in favor of the statute's validity is sometimes even greater. On the side of the lawmakers and the four outvoted judges of the Supreme Court may be a carefully prepared opinion of the attorney general advising that the statute is within the Constitution and opinions of one or more judges in the lower courts to the same effect. Under certain circumstances, an equal division of the Supreme Court judges at least confirms the nullification of a statute. When only eight or six judges sit in a case and they divide equally, the decision of the court below is affirmed; if the lower court ruled that the statute is invalid, the failure of the Supreme Court to reverse that ruling increases the presumption that the statute will be viewed as invalid in any later litigation.

When displeasure with the Supreme Court mounts to such a point that some influential political leaders and spokesmen of great interest groups propose to strip it entirely of power to invalidate legislation, a great many other influential people are ready to consider less drastic limitations on judicial power. It would seem feasible, at such a time, to unite critics of the Court in a demand that the statute be enforced as law unless more than a bare majority of the Supreme Court agrees that it violates the Constitution. A number of different formulas have been proposed—the statute stands unless six of nine judges concur in its invalidity, or seven judges, or eight, or even unanimity of a full court. All such drives against the Court have failed. Either those who wish to take the Court down disagree on how many notches to reduce it, or friends of the Court are too numerous and too strong for a united attack to prevail.

A *fourth* strategy for containing judicial power is to preserve the Court's power to decide any question, including the validity of legislation, by simple majority vote, but subject the decision to review by some other tribunal. This remedy has been proposed, rejected, and revived again and again.

For almost a century, the main complaint lodged against the Supreme Court was that it took authority away from state governments and gave it to the national government, contrary to the plain words or unavoidable implications of the Constitution. This cause of displeasure was reflected in the proposals which were made during that period for a further review of the Court's decisions. It was strongly urged in some of the ratifying conventions of 1787 that the president (or the president and Senate) be authorized to set up from time to time a special court to review any decision of the Supreme Court which he (or they) might think erroneous. This recommendation has more than once been renewed by resolution of a state legislature or constitutional amendment laid before Congress for consideration. In many cases, the proposal specified that the reviewing tribunal consist of one judge from each state; in some cases, the proposal was not for a special tribunal to review the Supreme Court but rather for a tribunal, sensitive to state rights, which would hear originally and adjudicate finally all disputes between national and state governments. The United States Senate, representing all states equally and until 1913 chosen by state legislatures, would seem a natural resort for those who contend that the distribution of authority between nation and states should be determined by a body highly sensitive to the interests of the American people oriented in part to their national existence and in part to their existence as separate states. More than one congressman has backed a constitutional amendment that would make the Senate the highest tribunal where this issue is involved, either to take the dispute as original jurisdiction or on appeal from the Supreme Court.

The Supreme Court still invites antagonism because its decisions breach state autonomy, as current reaction to the Segregation decisions reveals. But for several decades an equal or greater amount of antagonism has been generated by decisions which hold that certain kinds of regulatory action are forbidden to all governments, whether national, state, or local. Consequently, the character of the superior body proposed for review of the Supreme Court's decisions has changed. Theodore Roosevelt stirred up a small flurry about 1912 in favor of a procedure by which court decisions, including those of the Supreme Court, might be affirmed or overruled by popular referendums. Much more persistent and more favorably received have been proposals to allow Congress to overrule the Supreme Court as it overrides a veto by the president. In the main, proposals of this character provide Congressional review only for decisions that invalidate acts of Congress, not for decisions that hold state laws unconstitutional. These proposals differ also in the size of vote required to re-enact the statute. And they rarely get by the first hurdles that beset every proposal to add an amendment to the Constitution.

This brings us to the *fifth* category of efforts by congressmen and presidents to restrain judicial power. Here, the strategy is to let the judges keep their authority and exercise it in conformity with their customary procedures, but to increase the opportunities for elected officials to determine who may sit on the bench and possess that power. At present, the president and a majority of the Senate fill vacancies on the Court, and we saw above that they inquire into his convictions about constitutional obligation before they appoint a man to the Court. But, once appointed, a judge serves until death or resignation, impeachment having been found an impracticable means of removal. In the opinion of many political leaders, the power of Supreme Court judges is such that they should not be allowed to determine how long they will hold it. The corrective most favored is removal from office by some process requiring the approval of both the president and one or both houses of Congress. Proposals of this character date from 1805. They appear in Congress just as regularly as the decisions of the Court excite widespread resentment.

Amendment of the Constitution promises a lasting remedy for what one may think wrong with the Supreme Court, but it can be brought about only by a vast concurrence on the details as well as essential character of the remedy. Statutes are more easily enacted than amendments. They do not go to state legislatures (or state conventions) for approval, and, if the president does not apply his veto, they need only a simple majority in each house of Congress, not the two-thirds vote required for approval of constitutional amendments. Statutes cannot institute a new procedure for removing judges, however, and it has been supposed that the constitutional language, "judges . . . shall hold their offices during good behavior," precludes a statutory requirement that all judges retire at a specified age. But the Constitution does not say how many judges shall compose the Supreme Court, and the number of members was initially fixed by statute and has later been changed by statute.

Historians differ as to what objectives were behind some changes, achieved or unsuccessfully attempted, in the number of judges. For approximately a century, members of the Supreme Court were assigned to circuits where they sat with other judges as an intermediate court of appeal. Proposals to alter the number of Supreme Court judges, therefore, were affected by views about how many circuits were needed. Allowing for this involvement, there can be no doubt that some of the bills before Congress proposing to increase or reduce the number of Supreme Court judges got their support from men who wished to upset the dominant theories or policies of the Court. The most recent of these efforts, and one that set the nation thinking about the consequences of judicial power, ran its course in 1937. Pres. Franklin D. Roosevelt was its prime author, and many of his party's leaders in Congress did all they could to achieve his goal. One cannot ask for a better demonstration of how the two elected branches of goverment sometimes put the Supreme Court on trial. For that reason, this incident is worth a few pages here and several more in a later chapter.

3. PRESIDENTIAL CHALLENGE

The judges on the Supreme Court when Roosevelt became president in 1933 were old in years (averaging almost sixty-eight), and most of them held conservative views about the proper realm of governmental authority. Not one gave up his place during the first Roosevelt term, and during that period they struck down a great deal of the legislation which the President considered essential to his New Deal. Among the measures that went down were the National Industrial Recovery Act (authorizing codes regulating production, wages, marketing, and prices in a wide range of industries), an Agricultural Adjustment Act (regulating farm production, marketing of farm products, and other matters bearing on the income and security of farmers), and acts intended to stabilize production of oil and coal by comprehensive regulation of those industries. These and some other New Deal statutes fell because the judges held that they exceeded the authority delegated to the national government by the Constitution and therefore encroached on the reserved powers of the states. Other acts went down because at least a majority of the judges thought they attempted to do things which no government should attempt to do and therefore, insofar as they adversely affected anyone's life, liberty, or property, did so without due process of law.

The supporters of the New Deal were too numerous and too stubborn to acquiesce in judicial destruction of their legislative program. Several means for undoing the work of the judges were considered, and President Roosevelt finally decided on the strategy he called reorganization of the judiciary, but which his opponents labeled an effort to "pack" the Court. Under the legislation which was laid before Congress in February, 1937, an additional judge could be appointed for every federal judge who (having served for ten years) failed to retire at the age of seventy. Limits were set to the number of judges who could be appointed; for instance, the total number of Supreme Court judges, counting those above seventy who had not formally retired, could not exceed fifteen. The proposed law, if enacted, would have enabled Roosevelt to make substantial changes in the federal judiciary immediately, for there were at the time six judges on the Court who had arrived at seventy and approximately twenty-five judges of that age sitting in the lower federal courts.

The Roosevelt proposal for reorganizing the federal judiciary became a center of national attention and the eye of a political cyclone. The strategy was unsatisfactory to some of the most ardent New Dealers, for they felt that the power of judges to nullify federal legislation should be drastically limited, if not terminated altogether. The enlargement, or "packing," of the Supreme Court and lower federal courts seemed to them at best to apply a poultice where surgery was required.

The principal opposition to the President's plan, however, came from people who felt that the courts should not be tampered with in any way. Most severe and most persistent in opposition to the President were men who opposed the New Deal on principle. The judges had defended them from legislation they did not like; these men, in turn, defended the judges when they came under attack. But the defense of the judiciary from packing was in no sense confined to people who opposed the legislation which the judges had invalidated. When reorganization of the judiciary became a practical issue, many people realized that they were deeply committed to the principle that the courts ought to be "out of politics," and they saw this attempt to alter the composition of the courts as an effort to subject the judiciary to politics, no matter what evidence and argument was offered that the judges were already in politics and that this was a plan to get them out. Stirred by such convictions, many prominent people who had strongly supported Roosevelt's New Deal sided against him when he pushed his judicial reorganization measure.

The legislative branch rescued the judges from their adversary, the Executive. The President's bill was reported adversely by the Senate Committee on the Judiciary, and on July 22, 1937, was recommitted with instructions for that committee to report another bill for judicial reform.

It is too much to say that congressmen understood the Supreme Court to be on trial and found it not guilty as charged. The President's bill, if we pursue the trial analogue, was not a bill of indictment only; it was an indictment and a schedule of remedies to prevent future offenses. Congressmen in numbers to form a majority could not be found to accept the whole package. It may be that a resolution deploring the position of the Supreme Court in recent litigation and urging the judges to adopt new views of public needs and constitutional obligations would have been adopted by majority vote in each house of Congress. One would have to give strange meanings to familiar words if he could read the evidence and then deny that the judges of the Supreme Court considered themselves on trial in 1937.

CHAPTER FIVE
The Right to Decide

1. WHAT KIND OF UNION?
2. UNSTABLE ALLIANCES
3. WHOSE VICTORIES?

The figure of a Court on trial must not be carried too far, however. There are differences of vast significance among the many crises which have dogged the Supreme Court.

1. WHAT KIND OF UNION?

The first forty years of the Supreme Court's existence, roughly until 1830, was a period of fixing the character of the federal Union. One view of the new constitutional structure, strongly supported by many people in each of the thirteen original states, described the Union as a voluntary compact of sovereign states. For men of this view, the center of gravity in the new system lay, not in the general government at the top, but in near-autonomous states which constituted the base of the structure. Opposed to this position, and also favored by many people in all parts of the nation, was the contention that the American people, a population located within states but acting as a single united citizenry, had created a consolidated government which permitted limited governmental authority to rest within the states. For the latter group, logic required that the general or national government have every power essential for maintaining a united nation and for achieving the social goals on which people in all parts of the country might agree. For these people, therefore, the union was not a compact of states, the states were not near-autonomous, and the center of gravity in the new structure was not spread among the partners in a union.

This question of where authority or power was placed in the new system was one of basic importance. It was an issue to which men brought deeply embedded conviction and powerful, if not overpowering, emotion. It was necessarily a political issue that encompassed other political issues.

On the question of how authority was distributed, the statements in the Constitution were helpful, but not determinative. Men who sat in the drafting convention at Philadelphia stood far apart on where authority should be placed and later stood just as far apart on where authority had been placed. The same was true of the men who served in the ratifying conventions in state capitals. Historians and other students of law and the Constitution arrayed themselves in controversy over the location of authority. And judges sitting in high courts over the land reached differing conclusions as to what the Constitution permitted lawmakers to do and required courts to do.

Soon after the new Constitution went into effect, the American people had to decide who would authoritatively interpret the document—which men or institutions would finally say what the Constitution means when its words can be given more than one meaning and how the intent of the Constitution should be extended when issues arise which the language does not seem to cover. One man could reasonably believe that this would most satisfactorily be done by a national officialdom, either a political body free to respond to expediency or a judicial body bound to pursue logic and stand by precedent. But another man could reasonably believe that the states, which he held to be partners in a compact, ought to share in fixing the meaning of the compact into which they had entered. If he could not go to the extreme of some who argued that any state could finally determine the extent of national authority within its borders, he might agree with Calhoun that any state could interrupt the execution of national policy within its borders until it could be determined whether the process for restating the terms of the compact would be invoked.

As the arm by which national laws were judicially enforced, federal judges inescapably became identified with the national government whose bid for power was contested. Within a decade after the Union was created, federal judges, in inferior courts and in the Supreme Court, had refused to enforce and had ordered state judges not to enfore state laws which a large part of the population believed the state legislatures had a right to enact. All federal judges, and especially judges on the Supreme Court, became specific targets in a war that was fought on a broad front. One would distort the picture if he said that the Supreme Court was on trial every time it came under attack during the first forty years of its existence. Sometimes the Supreme Court as a particular institution was under reconsideration. More often, the entire national government was on trial, and the Supreme Court was selected to sit in the dock only because the prosecutors thought it offered their surest hope of getting a conviction from a jury that would like to sentence every branch of the national government.

Caution must also rule in interpreting attack on the Supreme Court during the two decades immediately preceding the Civil War. If one believed that the character of the federal Union had been determined and the distribution of authority within that structure decisively settled when President Jackson stood firm against South Carolina in 1832, he might still acknowledge that the slavery issue had protruded beyond the bounds of governmental or constitutional containment by 1840 or 1850. When officials and plain citizens of Southern states nullified national laws by refusing to permit entry of free Negroes into their states, were they not invoking law they thought superior to the Constitution? And, when the Wisconsin Supreme Court judges, in defiance of orders from the United States Supreme Court, released from custody a man who aided the escape of fugitive slaves, were they not invoking a law they thought higher than the words of the Constitution and the previous understandings about how those words would be interpreted? If this be a defensible explanation of why the Supreme Court was treated the way it was during the period when abolition challenged slavery, may we not conclude that a way of life was under attack and that the Supreme Court simply got knocked around because it was caught between the contestants?

Taking this view of the matter, some persons conclude that the outcome of the Civil War and the adoption of the Reconstruction amendments made illegitimate any further appeals to a law higher than the Constitution. By this line of reasoning, they strip any cloak of legitimacy from the outbursts against the Supreme Court and resistance to its orders in the Deep South in our own decade. Such a position, of course, has implications for other, and future, situations when conscience induces men to challenge the primacy of law and constitutional language, but this is a matter we need not go into here.

2. UNSTABLE ALLIANCES

The assertion that the Court from time to time goes on trial seems inappropriate to many people because the complaint against the judges is filed by a limited part of the nation and not by the whole of it. It is a fact that only a part of the population is at odds with the Court at any time. Furthermore, no sizable sector with an identifiable common interest has ever maintained a consistent and persistent opposition to the Supreme Court. The Court has been denounced and defied by spokesmen for nearly every type of common interest, but rarely have spokesmen for significantly differing interests denounced and defied the Court at the same time.

State judges, state legislatures, and congressmen from all sections of the country have refused to comply with the Supreme Court's orders, threatened or tried to prevent enforcement of its orders, moved in one way or another to strip the Supreme Court of power. If these many movements against the Court had come in unison, they might have forced a significant relocation of authority among the courts or even a major redistribution of authority among the political and judicial bodies.

But assault on the Supreme Court has been fragmented. When Kentucky and Virginia wanted to put a brake on national power in 1798 and 1799, not another state legislature came to their aid. When Pennsylvania was calling out troops to stand off the Supreme Court and asking for creation of a special tribunal to police the frontier between national and state authority, the Virginia legislature answered that the existing Supreme Court was perfect for the job. Ten years later, the Virginia legislature was urging a constitutional amendment to do just what Pennsylvania had recommended, and the Pennsylvania legislature had lost interest. Another dozen years found South Carolina pressing a right to nullify an act of Congress—old doctrine for Kentucky, Virginia, and Pennsylvania, but not one of those states was in a fighting mood. So it has been with the elected branches of the national government. Many congressmen and a few presidents have been willing if not eager to cut a few slices off judicial power. Not enough of them have been ready to do the cutting at the same time.

3. WHOSE VICTORIES?

This account of the experience of the highest tribunal invites one to conclude that, although the Supreme Court has suffered some setbacks, it has thus far been victorious in its long war with the elective branches of government and other opponents of judicial power.

To conclude this much is not necessarily to concede that the Supreme Court judges triumphed over their critics and assailants. To judge of defeat and victory, one must know what the protagonists conceived their objectives to be. One cannot know whether obstacles thrown in its path impeded the progress of the Court or altered the course of its development unless and until he knows what the development of the Court would have been if these obstacles had not been erected. But the latter cannot be known. One can only speculate as to what might have come to be if certain things had not been as they were. And one man's speculations are not likely to be convincing to another thoughtful person.

Allowing for uncertainties as to why men do what they do, it can safely be said that criticism of the Supreme Court and efforts to curb judicial power significantly affected the behavior of Supreme Court judges. Warren reports several occasions when the judges put off the painful day when they would hear argument or make a decision or announce a decision already made on an issue, and it is fairly clear that, in some of these cases, the delaying tactics were stimulated by bitter criticism to which the judges had recently been subjected. The decision of the judges in 1834 to enforce a statute unless a majority of all the judges agree on its invalidity might have come regardless of pressures on the Court, but it seems irrefutable that it came when it did because the judges were sensitive to criticism.

Two incidents in the history of the Supreme Court are worth special mention. On February 7, 1870, the Supreme Court held invalid (in *Hepburn* v. *Griswold,* 8 Wallace 603) certain acts of Congress which made issues of paper money legal tender in meeting various obligations incurred before the statutes were enacted. The Supreme Court consisted of eight judges at the time, and the vote for invalidity was five against three. Immediately thereafter, one judge retired, and two new ones took seats on the Court. On March 31, the Court announced that the litigation decided on February 7 would be opened for rehearing. The case did not come to a second decision because certain applicants promptly asked for dismissal of the case. But, on April 30, just a month after the decision to reopen *Hepburn* v. *Griswold,* the Court ordered a new argument of the "Legal Tender cases" (12 Wallace 457), a number of suits involving the same issues as *Hepburn* v. *Griswold.* On May 1, 1871, these cases were decided; *Hepburn* v. *Griswold* was reversed, and the legal-tender legislation was held valid and enforceable. The four sitting judges who found the legislation unconstitutional in February, 1870, were of the same opinion in May, 1871; they were overruled because the two new judges voted with the three who spoke in favor of validity in the original decision.

This entire dramatic episode took place in the midst of a raucous public clamor and at a time when the judges knew their actions were subject to sharp scrutiny by political leaders. One can hardly escape concluding that what happened in the courtroom was significantly influenced by what was going on outside.

We live today in the aftermath of another dramatic episode —the effort of Pres. Franklin D. Roosevelt to alter the composition of the Supreme Court in 1937. The dominating view of constitutional obligation presented in Supreme Court decisions in the past two decades differs significantly from the view prevailing when the President put his plan before Congress. Without question, the change in orientation was brought to the Court mainly by new personnel appointed by Presidents Roosevelt, Truman, and Eisenhower after the great Court fight was over. But the change began before President Roosevelt had made his first appointment, in fact while his proposal for reconstituting the Court's membership was under scrutiny in Congress. On this, probably all students of recent constitutional history agree, and they equally agree that the first shift in the Court's position was due mainly to change in position by one or two judges. There is no doubt that Associate Justice Owen Roberts changed in his views as to how certain provisions of the Constitution should be interpreted and applied; students disagree as to whether the views of Chief Justice Hughes also changed. One of the most highly regarded students of judicial power, Alpheus T. Mason, refers to these two men as "Justices on the flying trapeze" and refers to their behavior as "the somersault of 1937." Their course of action is seen as "a skilfully executed campaign," as a "decision to retreat in the immediate skirmish in order to win in the more crucial battle for judicial supremacy." Mason adds:

> For those bent on scuttling the President's plan the Hughes and Roberts switch came in the nick of time. But the victory was not unmixed. To defeat the President's plan, the Justices had to backtrack, and Roosevelt never doubted that his own [quoting President Roosevelt] "clear-cut victory on the bench did more than anything else to bring about the defeat of the plan in the halls of Congress." Before a single judge retired, before any appointment was made "the Court began to interpret the Constitution instead of torturing it." [1]

Robert H. Jackson, attorney general and later associate justice of the Supreme Court and one of the managers of Roosevelt's campaign against the Supreme Court, describes the events of 1937 in language fully in keeping with the remarks of Professor Mason. In a book written immediately after those events, Jackson differentiated two aspects of controversy—the proposal to reorganize the Court and an "intellectual revolt" against the philosophy dominating the Court during the first years of the New Deal. The intellectual revolt, he said, enjoyed a victory as great as the defeat suffered by the reorganization proposal.

> This paradoxical outcome is accounted for by the recognition on the part of some Justices—belated but vigorous—of the validity of the complaints against their course of decision. They united with long-protesting Justices and proceeded to weaken the President's political assault by acknowledging and correcting his grievances. They confessed legal error and saved themselves from political humiliation. They subdued the rebellion against their constitutional dogma by joining it.[2]

[1] Alpheus T. Mason, *The Supreme Court from Taft to Warren* (Baton Rouge: Louisiana State University Press, 1958), pp. 109–115.

[2] Robert H. Jackson, *The Struggle for Judicial Supremacy* (New York: Alfred A. Knopf, 1941), p. vi.

II • CONSTITUTIONAL LANGUAGE AND JUDICIAL REVIEW

The preceding five chapters show that the recent and current displeasure with the Supreme Court is not unique in American experience and that the sullen, stubborn resentment of the Supreme Court's actions on segregation has rich precedent in all formative periods of American history.

The five chapters ahead explore the foundations of the Supreme Court's power to give the Constitution its authoritative interpretation and to force other branches of government to comply with the Constitution as the Court has interpreted it. Chapter VI examines the Constitution to see what provision it makes for interpretation and enforcement of its contents and gives a brief account of how judges acquired the authority to say finally what the Constitution requires, permits, and forbids. Chapter VII announces a thesis—that distrust of the Supreme Court and readiness to decry and resist its orders are nourished by doubt that its power to nullify legislation was rightfully acquired—and draws evidence supporting that thesis from the great debate of 1937 on the Supreme Court's role. This supplies good reason for examining once more the reasoning by which John Marshall established the practice of judicial review—the subject of chapters VIII and IX. Chapter X offers an explanation of why many people find Marshall's reasoning unconvincing and his conclusion unsound.

CHAPTER SIX

The Constitution Becomes Law

The effect of a constitution lies wholly in the fact that men and women order their conduct according to what they read in the document. A constitution has influence only as men take care to find out what is written in the document and then behave in keeping with what the constitution says. Three steps are involved: The content of the document must be attended to; it must be accorded respect. The content of the document must be interpreted; the meaning of its language must be fixed. The mandates of the document must be enforced; men must voluntarily comply with the language of the document or they must be induced or compelled to do so.

The first step presents no problem in the United States today. The Constitution of the United States commands enormous respect. Arguments are won by citing its contents. Its authority is taken for granted by people who have not the slightest notion of what it says. Problems abound, however, at the second and third steps—deciding what the Constitution requires, permits, and forbids and making sure that men live up to the obligations which the Constitution imposes on them.

1. A DOCUMENT TO INTERPRET

The Constitution is expressed in language which ranges from statements so precise as to be nearly indisputable, through ambiguity and vague generality, to failure to say anything where one may think a statement is clearly needed.

It will be seen that men who fix meanings for the language in the Constitution face a variety of challenges to their ingenuity.

The framers of the Constitution wrote: "The Senate of the United States shall be composed of two Senators from each State, chosen by the Legislature thereof, for six years; and each Senator shall have one vote." This sentence comes close to being a model of precision. "The Senate" and "the United States" are clearly identified elsewhere in the document. "States" and "legislatures" are discrete institutions familiar to people in all parts of the country and everywhere labeled by these two words. The key adjectives are from the vocabulary of mathematics, and all Americans turn up one, two, and six in the same order. There could be some argument about what constitutes a vote, but not much about what is a year, all parts of the nation having the same calendar. There is, however, one striking imprecision in the sentence that could become the focus of great controversy: "chosen by the Legislature." What is to constitute a choice by the legislators of a state—what constitutes a quorum for making a choice, and what percentage of all legislators must agree—may purposely have been left unsettled on the supposition that each state legislature ought to decide these questions for itself. Can we say the same for the larger question: Did the framers want the choice made by the legislators or by the lawmaking process? Where the governor has a veto on enactments by the legislature, can he veto the election of a senator? We do not know whether the men who wrote the Constitution wanted the choice made by the legislators only, by the procedure locally fixed for the enactment of legislation, or by any procedure satisfactory to a state legislature which enabled the legislators to participate in the election.

The Constitution says that full faith and credit shall be given in each state to the public acts, records, and judicial proceedings of every other state and that Congress may enact legislation designed to facilitate and secure this giving of faith and credit. The Constitution also says that fugitives from justice who are found in any state shall be delivered on demand of the executive of the state in which they are charged with crime and from which they have fled, but the Constitution does not, as in the case of extending full faith and credit, say that Congress may enact legislation designed to secure the surrendering of fugitives. Why is there no provision for national legislation on the latter aspect of interstate relations? These are possibilities: (1) The point was simply overlooked; there is no way of finding an intention because it never occurred to anyone in the framing convention or ratifying conventions to mention the matter. (2) There was general agreement that Congress should have the power, but nothing was said about it because of a common presumption that the grant of power to regulate commerce among the several states conferred power to enact legislation on this point. (3) There was agreement that Congress should be able to enact legislation, but inability to agree as to how much power should be conferred or how the grant of power should be hedged. (4) There was agreement that Congress should not be able to regulate the matter, and silence of the Constitution on this point was thought the best way of getting that result. (5) The framers of the Constitution, because of inability of some to make up their minds and inability of others to agree, could not decide whether Congress ought to have the power, so the issue was left open with the expectation that it would be settled later by amendment of the Constitution or by other means. Still other explanations of the silence of the Constitution on this matter can be imagined.

Some language that is furthest removed from precision will complete these illustrations of style in constitutional expression. Article I, Section 8, of the Constitution closes with the assertion that Congress shall have power "To make all laws which shall be necessary and proper for carrying into execution . . ." the powers vested by the Constitution in the government of the United States. "Necessary," standing alone, does not have the same meaning for any man as "proper," standing alone. Used together, any man may well ponder before deciding what meaning to attach to the pair. And the number of meanings increases by leaps and bounds as additional persons come into the discussion. Your view of what is necessary is not the same as mine; your view of what is proper is not the same as mine; and when you put "necessary" and "proper" together you arrive at a state of mind which differs even further from mine.

Finally, consider equal protection of the laws and due process of law. State and local governments are forbidden to deny to any person the equal protection of the laws. The uncertainty that clothes this instruction to states and local officials was noted in the opening chapter. It is now established that people need not be treated absolutely alike, or even in essentially the same way. Classifications may be made, and laws may apply differently to different classes. What classifications are proper and how the application of law among classes may vary—these are not specified in the Constitution.

What is proper, in each case, will be determined by the man who is in a position to make his interpretation of the Constitution stick.

So it is with the two statements in the Constitution which forbid any government to deprive any person of life, liberty, or property without due process of law. In specifying that government shall act by "due process of law," one constitution-maker may have meant to say that judges and juries shall continue to decide cases in keeping with their practice in deciding cases in the past. But "due process of law," in the mind of another constitution-maker, may mean that lawmakers shall not enact legislation which attempts to achieve objectives not sought in legislation of the past or that lawmakers shall not adopt ends or means which would be offensive to a mythical person that the constitution-maker has erected as his image of a reasonable man. A later chapter will give some impression of the range of meanings which have actually been cemented to the term "due process of law."

Surely, Abraham Baldwin, delegate from Georgia to the Constitutional Convention of 1787 and later a member of Congress, was guided by accurate observation and great wisdom when he spoke as follows to the House of Representatives in 1796:

> . . . [I]t was not to disparage the instrument, to say that it had not definitely, and with precision, absolutely settled everything on which it had spoke. He had sufficient evidence to satisfy his own mind that it was not supposed [to do so] by the makers of it at the time, but that some subjects were left a little ambiguous and uncertain. It was a great thing to get so many difficult subjects definitely settled at once. . . . The few that were left a little unsettled might, without any great risk, be settled by practice or by amendments in the progress of the Government. . . . When he reflected on the immense difficulties and dangers of that trying occasion—the old Government prostrated, and a chance whether a new one could be agreed on—the recollection recalled to him nothing but the most joyful sensations that so many things had been so well settled, and that experience had shown there was very little difficulty or danger in settling the rest.[1]

2. JUDICIAL SUPREMACY ESTABLISHED

The framers of the Constitution did not write into the document a procedure for fixing its meaning when men disagree about it. It is certain that the framers expected issues of interpretation

[1] Quoted in Farrand, *Records of the Federal Convention,* Vol. III, pp. 369–370 (cf. Bibliographic Note 3).

to arise. Several members of the Convention appear to have taken it for granted that federal and state judges would not enforce a statute or executive order which the judges believed in conflict with the Constitution. But it remains a fact that the most careful reading of the document will not turn up so much as a hint as to who should finally decide whether senators were to be elected (prior to the Seventeenth Amendment) by the state lawmaking authority or by the state legislature alone, who should finally decide whether Congress may enact legislation designed to facilitate the surrendering of fugitives from justice when the officials of a state are reluctant to deliver them, or who should finally decide whether any particular act of Congress is sufficiently necessary to be regarded as "necessary and proper" for executing a power vested in the national government.

We partially explored one aspect of this question of authoritative interpretation in Chapter III—the right to say finally how the Constitution allocates power between the national government and the states. We noted the turbulent years of state interposition and efforts to nullify acts of the national government, of defiance by state judges who denied the right of the Supreme Court to review their decisions as to where the boundaries of authority had been drawn. Both the political and judicial branches of state government were subjected sufficiently for us to say that the authority of the Supreme Court has been secure in this area of conflict since the Civil War. It will not oversimplify to say that the Court gained its dominance over state authorities for two reasons. First, there was a widespread popular conviction that one national government rather than several state governments ought to decide controversies about boundaries between national and state power. Second, there was language in the Constitution which could be read as an invitation to the Supreme Court to make these decisions. We noted above (Chapter III) that this conclusion could be reached only by a considerable leap of inference. A nation sensitive to the need for a single arbiter was willing to make the leap.

It was also a bold leap of inference which found in the Constitution authority for the Supreme Court to say finally what the Constitution permits Congress, the president, and national administrative officials to do in matters that do not involve distribution of authority between the national government and the states. The Constitution states (Article VI) that members of Congress and all executive and judicial officers of the United States shall be bound by oath or affirmation "to support this Constitution." It specifies further (Article II) that the president shall swear or affirm that he will, to the best of his ability, "preserve, protect and defend the Constitution of the United States." It describes the authority of the national courts in a long sentence (Article III) which begins with the statement that: "The judicial power shall extend to all cases, in law and equity, arising under this Constitution, the laws of the United States, and treaties made, or which shall be made, under their authority; . . ." And it makes this announcement in Article VI: "This Constitution, and the laws of the United States which shall be made in pursuance thereof, and all treaties, made, or which shall be made, under the authority of the United States, shall be the supreme law of the land; and the judges in every State shall be bound thereby, anything in the Constitution or laws of any State to the contrary notwithstanding."

It was noted above that the foregoing language does not tell us which of the three categories of supreme law—Constitution, laws (presumably statutes), or treaties—is the "supremest" law and therefore that state judges are not clearly instructed as to which of the three sources of law they are to enforce if mandates in Constitution, statute, and treaty seem to them contradictory. It must be added now that there is no clear instruction to the judge in the national court as to which source of law he shall enforce if he is confronted by irreconcilable contradictions. And, finally, a third quandary is unresolved by constitutional instruction. If Congress, president, and judges disagree as to whether, in any particular instance, there is irreconcilable conflict between Constitution, statute, and treaty, is each to say finally for himself or for his branch of the government what he is permitted to do, what he is required to do, what he is forbidden to do? Or does one branch of the government make a final pronouncement on the issue with consequent obligation of the other two branches to accept the decision and act in conformity?

It is not too crude an evaluation of events to say that it took us eighty years to find a solution to these issues about supremacy among sources of law and supremacy among rival interpreters of law. It was a tumultuous eighty years that culminated in the rebellion, bloodshed, and bowing to force that we call the Civil War. In the resolution of issues about supremacy in law and placement of authority among interpreters of law, the Supreme Court played a leading role.

We shall note some main steps by which the Supreme Court marched to its present pre-eminence in constitutional interpretation. But that account must be prefaced by a summary statement of the solution which the nation appears now to have accepted.

The Constitution of the United States is the "supremest" law of the land, and statutes and treaties of the United States, like the constitutions and laws of any state, are lawful only in so far as they conform to the Constitution. Whether law that is subsidiary to the Constitution conforms to the Constitution or conflicts with it is a question for the judges to decide when the question confronts them in litigation. When judges disagree on this question, the final say is by the nation's Supreme Court on proper appeal.

When any act of the national government (including statutes and treaties) or any act of a state or local government is brought into a court for enforcement, any party involved in the legal proceeding may raise the question whether the act is in keeping with the Constitution. If the judge concludes that the question was properly raised and that he must answer that question in order to know what law to apply in the case, he will decide whether the act is in keeping with the Constitution, and he will not enforce the act if he finds that it conflicts with the Constitution.

In this fashion, several acts of Congress, many state laws, and many acts of state and national officials have been declared invalid by the courts, and treaties also may presumably be declared invalid, though none appears to have been held invalid yet. All public officials, including congressmen, state legislators, and governors, are expected to know how the judges have ruled and to refrain from doing anything in the future which a court of high authority (especially the United States Supreme Court) has said the Constitution forbids. But, until a court of high authority has ruled on a point, each public official decides for himself what the Constitution permits, forbids, or requires him to do. Congressmen, the president, state legislators, and governors may or may not ask the advice of lawyers as to what the courts are likely to hold if their acts are challenged as unconstitutional; lesser officials may be required by law to obtain legal advice and act accordingly. And judges may, where injunction is a proper action to avoid anticipated injury, enjoin a public official not to enforce a statute which the judge believes contrary to the Constitution.

The procedure by which the courts invalidate the acts of other branches of the government because of conflict with the Constitution became known as "judicial review." It is now established as a regular feature of government in all of the states as well as the national government.

It took the country, I have said, eighty tumultuous years to settle the two great questions: which one of several sources of law is the supreme law, and which one of many interpreters of the law is final in disputes about what the law requires, permits, or forbids. A quick look at three great decisions of the Supreme Court will tell us a great deal about how the two questions got answered and how the Supreme Court, in helping supply the answers, pushed its way to primacy in constitutional interpretation. These three great decisions came in 1793, 1803, and 1857.

3. THREE LANDMARK DECISIONS

The first notable step of the Supreme Court in establishing the practice of judicial review occurred in 1793. President Washington addressed a letter to the members of the Court asking them to tell him what they understood to be the authority given him by the Constitution to decide certain questions involved in our neutrality toward a war then in progress in Europe. Chief Justice John Jay replied for the Court that it would not tender legal advice, that it would only decide cases which arose in the course of litigation. The Supreme Court and all other federal courts have followed this policy ever since. Some state courts, however, will give state legislatures and officials advisory opinions stating what the judges consider the proper interpretation of state and federal statutes and of state and federal constitutions.

Ten years after Jay sent his letter to Washington, the Supreme Court announced the second of these landmark decisions when it stated categorically that it would not enforce a statute which the judges believed contrary to the Constitution. The declaration was pronounced by Chief Justice John Marshall, speaking for all members of the Court in the famous case of *Marbury* v. *Madison* (1 Cranch 137, decided 1803). (The most significant parts of Marshall's opinion are cited in the Appendix.)

The occasion for speaking arose out of a suit instituted by William Marbury and others against James Madison, then secretary of state under Pres. Thomas Jefferson. Among the last statutes passed by Congress before Jefferson became president were three which reorganized the federal judiciary, providing for additional judges, attorneys, marshals, and forty-two justices of the peace for the District of Columbia. One of the last acts of Pres. John Adams had been to appoint good Federalists to these positions. These were the "midnight appointments."

These appointments were consummated by the delivery of a commission to each appointee. But the commissions prepared for the forty-two justices of the peace had not been delivered to them when President Adams and Secretary of State John Marshall left office. These undelivered commissions had been signed by Marshall; the seal of the United States had been fixed. But, wholly because of the carelessness of Marshall, it appears, the forty-two commissions were still on his desk on March 4, 1801, when Jefferson became president. Reports differ as to what happened thereafter. According to one account, Jefferson ordered twenty-five of the commissions delivered; seventeen others, including one for William Marbury, were held up. These seventeen documents were still on the desk of the secretary of state in May, when James Madison assumed the duties of that office. There they were to stay until, a contemporary quoted by Charles Warren speculated, "they were disposed of with the other waste paper and rubbish of the office."

Marbury and three other would-be justices decided to go to court. They concluded that petition for a writ of mandamus was their proper action. If issued, the writ would require Madison to show cause to the court for not delivering the commissions; if the court found that he had an obligation to do so, the writ would order Madison to deliver them to the men who brought the suit.

The next question for Marbury and his associates was in which court to file the petition? The Judiciary Act of 1789 provided that the Supreme Court should have authority to issue the writ of mandamus "in cases warranted by the principles and usages of law, to any courts appointed, or persons holding office, under the authority of the United States." This seemed to them to indicate that the Supreme Court had authority to entertain their case; they filed their petition in that court.

John Marshall, who had become chief justice while he was still acting as secretary of state and before he signed the commissions in dispute, delivered the opinion of the Court. The judges found, he said, that the men who had brought suit had a right to their commissions. Also, a writ of mandamus to the secretary of state was the proper remedy. Furthermore, they were right in thinking that the Judiciary Act named the Supreme Court as the proper place in which to institute the suit; that statute had been intended to give the Supreme Court original jurisdiction in suits for mandamus directed to an officer of the United States government. But, Marshall said, the statute was in conflict with the Constitution on the latter point. The Constitution states in Article III that the Supreme Court shall have original jurisdiction in two kinds of cases (those involving representatives of foreign nations and those to which a state may be a party); in all other cases which are proper for the federal courts, the Supreme Court is to have appellate jurisdiction. Therefore, Marshall concluded, the statute, having attempted to enlarge the Court's original jurisdiction beyond the provision in the Constitution, was in conflict with the Constitution.

Should the Court, then, follow the statute and accept jurisdiction? Or should it follow the Constitution and refuse to do what the statute would require? Is the Constitution law? If it is law, is it supreme over all other law? If it is the supreme law, is it supreme in the sense that the courts must apply it in place of other law which conflicts with it? Marshall concluded, speaking for the whole Court, that the Constitution is law, that it is binding on the courts as well as on other branches of the government, that the courts must be guided by their own understanding of what the Constitution requires, and that if they find any other law to be in conflict with the Constitution they must refuse to enforce that law.

Having found, on their own examination, that the Constitution limited the original jurisdiction of the Supreme Court to two kinds of questions, which did not include the kind of question brought before them by Marbury and his associates, the members of the Court concluded that they could not take jurisdiction in the case; the Judiciary Act having directed them to do something which the Constitution did not permit, they had to ignore the requirements of that statute.

The reasoning by which Marshall arrived at the two great conclusions which he announced must be read to be fully appreciated. Enough of his opinion is quoted below to make clear how he established, first, that the Constitution is law supreme over all other expressions of law in the United States and, second, that the Supreme Court judges are to be guided by their own interpretation of the Constitution and to ignore every other expression of law which they are unable to reconcile with their interpretation of the Constitution.

It can be argued, and some writers have made a great deal of this, that the Supreme Court judges did no more in *Marbury* v. *Madison* than declare a right to stand by the Constitution when a statute commands the Supreme Court to do something the Constitution *expressly forbids* the Supreme Court to do. According to this view, the Court did not, in *Marbury* v. *Madison,* announce that it would refuse to enforce an act in which the lawmakers violate a constitutional provision fixing limits on what the lawmakers may do.

If there was uncertainty whether the Court would enforce laws which the judges think in excess of legislative power, that uncertainty was brought to an end by the third of our landmark decisions, the Dred Scott case (*Scott* v. *Sanford,* 19 Howard 393). This decision, announced in 1857, was the first after *Marbury* v. *Madison* in which the Supreme Court declared an act of Congress in conflict with the Constitution, and the point of conflict was not confined to the structure and jurisdiction of the judicial branch or the integrity of the Court itself. In this case, the Supreme Court held, by a vote of seven against two, that the statute known as the Missouri Compromise—which ruled slavery unlawful in certain territories of the United States—deprived slave-owners of their property without due process of law. Since the Fifth Amendment to the Constitution stated that the national government should not deprive any person of his property without due process of law, the statute was held in violation of the Constitution, and the Court must view the slaves who were taken into the "free" territory as still slaves, despite what the statute said to the contrary. Eight of the nine judges wrote separate opinions to express personal views about the power of Congress and the president to, by enactment of law, forbid slavery, regulate the movement of slaves, and fix conditions of property ownership in territory not then admitted to the Union as a state. But Chief Justice Taney spoke for seven judges when he said, ". . . it is the opinion of the court that the act of Congress which prohibited a citizen from holding or owning property of this kind [a slave] in the territory of the United States north of the line therein mentioned, is not warranted by the Constitution, and is therefore void. . . ."

The significance of the Dred Scott case for establishment of judicial supremacy in constitutional interpretation is affected by a number of considerations relating to the jurisdiction of the lower federal court which heard the litigation in first instance. Students of constitutional law are agreed, nevertheless, that this decision finally established the point that the Supreme Court will not enforce any act of the other branches of government which the Court finds on its own inquiry to be in conflict with the Constitution. When the Supreme Court ruled that the statute which purported to liberate slaves in "free" territory was not effective as law, slave-owners were informed that state and federal courts alike, on proper suit, would order public officials to protect the slave-owner in his control over his slaves, subject to whatever the effective law of a state might say on that subject.

4. A NEW PLATEAU OF JUDICIAL POWER?

The three decisions we have just discussed established the right of the Supreme Court to fix the meaning of the Constitution in disputes that are settled by litigation. They fixed the rule that judges will refuse to enforce a statute when they find that it requires an action or imposes a regulation that the judges believe to be forbidden by the Constitution. This is what the power of judicial review had become on the eve of the Civil War, and this is how the power of judicial review was described up to 1954.

In the Segregation cases, the Supreme Court took a further step in its march toward primacy in the interpretation and enforcement of the Constitution. A little thought applied to the facts presented in the first chapter of this book will make it clear that those decisions had social consequences unprecedented in the landmark cases we have examined. The impact of the Segregation cases was not limited to the invalidation of a statute. Those decisions declared a way of life unlawful and ordered a revision of law and governmental practice. They stand as the fourth in a list of landmark cases which have lifted the Supreme Court to the high level of authority where it operates today.

Cooper v. *Aaron* (358 U.S. 1), decided in 1958, requires fuller reporting at this point. The significance of this case lies not in the decision which determined what order would be issued, but in a declaration which the judges made concerning the relation of the Supreme Court to other public officials and branches of government in fixing the meaning of the Constitution's language. In the opinion accompanying this decision, the Supreme Court made a series of statements which were intended—I do not see how there can be any doubt about the intent—to force this conclusion: What this Court says the Constitution means is exactly what the Constitution does mean, and all other public officials and branches of government, national and state, shall respect this Court's statements of what the Constitution means, no matter what other interpretation may seem to them to be clearly implied by the words of that document.

The suit in *Cooper* v. *Aaron* began as an application by school officials in Little Rock, Arkansas, for permission to suspend action on their plans for termination of segregation in the schools of that city. Plans of the school officials for desegregation had been approved by the federal district judge, but, when Negro children arrived on the school grounds, they were denied entrance to the school by the

Arkansas National Guard, acting on order of the governor. Subsequently, the state military force was withdrawn, and military contingents of the national government provided protection which enabled Negro children to mix with whites in the classroom. But the "chaos, bedlam, and turmoil" which reigned in Little Rock created such obstacles and hazards that the school officials, at the end of the first semester, requested the federal district judge to permit a suspension of the plans for integration and allow the Negro children to be assigned to all-Negro schools for a temporary period. The district court authorized suspension of the plans, but this order was reversed by the federal circuit court, and the case came to the Supreme Court for final determination.

The Supreme Court ordered reinstatement of the school board's plans, thus requiring that Negroes be readmitted to classrooms with whites at the opening of the next school term. Reviewing events in Little Rock, the Supreme Court justices said in their opinion that the tumultuous conditions "are directly traceable to the actions of legislators and executive officials of the State of Arkansas, taken in their official capacities, which reflect their own determination to resist this Court's decision in the *Brown* case. . . ." After explaining their decision to order reinstatement, the justices turned their attention to the assumptions of the governor and legislature of Arkansas "that they are not bound by our holding in the *Brown* case." Quoting the language of Marshall in *Marbury* v. *Madison,* the Court said:

> This decision declared the basic principle that the federal judiciary is supreme in the exposition of the law of the Constitution, and that principle has ever since been respected by this Court and the Country as a permanent and indispensable feature of our constitutional system. It follows that the interpretation of the Fourteenth Amendment enunciated by this Court in the *Brown* case is the supreme law of the land, and Art. VI of the Constitution makes it of binding effect on the States "any Thing in the Constitution or Laws of any State to the Contrary notwithstanding." (P. 18.)

The remainder of the opinion is expressed in language which indicates that the judges regarded their statement as to what the Constitution means to be identical with the words of the Constitution itself in capacity to impose obligation on the rest of the nation.

The claim of *Cooper* v. *Aaron* to stand in importance with the other three landmark cases we have examined turns on one's evaluation of earlier pronouncements and actions. The opinion in *Marbury* v. *Madison* did not say that the federal judiciary has authority superior to that of the other branches of the government in deciding what the Constitution requires, permits, or forbids. Edward S. Corwin, writing in 1938, stated that he could find nowhere in all the decisions and opinions of the Supreme Court a statement to that effect. I do not find a firm statement to that effect between the time Professor Corwin terminated his search and the assertion in *Cooper* v. *Aaron*. Whatever a proper reading of the precedents may be, we do now have a firm pronouncement of the Supreme Court that it is above all other officials and branches of government in exposition of the Constitution.

CHAPTER SEVEN

The Great Trial of 1937

1. JUDICIAL REVIEW—
   CONFERRED OR USURPED?
2. "THE SOUND RULE . . . HAS
   BEEN CAST ASIDE"
3. DOUBTS HAVE
   CONSEQUENCES

The American people have put their blessing on the power of judges to declare laws unconstitutional and therefore unenforceable. But history shows that popular acceptance of the practice has been less than universal and that the process of legitimation has not yet run its course. The people have reserved the right to scream in anger, to denounce the judges as pawns in the hands of a part of the population, and to attempt by legislation or other means to hobble the Court so it cannot again dispense the same injury.

Some of the criticism which is heaped on the Supreme Court is limited to the wisdom of a decision. The right of the judges to decide as they did is not questioned; the critic asserts only that the judges did not understand what they were doing or displayed a social bias or opened themselves to some other charge of poor judgment. Criticism stemming from this base must always be expected and endured in a democratic nation. But many people take a different view of criticism which asserts that a high public official performs acts which he has no authority to perform at all or, having limited authority to act, goes beyond the bounds of the power given him. Criticism coming from responsible people which alleges lack or abuse of power calls for an investigation. If the criticism is sustained, the official should either be brought back onto his legal reservation or the scope of his authority should be enlarged.

The bitter attack on the Supreme Court which has marked so

much of our history has frequently included allegations that the Supreme Court itself violates the Constitution which it forces the other branches of government to obey. Prominent in this general charge is a contention that the power of judicial review was usurped by the judges. This is too restrictive a view of judicial authority for some other severe critics of the Supreme Court. They do not charge usurpation of power. They hold that the judges have been empowered to interpret and enforce the Constitution, but they contend that the power granted does not cover all that the judges have done. According to the latter group of critics, the judges have converted the occasion to interpret the Constitution into an opportunity to change its meaning and have transformed their power to nullify statutes into a power to pronounce and enforce public policies that ought to be fixed only by the elected lawmaking body.

Charges of lack of power and abuse of power have been directed at the Supreme Court throughout our history by thoughtful students of history and political institutions and by political leaders who enjoyed high prestige. These charges have been persuasive with great numbers of the population. They are entitled to a fair examination in this book. We shall, in this chapter, observe the charges as they emerged in one crisis situation—the effort to reconstitute the Supreme Court in 1937. This will prepare us for an inquiry into the dispute whether the power of judicial review was conferred by language adopted in 1787 or was usurped by the judges and for an evaluation of charges that the Supreme Court, by committing the nation to policies not implicit in the Constitution, has invaded the realm assigned to the lawmaking authorities.

1. JUDICIAL REVIEW—CONFERRED OF USURPED?

President Roosevelt's proposal to enlarge the membership of the Supreme Court was laid before Congress on February 5, 1937. The vote which decisively rejected it occurred in the Senate on July 22, 1937. Between those dates the Senate thoroughly examined the President's recommendations. The Senate Committee on the Judiciary conducted hearings which filled more than 2,000 pages. Senators praised and deplored the President's objectives and applauded and denounced the means by which he sought to achieve his objectives. Although the bill to reorganize the judiciary was not advanced to debate in the House of Representatives, members of that chamber made their judgments known in radio addresses and other speeches which, along with statements by people outside Congress, were crowded into *The Congressional Record.* An examination of the hearings and report of the Senate committee and of *The Congressional Record* during the period the President's bill was alive reveals that the following positions concerning the legitimacy of judicial review were taken.[1]

A. *Silence on the question of how the courts got their power of judicial review.*

Most of the men who spoke or wrote about the President's proposal, whether for or against it, said nothing about how the courts got their power to declare laws unconstitutional. It seems likely that nearly all of them supposed the power to have been conferred by the Constitution and saw no reason to mention it; it is possible that some believed the power had been usurped and thought it not good politics to say so.

B. *Positive statement that the power of judicial review was vested in the courts by the Constitution.*

This position came out in statements that the power to nullify national and state laws was undisputably provided by articles III and VI, that it was clearly implied by the character and content of the Constitution as a whole, that statements made by the framers show this to have been their intention, or that the framers took the power of judicial review for granted and left John Marshall the shallow honor of announcing the obvious. This group includes both proponents and opponents of the President's proposal. Some who boldly attacked the Supreme Court stated emphatically that judicial review is essential to our constitutional system. They insisted that the Supreme Court had abused this power in recent years, and they supported the President's effort to bring the Court back to its proper role by adding new members.

C. *Contention that the power of judicial review was usurped.*

My reading of *The Congressional Record* and the hearings and report of the Senate committee identified twelve men who declared unequivocally that the power of judicial review, at least as respects national legislation, was seized by the Supreme Court and not given to it. Two other statements, less precisely formulated on this point, seem to me to represent the same view. The fourteen statements came from three senators, four members and one former member of the House of Representatives, two judges in state courts,

[1] The hearings and the committee report are cited in Bibliographic Note 6. Debate in the Senate is reported in *Congressional Record,* Vol. 81, mainly in parts 2 and 3. Parts 9 and 10 of Volume 81 (the Appendix) contain statements not made on the floor of Senate or House.

three other lawyers, and one professor of political science. Thirteen of these fourteen endorsed the bill to enlarge the membership of the Supreme Court; the other statement was published before the President made his proposal and was read into *The Congressional Record* by a member of the House of Representatives. The fourteen men came from all parts of the country, residing in eleven states as widely scattered as New Jersey, Wisconsin, Tennessee, Texas, and California.

All I can say about these men as a group is that every one of them said that the Constitution did not provide for judicial review. Each contended that the courts got the power to nullify legislation because the Supreme Court, in 1803, seized that power without constitutional authorization. In view of what they expressly stated, it seems probable that some of these men, if questioned, would have said that the practice of judicial review has proven more harmful than helpful to the nation and ought to be terminated. Not all of the fourteen were of that opinion. At least one of the group, Sen. Kenneth McKellar (D., Tenn.) expressly stated that more than a century of acquiescence in judicial review had given that practice a constitutional foundation which the framers had denied it, and he implied, if he did not expressly say, that judicial determination of constitutionality was a valuable feature of our constitutional system, provided that the judges showed a proper restraint in the exercise of their power. My guess is that Senator McKellar spoke for several in the group of fourteen when he said the following in answer to another senator:

> I have already said, as the Senator would have heard had he been listening, that early in our constitutional history our Supreme Court assumed the power to declare void and invalid acts of Congress. It did not have the specific right to do it under the Constitution. There was no provision under the Constitution which authorized the Court to do it, but the Court assumed such power. That practice has been going on for 134 years and, in my judgment, it is imbedded in our Constitution just as if we had passed an amendment to the Constitution in the ordinary way making such provision. The Congress did not initiate such an amendment to the Constitution. The Supreme Court of the United States simply amended the Constitution by judicial dictum first and then decision. . . . The Constitution itself did not give that power to the Supreme Court specifically. In my judgment it ought to have done so. . . . If it had done so, and had hedged the power about with proper checks and balances, it would have been far better.[2]

[2] *Ibid.*, Feb. 17, 1937, p. 1286.

How shall we interpret this evidence of personal convictions drawn from the great debate of 1937? The clamor of fourteen men seems not very impressive when the literate population is as sharply divided as was the case when Roosevelt laid his proposal before the country. Should we dismiss their contentions as a tactical move for political advantage, obvious as such to the nation and therefore of no effect on the prestige of the Court or the outcome of the effort to control it? Some occurrences now to be noted indicate that the most extreme position which was taken by any of the critics of the Court in 1937 had a significance not suggested by the count of fourteen heads. Consider these items:

• Several who participated in the 1937 debate—on the floors of Congress, before the Senate committee, on radio, and in other forums that led to printing in *The Congressional Record*—referred to current charges that the power of judicial review had been usurped by the Supreme Court and replied to those charges with extended efforts to prove that judicial review was founded in the Constitution itself. In the Senate hearings, a professor of political science devoted nine pages of testimony to review of evidence in which he found proof that power to nullify legislation on constitutional grounds was intended by the framers and provided in language written into the Constitution. A Detroit attorney directed his whole presentation to American experience with an independent judiciary and proof that judicial review was established by the Constitution. Sen. Royal S. Copeland (R., N. Y.) while the hearings were in progress delivered a public address in which he went back to the debates of 1787 and found proof that judicial review was part of the fundamental constitutional design. A few weeks after the hearings ended, a member of the House put into *The Congressional Record* a memorandum in which a professor of social sciences, without taking sides, carefully inquired into the establishment of judicial review in this country.

• In the hearings of the Senate Committee on the Judiciary, senators for and against the President's proposal repeatedly turned the attention of witnesses to the question of how the Supreme Court acquired its power to declare statutes invalid. The most notable instance of this was the questioning of Edward S. Corwin, a distinguished student of the origins and the practice of judicial review. Senators in opposition to the President's court plan tried hard to get Professor Corwin to say unequivocally that, in his judgment, judicial review was intended by the framers and specifically provided for in the Constitution. They had to get along with a stubborn reiteration that the evidence as to intention was inconclusive and that the words of the Constitution seemed not well chosen for an indisputable placement of authority to say finally what the Constitution permits, forbids, and requires.

• The Senate committee decided that, at the close of the hearings, proponents and opponents of the President's bill could each file up to ten additional documents supporting their side of the argument. The first statement filed by the President's supporters was a letter by a lawyer in Clarksdale, Mississippi, which first declared and then sought to prove that the case against the President's plan rested on three fallacious suppositions. The first fallacy, he said, was a supposition either "that the Constitution has given to the Supreme Court jurisdiction to declare acts of Congress void as being unconstitutional, or that the Supreme Court has assumed that jurisdiction for such a length of time that it has become a rule of law, acquiesced in by all." After indicating two other fallacies underlying opposition to the President's proposal, he said: "As the Constitution is now written and by every construction thereof, whether 'adaptive' or 'historical,' the Congress of the United States is and was intended to be by the framers of the Constitution supreme master of the other two departments of government, and if Congress so desires, there is no appeal from its decisions except to the people for a constitutional amendment or by force."

The opponents of the President's bill filed as one of their ten statements a document prepared by the American Bar Association consisting of forty-four exhibits and a summary of the points made in these exhibits. Exhibit Five reviewed the testimony of Professor Corwin and argued that the available evidence should have convinced the professor that the Constitution without question did authorize the courts to fix the meaning of the Constitution and enforce that meaning by invalidating statutes when necessary. Exhibit Twenty was a studied effort to remove that question from further controversy. It did not dismiss as a crackpot proposition the contention of the fourteen men that judicial review was established by an act of aggression in 1803. Instead, it dignified their arguments by answering them in a scholarly essay that arrayed the relevant evidence and argued that the nation was presented with judicial review in 1787 when it was handed a new Constitution.

• The report of the Senate committee which conducted the hearings, signed by ten of the eighteen members, includes a full-page consideration of the source of the Supreme Court's power.[3] This discussion opens: "The assertion has been indiscriminately made that the Court has arrogated to itself the right to declare acts of Congress invalid. The contention will not stand against investigation or reason." Examining the evidence, debates in the Convention of 1787, and language in the Constitution, the committee concluded: "But, while carefully refraining from giving the Court power to share in making laws, the Convention did give it judicial power to construe the Constitution in litigated cases." A citizen "has a right to demand that Congress shall not pass any act in violation of that instrument, and if Congress does pass such an act, he has the right to seek refuge in the courts and to expect the Supreme Court to strike down the act if it does in fact violate the Constitution. A written constitution would be valueless if it were otherwise." And, at another place: "The right and duty of the Court to construe the Constitution is thus made clear."

2. "THE SOUND RULE . . . HAS BEEN CAST ASIDE"

Doubt about the constitutional basis for judicial review abets attack on the Supreme Court, but it is not a necessary condition of such attack. I have said that some of the men who took a front-line position against the Court in 1937 emphatically endorsed judicial power to declare laws invalid. Their complaint was, not that the judiciary had stolen a power which the nation had not given it, but that the men who then served on the Supreme Court had exercised an authorized power in a wrongful manner. In litigation involving New Deal legislation, judges had not confined their vetoes to statutes which, by a fair reading of the two documents, were demonstrably in violation of the Constitution; rather, a majority of the Supreme Court judges, and other judges following their lead, had declared statutes unenforceable simply because the judges thought they put greater burdens on people than they ought to be required to bear. This was the central charge against the Supreme Court in 1937—that the judges had converted their rightful power to say authoritatively what the Constitution forbids into a license to deny enforcement of any act of government they personally thought unwise.

Roosevelt stated his cause of complaint as precisely and as

[3] All quotations are from pp. 17–18 of Senate Report No. 711, 75th Congress, 1st Session.

succinctly as anyone could ask. Speaking to the nation by radio a month after he laid his reorganization bill before Congress, the President said:

> In the last four years the sound rule of giving statutes the benefit of all reasonable doubt has been cast aside. The Court has been acting not as a judicial body, but as a policy making body. . . .
>
> The Court in addition to the proper use of its judicial functions has improperly set itself up as a third House of Congress—a super-legislature, as one of the Justices has called it—reading into the Constitution words and implications which are not there, and which never were intended to be there.[4]

I know no reason to doubt that Roosevelt considered judicial review (when exercised in a way he thought proper) essential to our constitutional system and supposed it to have been authorized when the Constitution was adopted. Certainly, Sen. Carl A. Hatch (D., N. M.) was of that view. He signed the report of the Judiciary Committee and thereby endorsed a statement that the Constitution, in language that "was never more clear," authorized the Supreme Court to strike down an act of government "if it does in fact violate the Constitution." He opposed the President's bill in debate, condemning it as an assault on the independent status which judges must have in order to carry out their historic function of holding the other branches of government within their constitutional limits. Yet, Senator Hatch charged the Supreme Court judges with abuse of power in language as emphatic as that which the President had used.

> Mr. President, I am in agreement with much that has been said here today about the usurpation of legislative power by the judicial branch of the Government. I believe that the courts of the land throughout a long period of our history have constantly usurped legislative powers and have rendered policy-making decisions, which is something the courts have no right to do. I concede that to be true, and I concede that the Supreme Court has gone further than that. Not only has the Court, in my opinion, invaded the legislative power but in instances it has amended the Constitution of the United States. The Supreme Court of the Nation has usurped the powers reserved to the people of America. I believe that to be a fact.[5]

"Throughout a long period of our history . . . constantly usurped legislative powers" is strong language, and it may be that

[4] *Congressional Record,* 81 (1937), 469–471; reprinted in Commager, *Documents of American History,* No. 515 (cf. Bibliographic Note 4).

[5] *Ibid.,* p. 6798

no critic of the Supreme Court would seriously contend that usurpation had been constant even for a brief period. But it is undeniably a fact that the charge made by Roosevelt and Hatch has been made time and time again over many decades by men who at the time were prominent in political leadership or respected for scholarly study.

I may say now, even if it repeats what has been made clear before, that acts of the Supreme Court have been decried because men of prominence, usually speaking for substantial sectors of the population, believed that the high tribunal had issued orders and announced courses of action not warranted by a proper reading of Constitution or statute. If one strongly believes that a court has strained, distorted, or emasculated a statute, he is entitled to conclude that the court has entered an area assigned to the lawmaking authority. If one strongly believes that a court has given the Constitution an insupportable meaning, nullified one of its provisions, or made the Constitution authority for requirements and prohibitions which have no reference point in the language put into that document originally or by amendments—in that case the astounded observer is entitled to conclude that the court has assumed a role which the Constitution assigned to others in its provision for an amending process. Documents that record our history are sprinkled with declarations that these conclusions did, indeed, lie behind the recurrent attack on the Supreme Court.

3. DOUBTS HAVE CONSEQUENCES

There is a mood in much of the contemporary writing on constitutional law which is antagonistic to further inquiry into the origins of judicial review. Stated bluntly, the position seems to be this. Attacks on judicial power should be viewed only as expressions of repugnance for the consequences of a particular decision. Recurring charges that judges have usurped or abused power have exactly the same significance as recurring charges that Congress and the president, by enactment of statutes, have encroached on the reserved powers of the states. No thoughtful person supposes that criticism of a statute and denunciation of the lawmakers manifest a doubt that the Constitution gave Congress and the president power to make laws; nor will a thoughtful person construe criticism of the Supreme Court as evidence of an honest doubt that practice over time has incorporated the power of judicial review into the constitutional foundations. The loud declaration of a political leader that the Supreme Court ignored the Constitution or willfully violated the Constitution is a display of bad faith and an effort to deceive. What has in fact happened is that men were infuriated by a judicial decision that toppled their interests or frustrated their plans; they fought back with charges of usurpation or abuse only because these seemed to be their most effective weapons of defense.

From these suppositions of fact, if I read certain contemporary writers correctly, emerge these conclusions. The power of judges to invalidate legislation is legitimate today; no good, and possibly much harm, comes of assertions that the practice had an illegitimate birth. Experience has proven that a judicial check on legislative innovation is essential to the national well-being; the lid of history ought not be lifted if what one sees destroys public appreciation of the value of an institution.

I proceed, in this book, from a different view of the facts and different assumptions about the social significance of what I suppose to be the facts. A minimum confidence in the nation's scholarship requires one to suppose that, with few exceptions indeed, the books and articles that bear evidences of investigation and thought bespeak a worthy purpose on the part of the author. Our scholarly writing demonstrates that a significant number of careful and thoughtful analysts came to the end of their inquiries either uncertain that judicial review was intended by the Constitution's makers or convinced that it was not intended. The political speech is not entitled to the same presumption of scholarly integrity. The nation has licensed its political leaders to campaign for undisclosed goals, to be selective in choice of evidence, to exaggerate in the announcement of conclusions. The political leader may, indeed, charge a court with usurpation or abuse of power when his conviction can honestly support only an admission that the court did not see things his way. But unworthy purpose or motive does not strip a statement of social significance. The most extravagant attacks on judicial power merit serious investigation if there is reason to believe that they significantly affect public confidence in the judicial process.

My reading of the evidence convinces me that there has been, throughout our history as a nation and continuing today, a significant social doubt that power to overrule acts of Congress was conferred on the courts by the Constitution. Of equal if not greater significance is a persisting supposition that the Supreme Court, even if authorized to nullify legislation, has repeatedly exceeded its authority in doing so. I find this evidence, of course, in the nearly continuous combat that engaged the Supreme Court before the Civil War, in the debate of 1937 reported in this chapter, and in writing, speech-making, and formal resolutions which erupted in response to the Segregation decisions of 1954.

The social significance of a doubt, supposition, or conviction is not adequately measured by the number of persons who express it. Proof of significance is also found in the behavior of those who respond to the expression. Whatever be the reason for waging war on the Court, the number of combatants and the vigor with which they fight is affected by assurances that they fight in the public interest and not for personal advantage. It must be the case that many who are reluctant to attack a tribunal they have many times praised are emboldened to do so when they learn that a man who might be expected to know has questioned whether the Court holds a license that authorizes its actions.

By such reasoning, I conclude that doubts about the scope of judicial authority bear fruit in disrespect for judges and demands for limitation of judicial power. Believing this, I think it necessary to examine with some care the roots of judicial review in constitutional language and in the circumstances of its appearance in practice. We shall do this, not to prove that the power is founded in the Constitution and not even to reach a scholar's conclusion as to what the evidence most strongly purports. We shall examine the evidence in order to see whether men may reasonably doubt, and to inspect the grounds for doubting, that the power of judges to nullify statutes was vested in them by the Constitution.

CHAPTER EIGHT

How Firm a Foundation?

Marshall's opinion in *Marbury* v. *Madison* stands today as the main intellectual support for judicial determination of constitutionality. His reasoning charted that leap of inference which placed on judicial review the blessings of the men who wrote the Constitution. Alexander Hamilton traced out this connection between Court and Constitution a decade earlier in one of his *Federalist* essays, and there are scholars who contend that Hamilton did a better job of reasoning than Marshall. Beveridge says that all the reasons Marshall gave in support of judicial review in his Marbury opinion were uttered on the floors of Congress while Marbury's case was before the Court. Accepting these judgments about lack of originality on the part of Marshall, it must be admitted that Marshall's essay in *Marbury* v. *Madison* became, for the American people, the authentic justification of judicial power to interpret and enforce the Constitution.

1. A THESIS AND ITS PROOF

The argument by which Marshall justified the Supreme Court's decision in *Marbury* v. *Madison* is expressed in language readily comprehended by the layman. Every step which he took in marching from the question before him to the grand conclusion, in so far as he reported them, is recorded in the parts of his opinion printed in the Appendix. It seems to me that his line of march is clearly presented in the four sentences which follow.

> A. Courts are required to determine which provisions of law are applicable to the issues presented to them in litigation.
>
> B. When expressions of law applicable to a case before it are in conflict, the court will enforce the provision which is superior in authority.
>
> C. The Constitution is the highest law of the land and superior to conflicting expressions of law not in the Constitution.
>
> D. Conclusion: If the court finds that a provision of a statute is incompatible with language in the Constitution, the court will apply the provision of the Constitution and not the provision of the statute to the case before it.

Recurrent challenge of Marshall's reasoning centers on the relation of the third statement to the two which precede it. The trouble arises from ambiguity in use of the word "law."

Marshall did not say how he arrived at the view of judicial authority announced in sentences "A" and "B." We take it for granted that he found support for them in long-established practice in Britain and America. It is undeniable that judges did determine the applicability of law and the relative authority of conflicting expressions of law. Judges sometimes spoke of the law of God, and they frequently spoke of a law of nature. And frequently, if not nearly always, they characterized the law of God and the law of nature as superior to law announced by legislative bodies. But English judges did not pronounce acts of Parliament invalid and refuse to enforce them when the act could not be reconciled with the revealed will of God or the rules which the judge believed to be expressed in a law of nature. If Marshall understood that judges on the North American continent had on one or more occasions refused to enforce a colonial ordinance or state statute because the judge thought it incompatible with a law of God or nature, he must have recognized that this was indeed a rarity. It may be that some judges were ready enough to stretch or twist the meaning of a statute to make it accord with the law of God or nature; the cases were few, if indeed there were any, in which a statute was declared unenforceable for this reason.

If I am right on the facts about this, it follows that judges did not always enforce the law they spoke of as "superior" and refuse to enforce the conflicting law they spoke of as "inferior." Judges in

Britain and America differentiated law as to essential character, or quality. The laws of God and the laws of nature we may label "admonitory law." Those that emanate from legislative assemblies we may label "effective law." The admonitory law established norms which men said ought to guide the formulation and interpretation of effective law. Admonitory law was, in that sense, superior to effective law. But, if the language found in the effective law could not be reconciled with the norms found in the admonitory law, the effective law was none the less enforced.

To make Marshall's statements accord with historic judicial practice, therefore, one must insert the word "effective" in front of the word "law" in sentences "A" and "B." So modified, the two statements tell us that, in disposing of litigation, judges determine the applicability of expressions of effective law and the relative authority of conflicting expressions of effective law. To sustain the march from this point to the conclusion in Sentence "D," one must make the third sentence read: "The Constitution is the highest effective law of the land. . . ." Presuming that Marshall would have agreed with my differentiation of two kinds of law, admonitory and effective, we may be sure that he would have said that the Constitution is the highest effective law of the land. Believing that, he could logically proceed to his conclusion in Sentence "D." Precisely there, on the point that the Constitution is effective law, is where his critics part company with Marshall.

Marshall filed only two exhibits to support his contentions that the Constitution is law and that it is the highest law of the land: the intentions of men who had framed written constitutions and certain expressions in the United States Constitution.

It is a striking fact that Marshall offered, first, an appeal to generalized experience and turned secondly to the content of the document he was reading. *First,* "all those who have framed written constitutions contemplate them as forming the fundamental and paramount law of the nation"; and, *second,* "the peculiar expressions of the constitution of the United States furnish addiional arguments." Surely, one has to believe that Marshall considered the general history of government more persuasive than the words of the Constitution itself for determination of the legal character of the latter document, for he closed his argument with a statement that the language of the Constitution "confirms and strengthens" the principle which he found embodied in more generalized practice.

One must also believe that Marshall would have preferred to rest his conclusion on the plain meaning of plain words in the Constitution if such language, supporting his conclusion, could be found in that document. Unable to stand on the content of the Constitution, his next resort, one must suppose, would have been the declared intentions of the men who framed and adopted that document, if conclusive evidence of their intent could be found. Only if these two resources failed would he make his principal stand on the history of purpose incorporated in written constitutions.

2. THE PROOF QUESTIONED

In order to appreciate why Marshall constructed his argument as he did and in order to evaluate the position of students who contend that Marshall's opinion did not provide a sound intellectual base for judicial review, we must go back over the ground that Marshall presumably traversed. A few paragraphs will suffice for his recourse to the content of the Constitution and the intentions of the framers. We shall devote a full chapter to review of the general experience with written constitutions which Marshall appears to have found convincing.

It is common for writers describing our constitutional system to found the power of judicial review squarely on the description of judicial power in Article III, Section 2, of the Constitution and on the specification of the supreme law of the land in Article VI.

Marshall referred to Article VI, but I think that what he said about it may properly be viewed as a denial that it furnished any significant support for a judicial power to fix the meaning of the Constitution. "It is also not entirely unworthy of observation, that in declaring what shall be the supreme law of the land, the constitution is first mentioned. . . ." Does this mean worth a little but not worth much? Not worth much, perhaps, because, if the document, reversing the order of listing, had said that national treaties, national laws, and the Constitution of the United States shall be the supreme law of the land, one could well assert: "It is not entirely unworthy of observation, that, in declaring what shall be the supreme law of the land, the Constitution is mentioned last"—the final source of law in a hierarchy of sources.

Much more noteworthy than his little point about the order of the words in Article VI is Marshall's failure to mention the remainder of the same sentence, which says that "the judges in every State shall be bound thereby [by the Constitution, laws, and treaties of the United States], anything in the Constitution or laws of any State to the contrary notwithstanding." More than a few writers on our constitutional system have viewed this reference to obligation of state judges as clinching their argument that judicial review was intended by the framers of the Constitution. The statement that state judges are bound by Constitution, laws, and treaties is regarded as proof that the Constitution was intended to be effective law, interpreted and enforced in court just as laws and treaties have been enforced in court for centuries. According to this view, the fact that state judges are mentioned and national judges are not means only this: the framers felt the need of an explicit declaration that the Constitution and lawful expressions of the new national government are law superior to all the law of a member state; they did not need to say that national judges, like state judges, "are bound thereby," because they had already said in Article III that the judges of the United States have the historic power of a court of law or equity in all cases arising under the Constitution, national laws, and treaties of the national government.

Why did Marshall not make capital of this line of reasoning? We cannot believe his failure to do so was the result of oversight. We must believe he considered the point and rejected it. He did not reject it because he felt he needed no further support for his main contention; if that were his state of mind, he would not have made his little point about the order in which Constitution, laws, and treaties were listed. I think we are forced to conclude that Marshall thought the line of argument I traced in the preceding paragraph an unsound one. If he did think of this line of reasoning and rejected it, or thought of and rejected other lines of reasoning which make Article VI a positive support for judicial review, we do not know what considerations account for the rejection. For those who distrust judicial power and seek weaknesses in Marshall's argument in support of it, this bit of ignorance about Marshall's state of mind is unimportant. It is enough for them to be able to say: Marshall did not find in Article VI any positive support for a power of judicial review; we are obliged to conclude that he believed Article VI provided no such support.

Marshall thought Article VI of the Constitution not entirely unworthy of mention; he found in Article III positive support for a power of judicial review. Article III, Section 2, opens: "The judicial power shall extend to all cases, in law and equity, arising under this Constitution, the laws of the United States, and treaties made, or which shall be made, under their authority. . . ." This can be construed as nothing more than a specification of jurisdiction. A declaration that the circuit courts of Indiana shall have jurisdiction of probate matters says nothing about what is the law of probate; it says only that probate causes may be tried in circuit courts and that when they arise the judge shall proceed in their settlement in accord with whatever he finds to be the law of Indiana on that subject. Marshall, reading this statement about judicial power in connection with other statements in the Constitution, concluded that the framers had done more than specify the jurisdiction of the national courts. He thought it certain that, if judges of the United States were expected to decide cases arising under the Constitution, they were expected to look into the Constitution to see whether it gave them any guide as to how those cases were to be decided. He looked into the Constitution and found that it did contain guides for decision—provisions in the language customarily adopted to announce rules of law enforceable in courts. He cited three such provisions in his opinion: one forbidding the national government to lay a tax or duty on goods exported from a state; one forbidding the enactment of bills of attainder and ex post facto laws; and one specifying certain conditions which must exist in order for a court to pronounce a conviction of treason. "Here the language of the constitution is addressed especially to the courts," he said, speaking directly of the provision concerning trial for treason. "It prescribes, directly for them, a rule of evidence not to be departed from."

Lawyers of considerable renown have disagreed as to the most reasonable construction of the statement in Article III, some contending that it does nothing but specify a range of jurisdiction, others agreeing with Marshall that it clearly implies that the content of the Constitution is law which shall be applied in cases arising in national courts. This division of respected professional judgment gives comfort to those who wish to avoid a conclusion that the Constitution recognizes a power of judicial review. Comfort expands into assurance when the skeptic decides that Marshall did not think much of his own argument. Marshall certainly invited such a conclusion, for he placed the power of judicial review first on expectations commonly associated with written constitutions and, only after completing the case for judicial review on that ground, on the fact that "the peculiar expressions of the Constitution of the United States furnish additional arguments."

If, as seems an irresistible conclusion, Marshall was convinced that language in the Constitution did not establish a power of judicial review beyond need for further evidence, one would expect him to inquire next into the announced purposes of those who constructed that document. He gives us no report on the results of that inquiry. Neither in the Marbury opinion nor elsewhere does he tell us what was said about interpretation and enforcement of the Constitution in the Philadelphia convention or in the several state ratifying conventions. The journals of the drafting convention and the notes made by several members of that body on which we rely so heavily today had not been printed at the time of *Marbury* v. *Madison*. But Marshall may well have had access to much of this knowledge by word of mouth, and it is possible that he obtained by that route a great deal more knowledge about the intentions of the framers than has been available to later scholars. He certainly knew what was said in the Virginia ratifying convention about the fundamental character of the Constitution and about judicial power under the Constitution, for he was himself a member of that assembly.

Why, then, did Marshall make no reference to what was said in these constituent assemblies or to what members of these assemblies said about the nature of the Constitution and of judicial power during the years between 1787 and 1803? Most of the men who shared in making the Constitution were alive in 1803. No matter what Marshall might have reported as their collective purpose, his statement would have been open to challenge and refutation by a great number of men who participated in the framing and ratification. If he rested the case for judicial power on evidence which could be rebutted by men who stood to know as much or more than he about what the constitution-makers had intended, he took a chance that resort to this evidence would weaken the case for judicial review, no matter how strongly Marshall believed that evidence to run in his favor. Can this consideration alone account for Marshall's complete silence about the intentions of the men who wrote the Constitution and the men who voted for its approval or rejection? Or ought we to suppose that Marshall examined the statements of these men and concluded that they canceled out, that the evidence that some of them wanted the courts to interpret and enforce the Constitution was equalled by evidence that others wanted the courts to have no such power? Or even—could it be?—that Marshall examined the evidence, found that it ran heavily aginst a power of judicial review, and kept a discreet silence about what his investigation disclosed?

It would be interesting to know which of these considerations or what other considerations accounted for Marshall's failure to discuss the intentions of the men who made the Constitution. We do not need to know why he was silent, however, in order to appreciate how great a support his silence has given, over the years, to students and to political leaders who dislike the behavior of the Supreme Court and are looking for proof that the power of judicial review was grasped rather than conferred. Historians have not been able to supply the evidence of a predominating intention so patently missing from the Marbury opinion. In spite of a prodigious combing of the records and a bountiful ingenuity in reasoning, students of American history have been unable to reach agreement as to whether the Constitution's makers decided in favor of judicial review and thought they had provided for it, decided against judicial review and thought their choice of language would preclude it, or could not reach a decision and believed they were referring the issue of judicial power, without prejudice, to others.

CHAPTER NINE

"Principles . . . Long and Well Established"

1. TEST: EXPRESS PROVISION
2. TEST: STYLE OF EXPRESSION
3. TEST: JUDICIAL PRACTICE
4. TEST: CONTEMPORARY OPINION

"The constitution," said Marshall, "is either a superior paramount law, unchangeable by ordinary means, or it is on a level with ordinary legislative acts, and, like other acts, is alterable when the legislature shall please to alter it." This is the fundamental question which occupied Marshall's attention in his opinion for *Marbury* v. *Madison*.

If Marshall preferred to find the answer in the language of the document itself or in the statements made by the men who framed and adopted the Constitution, he was thwarted in his search. He found his answer in the experience we call history. The question is decided for you, he said, when you "recognize certain principles, supposed to have been long and well established." And where does one find the principles and proof of their establishment? "Certainly all those who have framed written constitutions contemplate them as forming the fundamental and paramount law of the nation, and, consequently, the theory of every such government must be, that an act of the legislature, repugnant to the constitution, is void."

Did history confirm Marshall's report of experience? Those who reject Marshall's reading of history answer this way: Yes, if by "law" one means admonitory law. No, if by "law" one means effective law, law which goes beyond admonition to establish mandatory rules enforceable in court.

I think all students of the subject are agreed that experience in Europe, wherever documents worthy of being called constitutions could be found, had to be counted as strong evidence against the proposition that written constitutions were treated as effective law. Marshall's appeal to history had to be appeal to experience on the North American continent.

The Articles of Confederation can have afforded little support for Marshall's proposition. They were a written constitution, but they created no court. They provided that Congress might appoint courts to try piracy and felonies committed on the high seas and establish courts to hear appeals in cases involving capture at sea, and such courts were in fact established. But the Articles contained no such language explaining the relation of its content to other evidences of law as the framers of the new Constitution put into Article VI.

This leaves experience with the colonial charters and early state constitutions to be examined. There appear to be four tests suitable to determine whether the men who framed them intended these documents to be effective law. *First,* and best evidence, would be language in the fundamental document declaring it the highest law for colony or state and asserting that acts of government in conflict with its provisions should not be enforced. If this test proves inconclusive, then, *second,* style of expression in a document may indicate whether it is designed to serve as effective law or only as admonitory law. *Third,* judicial orders and opinions in litigated cases will reveal that fact if courts did nullify ordinances or statutes on ground of conflict with the fundamental document. And, *fourth,* the remarks of contemporaries, especially the men who wrote the document, may provide a record of what informed persons thought to be expected or legitimate practice.

1. TEST: EXPRESS PROVISION

The first test, specific provisions for judicial review in written charter or constitution, proves inconclusive. If clear provision for judicial review in one state within a decade after the Philadelphia convention (Kentucky, 1792) convinces one that the framers intended courts to interpret and enforce the national Constitution, then Marshall's findings and conclusions are established. If, on the other hand, failure to make such provision in other constitutions convinces one that silence on that point implies rejection of judicial review, one should withhold approval of Marshall until other evidence is examined.

The Massachusetts Constitution, put into effect in 1780, contained this provision (Part the Second, Section I, Chapter I, Article IV):

> And further, full power and authority are here given and granted to the said general court [the legislative body], from time to time, to make, ordain, and establish, all manner of wholesome and reasonable orders, laws, statutes, and ordinances, directions and instructions, either with penalties or without; so as the same be not repugnant or contrary to this constitution, as they shall judge to be for the good and welfare of this commonwealth, and for the government and ordering thereof, and of the subjects of the same, and for the necessary support and defence of the government thereof. . . .[1]

Clearly, the men who wrote the Massachusetts Constitution wished to set limits to governmental action. But did they view the document only as a body of admonitions, guides and standards to which conscientious legislators would adhere, or did they intend more than this? Did they intend that judges who disagreed with the lawmakers should overrule the latter and refuse to enforce statutes which the judges thought repugnant or contrary to some provision of the constitution? The answer to this question will not be found by reading the Massachusetts Constitution (nor that of New Hampshire or Vermont, which had similar language), unless one can find it in the document's general style of expression, which is discussed below.

Pennsylvania may be thought to have edged somewhat closer to forthright provision for judicial review. Its first constitution (1776) asserted that the several paragraphs entitled Declaration of Rights "ought never to be violated on any pretence whatever"; asserted that the legislature "shall have no power to add to, alter, abolish, or infringe any part of this constitution"; and, after specifying certain authority for the judicial branch, added that the courts shall have "such other power as may be found necessary by future assemblies, not inconsistent with this constitution." This declares obligation, certainly, but does it necessarily imply that courts will force compliance by refusal to enforce statutes which the legislators think are consistent with the constitution but which the judges think are not? If this was not clear-cut endorsement of judicial review, did Pennsylvania take the crucial step in its new constitution of 1790, when it closed a listing of rights and liberties with this

[1] All quotations from state constitutions are as printed in Thorpe's collection, cited in Bibliographic Note 10.

statement: "To guard against transgressions of the high powers which we have delegated, we declare that everything in this article is excepted out of the general powers of government, and shall forever remain inviolate" (Article IX, Section 26).

Constitutions written after 1787 and before Marshall spoke in 1803 could not have influenced men who wrote and adopted the national Constitution, but their contents may reveal what was in the thinking of the times and may therefore enter into judgments as to what the constitution-makers of 1787 thought they were providing. If Marshall thought the language I have quoted, including the Pennsylvania addition of 1790, not sufficient to prove a constitutional grant of judicial power to nullify statutes, he must have found what he was seeking in the document with which Kentucky entered the Union in 1792. "To guard against the high powers which have been delegated, we declare that everything in this article [the 'Bill of Rights'] is excepted out of the general powers of government, and shall forever remain inviolate; and that all laws contrary thereto, or contrary to this constitution, shall be void (Article XII, Section 28).

Surely, this was an express provision for judicial review. If a measure which passed the legislature and escaped veto by the governor "shall be void," by what means could it be made void except by refusal to enforce it? And how can a statute be made void by refusal to enforce it, under Anglo-American practice, without allowing judges to determine whether it is valid and issue orders accordingly?

Of how much worth is one undeniable provision for judicial review? It proves that judicial review was conceived of and approved by constitution-makers in one state. It creates a presumption that judicial review was intended in other states only if you make prior assumptions that all states were moving in unison, that no state was ahead of the others, and that no innovation or invention was taking place. For, if one does assume that one state might be first to try out a practice, he must acknowledge that Kentucky may have introduced constitutional provision for judicial review to the nation in 1792, five years after the national Constitution was written.

2. TEST: STYLE OF EXPRESSION

If the evidence we have just examined did not prove to Marshall's satisfaction that the colonial charters and early state constitutions were generally thought of and in practice treated as effective law, he may have resorted to a second test—one of rhetoric, or style of expression. This class of evidence also fails to put an end to the argument.

It is undeniable that the colonial charters were expressed in language that only lawyers would compose and that this language was eminently suitable for interpretation by judges after listening to argument by attorneys trained in law. Charters were treated as legal instruments in English and colonial courts. But it must be appreciated that the charter of the colony differed greatly from the later state and national constitutions in essential purpose. The charter was a declaration of the king addressed to the founder or founders of the colony, and it ordinarily opened with a description of the land which the founder was to possess and the terms on which the wealth he extracted was to be divided between himself and the king. The language of the document was the language of contract and assignment, and it was sometimes the language of feudal relationships. My own view is that a colonial court decision declaring an ordinance of the colonial legislature invalid on the ground of conflict with the charter would not provide a persuasive precedent for judicial review under state or national constitution. Persuasive or not, we shall see immediately that such precedents were virtually unavailable to Marshall.

We come now to the constitutions adopted between 1776 and 1803, when Marshall announced his findings. The language in these documents varied enormously in precision of expression and in mandatory character. The Articles of Confederation, drafted in 1777, are remarkably precise in statement; it is a document of firm instruction, not one of admonition and appeal to reason. The earliest state constitutions tended to be quite specific as to how government should be organized and how each branch of government should proceed in performing its acts. When they mentioned relationships between government and the people who are governed, however, their content ranged from declarations which read like a sermon to pronouncements that government "ought" to do this and "ought not" to do that to a firm assertion that government "shall" or "shall not." The sermons and the oughts predominated, however; the mandatory statement that government "shall" or "shall not" was certainly not a common provision in the first round of constitution-making for the thirteen states. The sermon is well illustrated by the paragraph in its "Bill of Rights" by which New Hampshire declared its position on cruel and unusual punishment in 1784.

> All penalties ought to be proportioned to the nature of the offence. No wise legislature will affix the same punishment to the crimes of theft, forgery and the like, which they do to those of murder and treason; where the same undistinguishing severity is exerted against all offences, the people are led to forget the real distinctions in the crimes themselves, and to commit the most flagrant with as little compunction as they do those of the lightest dye: For the same reason a multitude of sanguinary laws is both impolitic and unjust. The true design of all punishments being to reform, not to exterminate, mankind.

This thoughtful lecture, slightly changed in language (the dye was extracted), has survived all subsequent revisions of the New Hampshire Constitution. But in other states the "oughts" and "ought nots" tended to be replaced by "shall" and "shall not" in the revision of state constitutions going on about the time the Philadephia convention was bringing forth the present national Constitution. Compare the language adopted by Virginia in 1776 with that approved by the Kentuckians when they emerged from Virginia as a new state in 1792.

> [Virginia] That excessive bail ought not to be required, nor excessive fines imposed, nor cruel and unusual punishments inflicted.
>
> [Kentucky] That excessive bail shall not be required, nor excessive fines imposed, nor cruel punishments inflicted.
>
> [Virginia] That the freedom of the press is one of the great bulwarks of liberty, and can never be restrained but by despotic governments.
>
> [Kentucky] That the printing-press shall be free to every person who undertakes to examine the proceedings of the legislature or any branch of government, and no law shall ever be made to restrain the right thereof. The free communications of thoughts and opinions is one of the invaluable rights of man, and every citizen may freely speak, write, and print on any subject, being responsible for the abuse of that liberty.

These few observations about style of expression will indicate why persons who distrust judicial power find this test of purpose in constitution-making insufficient to support Marshall's finding. The test of rhetoric reveals that there was language in each of the fundamental documents which a judge could take hold of in case he wished to decide whether a statute was in keeping with higher law. But, with equal force, the test of rhetoric proves that, in areas of affairs where litigation ordinarily occurs, the superior document frequently used language which the judge would have to rewrite if he wished to show that a statute was in demonstrable conflict with the constitution.

The student who is unwilling to concede to the great Chief Justice any more than he must thus finds ground for insisting that the framers of those documents thought they were formulating admonitory law or, at best, a combination of admonitory and effective law. In support of this conclusion, he can cite at least one of the nation's founders. "There are certain maxims by which every wise and enlightened people will regulate their conduct," said Patrick Henry, speaking in the Virginia ratifying convention. "There are certain political maxims which no free people ought ever to abandon—maxims of which the observance is essential to the security of happiness." The Bill of Rights of the Virginia Constitution, he continued, "contains those admirable maxims." [2]

3. TEST: JUDICIAL PRACTICE

The third test which Marshall could apply, experience in actual practice of judicial review, looks especially promising. If judges were accustomed to invalidating legislative acts on grounds of conflict with higher law, one could assume that men who framed the fundamental documents expected them to be read critically by judges and enforced in litigation. The proof would be overwhelming if judicial review were a frequent practice under charters and constitutions that contained no express provision for judicial review. Again, however, application of the test has provoked opposing conclusions rather than agreement among scholars.

Records of litigation in early days are meager, but we know enough about the performance of higher courts to say with confidence that instances of judicial nullification of colonial ordinances and state statutes prior to *Marbury* v. *Madison* were rare indeed. Squeezing everything he could out of a case, Charles G. Haines was able to find only eleven court decisions, prior to the Philadelphia convention in 1787, which in one way or another endorsed judicial review. Two of his cases were in Massachusetts during the Colonial period; nine cases came after statehood—two in Virginia and one in each of seven other states. But Professor Haines, by his own admission, was most liberal in what he identified as a precedent

[2] Elliot, *Debates*, Vol. 3, p. 137 (cf. Bibliographic Note 3).

for judicial review. Other students, setting stiffer requirements for selection, whittle Professor Haines's eleven cases down to three, or two, or one, or even to no case where a statute was declared unenforceable in court because it violated a charter or a constitution.

The sixteen-year period from 1787 until *Marbury* v. *Madison* in 1803 produced, as far as I can tell, at most one New Hampshire decision, two Virginia decisions, and three Kentucky decisions in which a court cited constitutional provisions as reason for refusing to enforce a statute. The Kentucky Constitution in force at the time specifically provided that laws contrary to that document "shall be void."

This brief account of the practice of judicial review in early days discloses why conservative historians find in that practice little support for a thesis that judicial power to nullify statutes was generally acknowledged and was taken for granted by the men who drafted and ratified the national Constitution. The period from 1776 to 1803 was one of intense legislative activity. Legislation which imposed rigorous regulation of personal conduct, provision of services to the public, quality and price of commodities, and the like was put into the statute books of all the Eastern states during this period. We know from indisputable evidence that there was great unhappiness with such legislation in many sectors of the population. Constitutional provisions labeled "Declaration of Rights" reached out to such a broad range of affairs and were expressed in such flexible language that we may be sure lawyers would have argued for invalidation of unpopular laws if they had generally understood that judges were expected to determine their validity. Why, then, were there so few instances in which a judge talked about power to nullify a statute and why were there no more than three cases (the maximum included in the count of conservative scholars) in which a statute was actually refused enforcement in court before the national Constitution was ratified? It will come as no surprise to learn that many students draw from this dearth of precedents a presumption that the early American constitutions were not intended to serve as effective law enforceable in court.

4. TEST: CONTEMPORARY OPINION

We need not dwell on the fourth test which Marshall must have applied in making up his mind that our early constitutions were thought of and treated as effective law—the testimony of contemporary observers of constitution-making and of political and judicial action under constitutions. Like the three tests already examined, this one is inconclusive; the evidence can be read both ways. One can find in the writings of informed and thoughtful people proof that some of them viewed their constitutions as legal documents enforceable in courts, expected judges to nullify acts of government which the judges believed inconsistent with the constitution, and thought constitutions would impose little restraint on public officials if the judiciary did not make them effective by voiding inconsistent legislation.

On the other hand, some of the writing which strikes one as careful description of the structure and processes of government makes no reference to judicial review where, one feels sure, it would have been emphasized if the author understood it to be expected practice. In still other records of contemporary opinion, persons active in public affairs and enjoying high prestige expressly stated that judicial nullification of statutes was not provided for in state or national constitutions and clearly implied or positively asserted that, if judicial review were provided for, it would negate progress toward those very principles of republican government which the constitutions were designed to enthrone.

I have not searched the source materials of American history for all the available evidence of what, prior to 1803, men thought to be actual practice and what they thought to be desirable practice in interpretation and enforcement of constitutions, but I have read a good many of the early statements and most, if not all, the principal writings which review and evaluate those statements. My personal conclusion is that the statements made by Americans up to 1803, viewed as evidence of what men believed to be actual practice or justifiable expectation of action, fail by a wide margin to constitute proof that the early constitutions were viewed and treated as effective law, enforceable in courts. Viewed as evidence of what was thought to be desirable practice, I think they fall short of proof that informed, thoughtful, politically active men were preponderantly of the opinion that judges ought to deny enforcement to acts of government which the judge believes contrary to the constitution.

But, even if one concludes that men who put their opinions in print were in agreement as to what was desirable, what light would this throw on actual practice, expected practice, or probable intent of men who framed written constitutions? If one believes that enlightened thought and persistent advocacy ordinarily precede the creation of new institutions and innovation in governmental practice, he must acknowledge that approval and recommendation of judicial review might have been widespread and persistent for many years before judicial review became a feature of government in operation.

If the foregoing analysis is valid, it follows that Marshall did not establish beyond reasonable doubt his contention that all who have framed written constitutions contemplated them as forming the fundamental and paramount law, enforceable in court at the cost of nullifying the inconsistent expressions of elected officials. Add to this Marshall's failure—failure, if my analysis in the preceding chapter is convincing—to wring out of the words in the document or the declared intentions of the men who drafted and ratified it irrefutable proof that the Constitution is effective law binding on judges. Put together these efforts to persuade which definitely fell short of full persuasion and one reaches a grand conclusion that the power of judicial review was not established in 1803 beyond refutation by a fair resort to evidence and reasoning. One may conclude that it was a superb stroke of statesmanship which gave judges the power of judicial review. One may also conclude that Marshall made as good a case by fact and logic for judicial review as any of his critics has ever been able to put up in support of an opposite conclusion.

But what one cannot conclude, it seems to me, is that Marshall set forth in his opinion everything that is required to bring all thoughtful, inquiring men to the position which Marshall and his colleagues announced in *Marbury* v. *Madison*. It must be acknowledged, I think, that men who fear extensive judicial power may reasonably cling to a conviction that a doctrine of judicial review was not originally incorporated in the Constitution but was grafted onto it by subsequent practice. A doubt that the whole package of present judicial power was legitimately conferred consequently lurks in the background of American politics and emerges to help convert grievance into passion when any sector of the population is greatly disappointed with the behavior of the Supreme Court in constitutional cases.

CHAPTER TEN

Judicial Review under Review

1. OBJECTIVE: COMPLETE LEGITIMATION
2. RESULT: STILL NOT CONVINCED

The burden of the two preceding chapters was to show that John Marshall did not provide a near-perfect intellectual support for his conclusion that judges should not enforce statutes which they believe to violate a written constitution. I asserted my own conviction that his reasoning is bound to be unconvincing to a man who is reluctant to be convinced. The skeptic who depends on Marshall's opinion for legitimation of the power of judicial review comes out of the reading with doubt that a power to nullify laws was conferred on any court.

1. OBJECTIVE: COMPLETE LEGITIMATION

As would be expected, many scholars have set themselves the goal that Marshall failed to achieve—to remove all doubt from reasonable minds that the power to determine constitutionality was conferred on the courts by the Constitution itself. These efforts vary in quality, of course, but the most fully developed arguments are alike in reliance on four main points: (1) some specific language in articles III and VI, (2) the legal character of the Constitution, (3) the doctrine of separation of powers modified by provision for checks and balances, and (4) statements by men who shared in framing and ratifying the Constitution. Reasoning which extends from each of these four points has been welded together by several writers to form one secure pillar on which to rest judicial power. The next several pages sketch out the reasoning which scholarly literature shows to be preferred.

Both articles III and VI make it clear that the Constitution is law, and law in the same sense that statutes and treaties are law. The three sources of law are twice put in the same sentence. In Article III, they appear without any differentiation as to character, quality, or status; as foundation for litigation, they are put on exactly the same plane. In Article VI, which speaks of supremacy of law, there is an indication that the Constitution is a source of law superior to statutes, but nothing to indicate that the Constitution is any less judge-enforceable for that reason. Nor is the legal character of the Constitution brought into question by the reference to state constitutions, state laws, and the obligations of judges in the states. The purpose of Article VI was not to differentiate among or to establish the equality of the three sources of national law; Article III says all that the framers thought necessary to say on that point. The purpose of the language in Article VI was simply to establish the facts that national law, whether expressed in Constitution, statute, or treaty, is superior to state law, however state law may be expressed and that no effort of a state to make judges act differently in that state should be effective. This being the purpose of Article VI, it was not necessary, and perhaps it would have been improper, to say anything in that paragraph about the obligation of federal judges to put the three sources of national law above any and all sources of state law.

The effect of the reasoning thus far is to establish that the Constitution is law in the same sense that national statutes and national treaties are law and that all three expressions of national law are superior to any expressions of state law. If the Constitution and treaties are law in the same sense that a statute is law, then courts will enforce the Constitution, statutes, and treaties, and, in case of conflict among them, the court will decide which statement of law will prevail and determine the outcome of the litigation. But which statement is to prevail? May the judge find the statute or a treaty more precisely applicable to the case before him and ignore contrary declarations in the Constitution? Or is there somewhere in the Constitution an indication that, in all cases of conflict, the judge shall obey the Constitution? Not in articles III or VI. In each case, the order of listing is Constitution, laws, and treaties, but that order provides weak support for a conclusion about order of priority in legal effect. Further, if order of listing fixed order of superiority, then statutory language would always be supreme over treaties, and the House of Representatives, by refusing to agree to changes in statutory language, could defeat the efforts of the president and Senate to regulate a matter by treaty. Our confidence that the founders intended to make the Constitution supreme should not be tempered by the degree of our confidence that the founders intended to make the lawmaking process superior to the treaty-making process. Article VI does speak of laws made "in pursuance of" the Constitution and treaties made "under the authority of" the United States. But this paragraph, it has already been said, was designed to establish the supremacy of national law over state law; if the intent had been to establish the supremacy of the Constitution over national statutes and treaties, it would be unreasonable to add that state judges are bound by the declaration and make no mention of obligation on the part of federal judges. The paragraph of Article VI can be made wholly reasonable by reading it only as a provision which subordinates state law to the Constitution and to all other expressions of the national government which are compatible with the Constitution. So read, the paragraph does not incontrovertibly establish the supremacy of the Constitution over national statutes and treaties, but it does anchor that implication and instruct one to infer that every other evidence that the Constitution is law means that it is law superior to statutes and treaties.

What other evidence is there that the Constitution is law? All of the Constitution when it is read in its entirety. Every paragraph of the Constitution but one contains a "shall" or a "shall not." The exceptional paragraph, the second of Article I, Section 5, says that each chamber of Congress "may determine the rules of its proceedings, punish its members for disorderly behavior, and, with the concurrence of two-thirds, expel a member." Elsewhere, a permissive "may" appears in the Constitution about a dozen times, but there is not an admonitory sentence or phrase in the entire document. The words "ought" and "ought not" which spotted the early state constitutions do not appear once in the Constitution of the United States. True, most of the "shalls" and "shall nots" appear in statements that are not likely ever to be involved in litigation. But they support a conclusion that the provisions which will be at stake in litigation were intended to be viewed as law before which all acts of government must bow. Indeed, they force that conclusion, for they make it undeniable that the men who made the Constitution intended it to be a document which imposes limitations on government and controls government, to be an authoritative charter to which any part of the nation might appeal when convinced that government is not in fact staying within the bounds which a national agreement has set for it.

If careful study of the substantive content leaves any doubt that the Constitution is law binding on all governments in the United States, examination of the procedures for amending the document will remove it. A system of law must provide for its own reconsideration and revision. The Constitution sets forth a procedure which permits its revision but removes the power of revision from any combination of officials that might chafe at the Constitution's restrictions. So elaborate a procedure for altering or augmenting the content of the Constitution could have been stipulated only by men who were determined to circumscribe governmental authority by barriers which the wielders of that authority could not circumvent.

Still another stretch must be traversed by those who seek to remove all doubt that power to enforce the Constitution was conferred on the courts by the Constitution itself. Assuming that the argument to this point brings conviction that the Constitution is law binding on all branches of the government and is superior to all other expressions of law, where is proof to be found that the framers intended the courts to have uniquely the power to determine what the Constitution means when its meaning is in dispute? Not just in the facts that the Constitution is the supreme law and that the courts interpret and apply law, for experience prior to 1787 showed that legislative bodies were not confined to enacting law of a subsidiary character. In England and in North America during the early period of statehood, it was not uncommon for legislative assemblies as well as the judges to interpret, explain, and apply the law in specific cases of litigation. Why, then, must we conclude that the Constitution authorized the judicial branch to fix the meaning of the Constitution finally and without appeal for application to specific cases of litigation?

The proof is found, insofar as proof can be established, in the Constitution's provisions for separation of powers and in the words and acts of men who shared in making the Constitution. The Constitution erected a national government of three branches, distributed power among them, and specified checks which one branch might impose on another. The Constitution does not say that the three branches are to be coordinate, at the same level of authority, and it does not specify checks which the judicial branch may exert on the other two branches. Testimony by men who helped bring the Constitution into being leaves no room for doubt that they intended the three branches to be coordinate. Statements about specific intent to authorize judicial review may be inconclusive, but there is no conflict in the testimony about intent to put the judiciary on a level of authority equal to that of the Executive and the legislature.

Could the judicial branch have won a place in our system of government coordinate with that of Congress and president if it had not acquired the power to fix the meaning of the Constitution and enforce that meaning in litigation? Two facts of the national experience support a conclusion that, lacking a power of judicial review, the judiciary would have been notably weaker than the other two branches. *First,* in nearly two centuries of experience, the courts have found no way to make a significant impact on the basic character of our constitutional system except by refusing to enforce legislative and executive acts which they believe to violate it. *Second,* the first Congress assembled under the Constitution apparently believed that it could not make articles III and VI effective without providing for the Supreme Court to determine the validity of statutes. Article III says that the judicial power of the United States shall extend to cases arising under the Constitution, law, and treaties of the United States. In the same article, the Constitution cites two types of case over which the Supreme Court shall have original jurisdiction and then states that, "in all the other cases before mentioned, the Supreme Court shall have appellate jurisdiction, both as to law and fact, with such exceptions, and under such regulations as the Congress shall make." In whatever way one interprets the phrase, "all the other cases before mentioned," the Supreme Court is bound to hear cases involving the validity of national statutes unless a law is passed excepting them from the Court's jurisdiction. The Supreme Court will get them because they will come up on appeal from the state courts. The Constitution did not say, in Article VI, that judges in the states are forbidden to pass on the validity of national statutes; it said only that judges shall "be bound" by the Constitution, laws made in pursuance thereof, and treaties made under the authority of the United States. It follows that the makers of the Constitution expected state judges (and perhaps federal judges sitting out of the national capital) to rule on the meaning and application of national statutes and therefore to rule on the compatibility of the language of the statute with the language of the Constitution. The founders did not instruct judges in the states to refrain from such rulings; they required only that the Supreme Court be final on such issues, subject to any legislative provision that might limit and regulate the Supreme Court's appellate jurisdiction.

Considering the language of articles III and VI together, one must admit that power to fix the meaning of the Constitution and enforce that meaning was conferred on the Supreme Court by the Constitution itself in respect to cases coming to the Supreme Court on appeal. The most that can be said in opposition to a power of judicial review is that this reasoning does not apply to cases that come originally to the Supreme Court and that, as respects cases received on appeal, Congress and the president may enact legislation restricting the cases that get to the Supreme Court and how it may deal with the cases that do get there. Whether the nation's lawmakers are authorized to cut off completely appeals to the Supreme Court on cases involving constitutional issues need not be argued here. But it is relevant to point out that the first Congress under the Constitution, in a statute strongly supported by men who had served in the Philadelphia convention or a ratifying convention, specifically provided that the Supreme Court should hear on appeal and decide finally: (1) cases in which the highest court of a state holds that a national statute or treaty is invalid; (2) cases in which the highest court of a state upholds the validity of a statute or other act of a state, overruling a claim that such statute or act is in conflict with the Constitution or with a law or treaty of the United States; (3) cases in which the highest court of a state rules against the claim of a party basing his claim on a construction which he gives the Constitution or a statute or a treaty of the United States. Nor is it irrelevant to point out that this enactment of 1789 remains on the statute books, has been the charter for assertion of rights before the Supreme Court in a great volume of litigation, and has been reinforced and expanded by subsequent enactments of Congress and the president.

Finally, if the Constitution's own content is not sufficient to sustain a power of judicial review, supporting evidence which John Marshall did not cite can be introduced. The distinctive character of a written constitution was discussed in the Philadelphia convention. Men who participated in writing the new constitution spoke of it as a legal document. Some expressly stated the judges would refuse to enforce state and national statutes that conflicted with it. Other members of the convention said things which indicated that they took for granted a power of judicial review. No member, so far as the records show, presented an argument designed to show how the Constitution could be made effective if judges did not enforce it when it is violated. Debate in the ratifying conventions and statements made on other occasions by men who participated in writing and ratifying the document offer similar support for the view that the Constitution was intended to be a judicially enforceable document.

2. RESULT: STILL NOT CONVINCED

The preceding section condenses the best argument I have found in support of the position that a power of judicial review was established by the Constitution itself. I did not undertake to reproduce the reasoning of any one man who has written on the subject, but rather to identify the points in the writings of many men that seem most convincing.

The case I have made for judicial review is, therefore, not a new one. Scholarly inquiry into the genesis and legitimacy of judicial review may be said to date from about 1885. Nothing that I put in my statement was overlooked by Edward S. Corwin in his *The Doctrine of Judicial Review* (1912). Writers have differed substantially in the evaluations they have placed on the various considerations presented, and they have differed in the conclusions they have derived from them. But the array of evidence and reasoning has been before the American people in its best form for half a century. It has not laid to rest a widespread suspicion that our judges have taken upon themselves a role which the founders of our constitutional system did not intend them to have.

A number of studious efforts have been made to prove that the men who participated in making the Constitution gave thought to the usefulness of judicial review, decided not to provide for it, and understood that the document they produced did not authorize judges to exercise this power. Such writing has undoubtedly helped nourish doubt about the legitimacy of judicial review, but we shall not examine that line of reasoning here. It will be sufficient to note why the opposite contention, the arguments of careful students that judicial review is rooted in the Constitution, has not removed all doubt on this point.

The reasoning which I have presented as the classic argument that judicial review was established by the Constitution encounters three main objections.

First is the counter: You ask too much when you ask us to believe that the framers of the Constitution would have agreed to authorize a power of judicial review but refrain from establishing it by specific provision. The power was too important and too novel in practice to be left to assumption. The desirability of providing for judicial review was debated in the Philadelphia convention. Some delegates thought a statement should be inserted in the Constitution saying that judges would refuse to enforce statutes and other acts in conflict with the fundamental document. Other delegates thought such a power should not be exercised by judges. No delegate appears to have taken the position that judicial review ought to be practiced, but should not be specifically provided for. The evidence is overwhelming that judicial review was not a firmly established practice familiar to the people of North America in the period prior to 1787. Although the impact of judicial power as we have witnessed it since their day may not have been envisaged by the framers, they undoubtedly realized that a right of judges to nullify statutes would have significant consequences for the constitutional system. We are forced, therefore, to assume that the absence of specific provision for that power in the fundamental document means that the men who wrote and adopted the document had not agreed that judicial review should be exercised. Only direct proof to the contrary can overcome that assumption, and direct proof has not been supplied.

Second, as a substitute for this direct proof, we are offered inferences from evidence that the Constitution was intended to have the effect of law and from statements about the nature of judicial power found in articles III and VI of the Constitution. These inferences extend too far from their base. The reasoning which supports them depends too much on imagination, too little on the plain meaning of plain words. The treacherous character of such reasoning is made manifest by the differences in the ways it is developed by writers of good repute. In order to find in Article III a meaning which he is determined to extract from that language, one scholar denies that Article VI has a meaning which another scholar has credited to the article and has indeed relied on as his main proof that the Constitution itself vests the courts with a power of judicial review. Further, we cannot overlook the fact that Marshall, in his Marbury opinion, used language contained in the document only as a secondary defense of the judicial power he had asserted. We cannot believe that he thought the content of a written constitution to be of secondary value for ascertaining what institutions that constitution was designed to erect. We must believe that he thought the framers had failed to write into the document the statements which would clearly imply that judges were required to put the Constitution above statutes. He put first reliance on another kind of proof because he thought that Article III, Article VI, and other internal evidence that the Constitution was intended to be law did not combine to form good proof that judicial review had been authorized.

The *third* main contravention of the classic argument for judicial review is a denial that support for constitutional establishment of that power can be found in a general commitment to separation of powers and checks-and-balances. This counterargument runs as follows. The doctrine of separation of powers is a more basic theoretical position than any endorsement of arrangements for one department of government to check another. Indeed, the arrangements called checks-and-balances were explained in *The Federalist* as modifications of an idealized separation of powers. This being the case, one should not assume that men who are committed to separation of powers will establish arrangements which modify the separation they seek to achieve. Only when evidence is clearly before him should one conclude that powers which have been generally separated have also been specially mixed to provide a check on exercise of power.

The Constitution expressly endows the president with powers to restrain Congress and the judiciary in the exercise of their powers. It expressly endows Congress (either one chamber or both in cooperation) with powers enabling it to check the president and the judiciary. But it contains no provision which asserts that the Supreme Court or any other court may exercise a specific power which would restrain the president or Congress in the exercise of their powers. It has been argued that the placement of restraining power in two departments of government implies that the third department is to enjoy an equal power of restraint. It seems more reasonable to contend that silence about a restraining power for the third reflects a conclusion that the third department should not exercise significant restraint on the other two.

The indicated presumption, therefore, is that the men who wrote and adopted the Constitution did not intend the judicial branch to exercise a check as great as the power of judicial review was bound to be. This presumption is moved close to conclusion by arguments in the *Federalist* papers. In the essays which are addressed most directly to separation of powers and checks-and-balances as general theory (numbers 47 and 48), great emphasis is placed on the need for the Executive to check the legislature and for the legislature to check the Executive. No reference at all is made to need for the judiciary to check either the Executive or the legislature. In a discussion of the need in a representative republic for restraints on the legislative body, there is no reference to a power of the courts to declare laws or executive acts unconstitutional and no reference to any other powers which courts might use to restrain either of the two other branches.

In Number 78 of *The Federalist,* Hamilton opens an extensive discussion of judicial power in the new system of government to be established by the Constitution. Most of this essay is devoted to explanation of why judges must have the power to pronounce legislative acts void because contrary to the Constitution. This consideration is introduced because it, in turn, explains why federal judges should hold their offices on permanent tenure. Hamilton spoke of the courts as "bulwarks of a limited Constitution against legislative encroachments," but he did not relate judicial review to a general doctrine of separation of powers or place judicial review in an array of checks to be exerted by one branch of government on another. His justification of judicial review was preceded, however, by two paragraphs relating the courts to the other two branches of government, and at this point he referred to the judiciary as "beyond comparison the weakest of the three departments of power; . . . it can never attack with success either of the other two." To this characterization he added a quote from Montesquieu: "Of the three powers above mentioned, the judiciary is next to nothing." Whatever reasons Hamilton had for believing that the new constitutional system made it necessary for courts to enforce the Constitution above statutes, he did not rely on a commitment to separation of powers and checks-and-balances to reinforce his reasoning.

III • THE SUPREME COURT AND PUBLIC POLICY

Part II explored the origins and foundations of judicial review in order to better understand the persisting doubt that the power to invalidate legislation was lawfully conferred on the Supreme Court. Part III is designed to help the reader understand why the Supreme Court has repeatedly been accused of crossing the boundaries of judicial power and invading a realm intended exclusively for the political branches of government. This look at how the Supreme Court has used its power should prepare the reader for critical evaluation of my appraisal of the Segregation cases, which is the subject of Part IV.

The only way one can make up his mind as to how the Supreme Court has used its power is to see what the judges did when they had a choice as to what ends the Constitution would serve. Unfortunately, this necessitates close attention to what the judges said and did in a series of cases. The following four chapters report some principal choices which the Supreme Court made in fixing the meaning of some constitutional provisions that set limits to governmental regulation of economic and social problems.

CHAPTER ELEVEN

The Elastic Clauses

The constitutional provisions which offer good handles for judges are of three types: (1) Some general provisions which serve as guides for dividing authority between national and state governments and give instructions for interpretation of the specific grants of power to the national government; (2) language which makes specific grants of power to the national government; (3) several provisions which place restrictions on the national government, or on state governments, or on both, either denying power to act at all or putting limitations on the way in which power can be exercised.

A fair view of how the Supreme Court judges have used their power to fix the meaning of constitutional language can be arrived at by examining a few of their acts relating to each of these three types of constitutional provision. We shall proceed in this order. In this chapter, we will note the use which has been made of the three instructions for interpreting specific grants of power (Type One). They are commonly referred to as elastic clauses. The next chapter will examine the interpretation, during John Marshall's time and later, of one specific grant of power (Type Two). The grant to be noticed is the power "to regulate commerce . . . among the several States" vested in the national government by Article I, Section 8. Further definition of this grant after Marshall's day and its use by the Supreme Court during the Great Depression and period of the New Deal will be examined in Chapter XIII. The next two chapters will explore some of the main demonstrations of judicial power under two great limiting clauses of the Constitution (Type Three)—the due-process-of-law clause in Chapter XIV and the guarantee of equal protection of the laws in Chapter XV.

1. THE GENERAL-WELFARE CLAUSE

Section 8 of Article I opens with a statement that the national government "shall have power to lay and collect taxes, duties, imposts, and excises, to pay the debts, and provide for the common defense and general welfare of the United States; but all duties, imposts, and excises shall be uniform throughout the United States." This language appears to invite three differing interpretations. *First,* it may contain four separate grants of power to the national government: to raise money, to pay its debts, to provide for the common defense, and to provide for the general welfare of the nation. *Second,* it may contain a single grant of power, but one of immense proportions—the power to raise money and spend it for any purpose which will achieve the common defense and general welfare of the nation. *Third,* it may be a single grant of power, but one more limited than the second alternative; the provision may authorize the national government to raise money and spend it in exercise of the powers delegated to the national government here and there in the Constitution, provided that in so doing it is acting for the common defense and general welfare.

An occasional voice has been lifted in favor of the first interpretation, but it has never received much support. Alexander Hamilton championed the second interpretation. James Madison was a prime spokesman for the third. The second interpretation won out. From an early day, Congress and the president levied taxes which they viewed, not as measures to raise revenue, but rather as impositions of cost which would induce businessmen or someone else to alter or terminate certain activities. The imposition, in form a tax, caused those who were subjected to it to pursue conduct which the lawmakers understood they lacked power to command by legislation and enforce with criminal penalties. Shortly after the Civil War, the national government entered on a program of grants-in-aid designed to induce state governments to carry out policies they would not otherwise adopt. Supposing that they could not directly control public education or regulate some practice affecting public health, Congress and the president could raise money by taxation and give it to state governments on condition that they adopt and enforce the policies which the national lawmakers preferred but could not impose on the nation.

The Supreme Court did not play a principal role in fixing the bounds of national power to tax and spend. Congress and president extended their power in successive steps that enjoyed general public approval, and the courts were not urged to nullify the action taken. So it was, in the main, until the inauguration of the New Deal. In 1936, the Supreme Court held a federal tax invalid on the ground that, in levying the tax and spending its proceeds, Congress and the President intended to induce farmers to pursue agricultural practices which the national government could not require them to pursue by legislative command and criminal penalties (*U.S.* v. *Butler,* 297 U.S. 1). Perhaps no other decision of the Court adverse to the New Deal excited greater anguish and indignation. There was no contention that the Court had incorrectly described the purpose and effect of the statute. The offense, in the eyes of the New Dealers, was that the Court had interpreted the Constitution to forbid a form of federal action which had been long honored, one which the President's supporters believed to be essential equipment for dealing with national problems and one which they thought authorized by a reasonable reading of the Constitution.

Three members of the Supreme Court disagreed with the majority in the Butler case. Less than eighteen months after it was decided, the interpretation of the Constitution on which that decision rested was largely, if not wholly, abandoned. The later view was announced in two decisions holding valid the national Social Security Act, a statute which made use of the taxing power to induce state governments to establish compulsory unemployment compensation programs (*Stewart Machine Co.* v. *Davis,* 301 U.S. 548; *Helvering* v. *Davis,* 301 U.S. 619). Between the announcement of the Butler decision (January 1936) and the announcement of the two later decisions (May 1937), the President had placed before Congress his bill providing for reorganization of the federal judiciary.

2. THE NECESSARY-AND-PROPER CLAUSE

After listing in seventeen paragraphs a series of specific powers that are vested in the national government, the constitution-makers brought Section 8 of Article I to a close with this statement: "The Congress shall have power . . . to make all laws which shall be necessary and proper for carrying into execution the foregoing powers, and all other powers vested by this Constitution in the government of the United States, or in any department or officer thereof."

We cannot be sure what reasons the framers had for putting this statement into the Constitution at this precise place. The clause is treated today as a guide to interpretation of the specific grants which precede it. We ask what could have been meant by the word "necessary," the word "proper," and the words "necessary and proper" combined into a phrase. If we find the right meaning of the phrase, we suppose we have a key to the extent of the power given to the national government to borrow money, establish a postal system, build and operate a navy, and so on.

My reading of the fragments of evidence that have survived makes me most doubtful that the framers intended the clause as a guide for interpreting the grants of power. They seem to have attached no special significance to the words "necessary" and "proper." Their purpose seems to have been to say, at the end of the main enumeration of powers given the national government, something like this: Legislation will be required for carrying into effect any of the powers given the national government; whatever legislation ought to be enacted, Congress is the body to enact it. Their purpose would have been fully served if they had left out the words "necessary and proper" and simply said: "Congress shall have power to enact laws carrying into execution the foregoing powers and all other powers vested . . ." etc. This is the conclusion I reach after reading notes on the debate in the convention, what Hamilton and Madison said in *The Federalist,* the debates on establishment of a national bank in 1791, and such other relevant information as I have found.

It is commonly said by students of constitutional law that the phrase has been given an expansive meaning, that the word "necessary" has been erased and the word "proper" has been made a synonym for "convenient." It is also said that this has been the handiwork of the Supreme Court and that Marshall laid the groundwork for this development in his opinion in *McCulloch* v. *Maryland.* I am not convinced that these conclusions are justified.

Note, *first,* that the Supreme Court has nullified very few national statutes on the ground that they went beyond the bounds of authority given the national government. In these few decisions, the necessary-and-proper clause got scant mention, indeed. The judges did not say, typically, that the statute went down because the regulations it imposed were not necessary and proper means of taxing or necessary and proper means of regulating commerce. Instead, they said that the statute went down because it did not have a constitutionally authorized objective, that the statute went down because it was not in fact an exercise of "the taxing power" or an exercise of "the commerce power." If the Court is going to dispose of a law by saying that it is not an exercise of any power given the national government, it need not inquire whether the contents of that law are a necessary and proper means of exercising any of those powers.

It should be observed, *second,* that the Supreme Court does not deserve all the credit for expanding national power, even in those areas of public life where national laws are allowed to operate. When the Supreme Court holds, as it has in most cases before it, that the objectives and means incorporated in the statute do fall within the bounds of national authority, it confirms an interpretation of constitutional power which the makers of the statute had previously asserted or presumed. If these interpretations result in a surprising enlargement of federal power, should one conclude that the enlargement is the handiwork of the Supreme Court?

There is a *third* point to consider in appraising the Supreme Court's impression on national development through its power to expand or contract the meaning of "necessary and proper." When the Court has justified a decision by arguing that the means adopted by a particular statute are necessary and proper for carrying out an enumerated power, does the explanation open or close any gates for later legislative experimentation? Examine the little essay by Marshall in *McCulloch* v. *Maryland* (4 Wheaton 316, decided in 1819), the early case in which the Court found the incorporation of a national bank a necessary and proper means of borrowing money, collecting taxes, and carrying out other enumerated powers. Here are the key sentences in Marshall's "ever immortal words" (Warren), Marshall's "ablest exposition of the Constitution" (Beveridge), the "definitive statement of the broad and liberal interpretation" (Pritchett):

> We admit, as all must admit, that the powers of the government are limited, and that its limits are not to be transcended. But we think the sound construction of the constitution must allow to the national legislature that discretion, with respect to the means by which the powers it confers are to be carried into execution, which will enable that body to perform the high duties assigned to it, in

> the manner most beneficial to the people. Let the end be legitimate, let it be within the scope of the constitution, and all means which are appropriate, which are plainly adapted to that end, which are not prohibited, but consist with the letter and spirit of the constitution, are constitutional. (P. 421.)

Does one know any more about what is necessary and proper when he has finished reading these words than before he started? Two points which Marshall made were not disputed. *First,* the end must be legitimate; the object must be to carry out one or more of the powers given the national government by the Constitution. *Second,* the means which are adopted for achieving the end must not conflict with a prohibition in the Constitution; no matter how legitimate the end, it may not be achieved by an ex post facto law or a bill of attainder.

Marshall did not win his great praise for saying this much; he is praised because of what he said on a third, disputed, point. If Marshall's words deserve to be immortalized, it is because of the wisdom they bring to decisions about the legitimacy of means for achieving legitimate ends.

The national government, said Marshall, must be allowed a choice among means which will enable it to perform the duties assigned it in the manner most beneficial to the people. Do the persons who have gone to court to find out whether this statute is valid have a common understanding of what is most beneficial to the people? Any means for accomplishing a legitimate end is necessary and proper if it is plainly adapted to that end. Does "plainly adapted" mean "absolutely indispensable," or "anything that comes in handy," or something in between? Any means is necessary and proper if it is consistent with the letter and spirit of the Constitution. But what does consist with the letter and spirit of the Constitution? Isn't that what the argument was about in the first place?

One cannot credit the Supreme Court judges with much statesmanship or debit them for lack of it because of what they have said about the meaning of the necessary-and-proper clause. But one can examine the means we have adopted in legislation and administrative devices for carrying out the battery of powers given the national government in the Constitution and can observe what the Supreme Court has done when urged in litigation to uphold or invalidate those means. He can evaluate what has been tried, what has been struck down, and what has remained effective. He may conclude that the net result is expansion of national power beyond what most of the constitution-makers would have approved, or he may conclude the opposite; thoughtful students have come up on both sides of this question. Whichever way one does come up, he is likely to conclude that the congressmen and the president had as much to do with the establishment of the range of national power under the Constitution as the judges had. And where one attributes a definitive influence to the judges, he is more likely to connect it with the judges' interpretation of the words which specify the delegated power (the end) than with the judges' interpretation of the necessary-and-proper clause.

3. THE TENTH AMENDMENT

This is the third of the general provisions relating to division of authority between nation and states. It reads as follows: "The powers not delegated to the United States by the Constitution, nor prohibited by it to the States, are reserved to the States, respectively, or to the people."

This amendment, like the nine which precede it, was submitted for ratification by the first Congress elected under the new Constitution. It is supposed that this amendment was not intended to change the Constitution in any way, that its purpose was simply to put into express language the understanding the framers had about where authority lay in the new governmental system they had designed. Supreme Court judges have been charged by some students of constitutional law with having used this language to alter the division of authority which the framers intended.

One way to give effect to the Tenth Amendment is to start with the specific grants of power to the national government and to stop with the necessary-and-proper clause. To illustrate: Congress and president might enact a law making it illegal, in the case of railroads carrying interstate trains, for anyone to cross the tracks except on highways designated by the Interstate Commerce Commission, these highways always to be at least twenty-five miles apart. Clearly, in Marshall's words just quoted, the end is legitimate. The purpose is to facilitate commerce among the states, and the statute is a regulation of commerce among the states. Is it necessary and proper for carrying out the power to regulate commerce among the several states? If one considers nothing but the relation of the means to the end, the statute appears to have its rationale; it can reasonably be expected to facilitate the movement of goods from state to state and therefore is authorized by the Constitution.

But the Tenth Amendment may be read in such a way that one does not stop with the necessary-and-proper clause. All powers not delegated to the national government are reserved to the people or the states. The power to develop the land in all ways appropriate for making a living and making living a pleasure was not delegated to the national government. Presumably, the framers understood that they were reserving to the people a wide range of choice in how to develop the land and were reserving to the state governments authority to protect, regulate, and facilitate the pursuit of these ends. Acting within its reserved powers, a state lays out highways in a fashion which provides for crossing interstate railroads between the spots designated by the Interstate Commerce Commission. Has the Tenth Amendment reserved to the states the power to locate highways within their borders, including the authority to mark the spots at which highways shall cross railroads as well as rivers? Whose law stands—the national law carrying out a delegated power or the state law carrying out a reserved power?

The question is not answered by saying that Article VI of the Constitution makes national law supreme over state law. The Supreme Court has said that the Constitution is supreme over both national and state statutes. It has said that, when there is a dispute as to where the line falls between the two systems of power, the judicial branch will answer the question if it is properly raised in litigation. So the Court could not say, in the illustrative case, that the national statute displaces the power of the state to locate its highways until it had first decided whether the Tenth Amendment reserves to the people or to the state governments some powers which the national government cannot displace.

The Supreme Court has, in fact, played the Tenth Amendment both ways. Sometimes it says in effect: "The provisions of the act of Congress are necessary and proper for carrying out a delegated power. This is all we need to know; the act must be enforced." In another case, it says in effect: "We cannot decide whether the act of Congress lies within the power granted to the national government until we determine the cost to our whole governmental system in terms of the erosion of powers reserved to the states." This practice of playing it both ways has been labeled "the doctrine of dual federalism."

The significance of the Tenth Amendment, like that of the necessary-and-proper clause, can be appreciated only when we see how it is applied in connection with one or more of the specific powers granted the national government. The power of the national government to regulate commerce among the states affords excellent material for our study, since it inevitably brushes against the power of the states to regulate commerce within their borders and to pursue a variety of policies intended to advance the welfare of their citizens.

CHAPTER TWELVE

What Is Commerce?

1. A SEARCH FOR MEANING
2. "AMONG THE STATES" BECOMES "BETWEEN STATES"

The foundation of national power in respect to commerce is a short sentence in Article I, Section 8, of the Constitution: "The Congress shall have power . . . to regulate commerce with foreign nations, and among the several States, and with the Indian tribes." This grant of power is followed, in sections 9 and 10, by four limitations on its exercise and one limitation on the power of the states in respect to commerce. They relate to importation of slaves and migration of other persons into a state, imposition of taxes on imports and exports, and discrimination against one state in favor of another in ocean shipping.

We shall confine our attention to one part of the basic provision—that Congress shall have power to regulate commerce among the several states. This grant of authority is in the simplest of words, yet these words have unfolded into a body of propositions and explanations that constitute at least one half of the constitutional doctrine pronounced by the Supreme Court. "Congress shall have power" seems not to have excited significant dispute. It means: Congress, subject to the veto power of the president, may enact laws. "The several States" seems to mean, without serious question as yet, the original thirteen states and all other states subsequently admitted to the United States. But "regulate," "commerce," and "among the several States" quickly proved to lack an agreed content and have been at the center of dispute in the political branches of government and in the judiciary almost continuously since the Constitution went into effect.

1. A SEARCH FOR MEANING

The Supreme Court made its first important statement about the power to regulate commerce in 1824 in the case of *Gibbons* v. *Ogden* (9 Wheaton 1). The point at issue was the respective rights of two steamboat companies to engage in the coasting trade of New York, in waters wholly within the state of New York and between ports in New York and other states. Ogden asserted an exclusive right to engage in this trade; Gibbons asserted a right to enter into competition with Ogden. Ogden's case rested on the validity of a New York statute which granted to certain persons an exclusive (but a transferable) right to engage in the New York coasting trade by means of steam-propelled boats. A part of this monopolistic business had been assigned to Ogden, as the statute permitted, and he therefore claimed the exclusive privilege of operating by steam between ports of New York and New Jersey. Gibbons' case for breaking into the trade rested on a license to engage in the coasting trade which had been issued by the national government under the authority of an act of Congress. Ogden's claims had been upheld in the courts of New York, but the decision of the United States Supreme Court was in favor of Gibbons.

The opinion, written by Marshall, said that Ogden's rights under the New York statute were superseded by the rights of Gibbons under the act of Congress. To support this conclusion, Marshall had to establish the authority of the national government to make law governing participation in the coasting trade. Having established this point and finding conflict between rights asserted under that law and those asserted under a state law, he did not have to inquire whether a state had a right to regulate the coasting trade in the absence of any conflicting action by Congress. Gibbons won the suit because the national law was supreme over the conflicting state law. Nevertheless, Marshall did say a good deal about the extent of state power over commerce.

In spite of the apparent simplicity of the words "to regulate commerce among the several States," the Supreme Court had a wide range of choice in deciding what the national government was authorized to do. There was support, in the informed opinion of the day, for almost every imaginable definition of national power. It was argued by some that "commerce" covered all of business activity from original production to ultimate delivery of goods; by others, that "commerce" covered such business activity as trading or traffic, but not transportation of goods or the carrying trade; by still others, that "commerce" covered the carrying trade, but not trading or traffic.

"Among the several States" was thought by some to mean that the national government could regulate commerce (whatever that might be) wherever it went on among the people scattered throughout the states; by others, to mean that the national government could regulate only commerce that in some way involved people who lived in different states; by still others, to mean that the national government could regulate only commerce that was related to the movement of goods from one state to another.

The meaning of "regulate" was also in dispute. At the broadest, it was interpreted to allow the national government to do whatever good sense saw as needful to stimulate, promote, stabilize, protect; at the narrowest, it meant only that the national government could remove barriers which any state might erect against the movement of goods from one state into another.

In his opinion for *Gibbons* v. *Ogden,* Marshall addressed himself first to what was covered by the word "commerce," then to the limits fixed by the words "among the several States," and finally to the authority that was conferred by the phrase "Congress shall have power to regulate." Here are his most definitive statements on each point.

On "commerce":

> The counsel for the appellee would limit it to traffic, to buying and selling, or the interchange of commodities, and do not admit that it comprehends navigation. This would restrict a general term, applicable to many objects, to one of its significations. Commerce, undoubtedly, is traffic, but it is something more; it is intercourse. . . . All America understands, and has uniformly understood, the word "commerce" to comprehend navigation. (Pp. 189 f.)

It is clear from the context that, for Marshall, "traffic," "buying and selling," and "interchange of commodities" were nearly synonymous terms. For his word "navigation," we may substitute "transportation" or "movement." Marshall repeated the word "navigation" many times in his long opinion and did not even once say "transportation" or "movement." There can be no doubt that what he said about carrying goods by water was fully applicable to carriage by land vehicles; otherwise, many of his comprehensive statements about national power over foreign commerce and commerce among the states would have made no sense.

On "among the several States":

> The word "among" means intermingled with. A thing which is among others, is intermingled with them. Commerce among the states cannot stop at the external boundary line of each state, but may be introducted into the interior.
>
> It is not intended to say that these words comprehend that commerce which is completely internal, which is carried on between man and man in a state, or between different parts of the same state, and which does not extend to or affect other states. Such a power would be inconvenient, and is certainly unnecessary.
>
> Comprehensive as the word "among" is, it may very properly be restricted to that commerce which concerns more states than one. . . . The genius and character of the whole government seems to be, that its action is to be applied to all the external concerns of the nation, and to those internal concerns which affect the states generally; but not to those which are completely within a particular state, which do not affect other states, and with which it is not necessary to interfere, for the purpose of executing some of the general powers of the government. The completely internal commerce of a state, then, may be considered as reserved for the state itself. (Pp. 192, 194 f.)

On "power to regulate":

> We are now arrived at the inquiry, What is this power?
>
> It is the power to regulate; that is, to prescribe the rule by which commerce is to be governed. This power, like all others vested in Congress, is complete in itself, may be exercised to its utmost extent, and acknowledges no limitations, other than are prescribed in the constitution. . . . If, as has always been understood, the sovereignty of Congress, though limited to specified objects, is plenary as to those objects, the power over commerce with foreign nations, and among the several states, is vested in Congress as absolutely as it would be in a single government, having in its constitution the same restrictions on the exercise of the power as are found in the constitution of the United States. The wisdom and the discretion of Congress, their identity with the people, and the influence which their constituents possess at elections, are, in this, as in many other instances, as that, for example, of declaring war, the sole restraints on which they have relied, to secure them from its abuse. They are the restraints on which the people must often rely solely, in all representative governments. (Pp. 196 f.)

Marshall's opinion in *Gibbons* v. *Ogden* has been praised by one Supreme Court justice for its "close and precise discrimination of most difficult points" and characterized as "either unconsciously or calculatedly confused" by a law teacher who later became a Supreme Court justice. It must be recognized that the hard questions about placement of authority were by no means completely answered in that opinion, if, indeed, they were even partially answered. The national lawmakers, according to Marshall's statement, may prescribe the rules by which buying and selling are to be governed where buying and selling concern more states than one. People in all states, then as now, had a vital interest in cotton grown in the Southern states. Where would one, having Marshall's view and being reasonable about it, set the limits to national authority to regulate the production, sale, and shipment of cotton? Clearly, national legislation could regulate brokerage of cotton, and, if such regulation appeared necessary to ensure the availability of cotton and cotton goods in other states, it seems that national legislation could control warehousing, price and other terms of sale, and the transportation of cotton. Could the national government also regulate the sale of slaves used in the production of cotton or prohibit the use of slaves altogether? Professor Crosskey, whose prodigious research is discussed later in this chapter, finds that the meaning commonly attached to "the regulation of commerce" in Marshall's day extended its comprehension to "agriculture, manufactures, innkeeping, horse-keeping, and every other branch of the internal business of the country." [1]

A high estimate of Marshall's legal ability and political acumen requires one to conclude that Marshall did not intend to suggest answers to these questions. The generality of his language in *Gibbons* v. *Ogden* is paralleled in other opinions he wrote. Note the indefinite character of his statements in *McCulloch* v. *Maryland* quoted in the preceding chapter. It seems an obvious conclusion that Marshall made a deliberate effort to avoid close, precise discriminations in the little essays he wrote on the meaning of constitutional language conferring authority on the national government. This practice could not have been due to conviction that dicta should be limited to explanation of the Court's decision, for his greatest admirers admit that many of Marshall's opinions ran far beyond what the decision required. It is possible that Marshall avoided precise statements about limits of national authority because he personally favored an expanded national power and thought that a free hand for the national lawmakers was the best way to ensure that result.

1 *Politics and the Constitution . . .*, pp. 290–291 (cf. Bibliographic Note 9).

Finally, the evidence we have does not preclude a conclusion that Marshall believed that the makers of the Constitution intended the national lawmakers to have final authority in choice of means for executing the delegated powers. In *Marbury* v. *Madison,* where the Supreme Court demonstrated that it would void a statute that undermined its own constitutional position, Marshall said that, "in some cases . . . the constitution must be looked into by the judges," and he asked: "If they can open it at all, what part of it are they forbidden to read or obey?" He then cited three constitutional provisions which, he said, were "addressed especially to the courts," but none of his illustrations came from the parts of the Constitution which conferred authority on the national government; all were drawn from the section which announced limitations on the national government or from the article entitled "Judicial Department." Marshall's language in both *McCulloch* v. *Maryland* and *Gibbons* v. *Ogden* gave a strong implication that the Court would not overrule the lawmaking authority in the choice of means by which a delegated power would be carried out. The implication is strengthened, one can argue, by other remarks in these two opinions which suggest or assert that the Court would refuse to enforce a statute if the judges were convinced that it was defective in its purpose, that it was not in fact an effort to carry into execution one or more of the delegated powers.

Marshall, on other occasions, made remarks that bear on a concept of judicial review. If they do not add force to the implication noted above, they certainly do not weaken it.

2. "AMONG THE STATES" BECOMES "BETWEEN STATES"

Commerce among the states, as Marshall described it in *Gibbons* v. *Ogden,* is intercourse that concerns more states than one. Intercourse embraces both traffic and transportation, and traffic includes buying and selling, or the interchange of commodities. Marshall wrote two other opinions in which he discussed the placement of power to regulate commerce; what he said in each of them is consistent with what he said in *Gibbons* v. *Ogden.*

Marshall's expansive conception of the power delegated to the national government was gradually narrowed by his successors on the Supreme Court. The more restricted conception took the label "interstate commerce," and the distinctive characteristic of interstate commerce turned out to be, not buying and selling or intercourse, but a movement of things (of commodities, of people, of energy) from one state to another. An authoritative digest of constitutional law describes the scope of national power in this complicated but precise statement:

> Today "commerce" in the sense of the Constitution, and hence "interstate commerce" when it is carried on across State lines, covers every species of movement of persons and things, whether for profit or not; every species of communication, every species of transmission of intelligence, whether for commercial purposes or otherwise; every species of commercial negotiation which, as shown "by the established course of the business," will involve sooner or later an act of transportation of persons or things, or the flow of services or power across State lines.[2]

It would strain Marshall's words too much to hold that he viewed movement across state lines as the distinctive characteristic of commerce among the states. His references to buying and selling, to interchange, to intercourse, to commerce which concerns more states than one, to concerns which affect the states generally—these ways of disclosing his mind were made too prominent to permit one to believe that he would have endorsed this formulation: Commerce among the states actually comes to pass only when commodities, people, or energy move across the line which separates two states.

The transition from Marshall's conception to the ideas encased in the term "interstate commerce" was not thrust on the nation by a bold assertion of policy; it was accomplished by the accretion of small advances in successive suits which the Supreme Court was called on to decide. Nearly all the early cases involved the validity of state legislation, rather than acts of Congress. Some state laws were challenged on the ground that they were in conflict with national legislation, and the issue as to conflict could not be determined, of course, until the Court first decided what activities were covered by the act of Congress. In many of these cases, the Court was unable to decide what activities had been brought under the national law until it first made some inquiry into the question: How far does the Constitution authorize the national government to go under its grant of power to regulate commerce among the states? In other cases, where the parties challenging the state law could cite no conflicting national legislation, they contended that national power over commerce among the states was exclusive and

2 *The Constitution of the United States of America,* "Analysis and Interpretation," ed. Edward S. Corwin, pp. 119–120 (cf. Bibliographic Note 14).

that the state law was void because it attempted to invade an area from which the states were barred by the Constitution itself. Again, the Court could not decide whether the state law must be obeyed until it first decided whether the national government had exclusive power and, if it did, whether this exclusive power extended to the activities covered by the state statute. Decisions fixing limits to state authority also helped fix bounds to national power, even though the latter question did not come up for consideration in the case. If, for instance, the Court ruled that a commodity was subject to regulation by the state up to the point where it was delivered to the carrier who moved it across the state's boundary, that ruling became a guide in the later litigation which asked the question: When does an article enter interstate commerce and become subject to regulation by the national government?

Thoughtful students differ as to how greatly the present definition of interstate commerce varies from Marshall's concept of commerce that concerns more states than one. There can be no confident estimate as to how far the later judicial doctrine departs from the intentions of the men who wrote the Constitution, for we cannot be certain that the constitution-makers were in substantial agreement as to what the scope of national power should be, and we are therefore the further removed from knowing what that intention was if agreement did in fact exist. Uncertainties about original intentions became greater than ever when a University of Chicago law professor dropped a bomb into the literature of American constitutional history and constitutional law in 1953—William W. Crosskey, *Politics and the Constitution in the History of the United States*.[3] Among the consequences was a rude shock to the confidence that formerly ruled when scholars announced the meaning of language in the Constitution. Crosskey contends that, when one applies to the plain words of the Constitution the plain meaning which those words had in 1787, he must inescapably conclude that the constitution-makers supposed they had created a governmental system vastly different from the system which in fact developed and exists today. When one applies to the document the contemporary meaning of its words, "the meaning of the Constitution . . . is one utterly inconsistent with much that has long passed among us as history" (p. 6). "In this whole sorry development, the Supreme Court's theories of the national commerce power have, unquestionably, been the most important causative factor"

[3] Cf. Bibliographic Note 9.

(p. 46). The examples which he offers of "the evil consequences of the Supreme Court's theories" indicate for Crosskey "how the Court's theories have long operated to hamstring and defeat effective government; to prevent the making of a vast number of much-needed reforms; to produce injustice; and to waste, in a never ending process of useless litigation, not only the public funds of our national and state governments, but the private funds of civil litigants as well" (pp. 46–47).

Although Supreme Court judges have been the main contributors to distortion of the Constitution, in Crosskey's view, our most respected political leaders have done their bit. The "sophistries and inconsistencies" presented by John Adams, John Dickinson, and Alexander Hamilton are "typical of the sophistries and inconsistencies that political bias, or preference, as to the meaning of the Constitution, has produced in the pronouncements of politicians about that document, throughout our national history" (p. 290). James Madison is found to have been facile and prolific in deceit, and so his "Notes" on the debates and actions of the convention of 1787 and other writings which have been a main reliance of historians are declared next to useless as guides to the meaning of the Constitution and the intentions of its framers (pp. 1009 ff.). For the same reason, *The Federalist* goes down, too. The main thing it did was make available, "in permanent form, a body of sophistry, innuendo, and near-falsehood, as to the meaning of the Constitution" which proved of unique value to the political leaders who opposed adoption of the Constitution (p. 10).

The fundamental error in constitutional interpretation, according to Crosskey, was the classification of the domestic commerce of the country—that is, the commerce which is not with foreign nations or with Indian tribes—into two categories, that which is localized within a single state and that which involves people living in two or more states. Read into the words "power to regulate commerce among the several States" the meaning which those words were commonly given in 1787, and one comes up with something very different, says Crosskey. What emerges when the words are read correctly, he argues, is this: "The national government shall have power to regulate the gainful business, commerce, and industry of the American people." "Commerce among the several States," in this view, is the business activity that goes on among people located in the several states of the nation.

Having arrived at such a conclusion, Crosskey necessarily concluded further that the now-familiar terms, "interstate commerce" and "intrastate commerce," are labels for an allocation of power between national and state governments that does violence to the general design for government and to the contemporary meaning of the words which the framers chose in providing for national power over commerce. And, similarly, he had to conclude that John Marshall started the judicial branch and the lawmakers down the path of error when he said that the national power "may very properly be restricted to that commerce which concerns more states than one."

Nearly all serious students of our constitutional development acknowledge admiration for the rare ingenuity which Crosskey brought to the formulation of crucial questions and for his prodigious research in trying to answer those questions. Although many highly regarded scholars have said that he is wrong on this or that and that he cannot be right in the main, I think none of them will say that he ought to be ignored. And at least a few men who stand up under other tests of scholarship have announced their conviction that Crosskey is basically right.

I present this view about what some of their words may have meant to the men who wrote the Constitution because Crosskey's extreme position shows the risk one assumes in evaluating the Supreme Court's use of its power. Surely one should be confident that he knows what the framers intended their words to mean before he accuses judges of distorting the meaning of constitutional language, nullifying provisions of the Constitution, and adding to it requirements and prohibitions not put there by the framers or by the amending process. Scholars who examine the Constitution's language and the circumstances of its origin seek to establish guides for interpreting the Constitution and criteria for evaluating interpretations which are made. The great distance which separates Crosskey and his supporters from those scholars in sharp opposition is proof that all critics of the Supreme Court measure from a precarious point when they conclude that the Supreme Court has extended, contracted, or twisted the Constitution's meaning.

CHAPTER THIRTEEN

To Regulate Commerce among the States

1. FROM "IN COMMERCE" TO "EFFECT UPON COMMERCE"
2. SHUFFLE AND NEW DEAL
3. REGULATION EMBRACES EXCLUSION

Within a few years after death removed John Marshall from the Supreme Court, that tribunal wrote into the Constitution two doctrines concerning national authority over commerce which were mentioned in the preceding chapter—that commerce among the states is better termed "interstate commerce" and that national power to regulate such commerce is confined to action that has an observable relation to movement of things (commodities, persons, and energy) from one state to another. Slower in coming was doctrine on a third point—in what manner and how closely must a particular regulation be related to interstate movement in order for the Court to hold that it is a regulation of interstate commerce.

It is the elaboration of constitutional doctrine on this third point which we shall now examine—the specification of boundaries within which the national government must contain itself in its effort to regulate interstate commerce. A good understanding of how the judges have used their power can be had by examining two questions to which many of their decisions and opinions have been addressed. (1) How far out from the actual movement of things may the national government reach in its effort to control interstate commerce? (2) How much power does the national government have to determine what things may move in interstate commerce?

1. FROM "IN COMMERCE" TO "EFFECT UPON COMMERCE"

The evidence is overwhelming that, when one spoke of commerce in 1787 and for three or four decades thereafter, he certainly included something then called traffic. Furthermore, Marshall seems to have followed the common usage when he said that traffic includes "buying and selling, or the interchange of commodities." It surely follows from this that the Constitution endowed the national government with authority to regulate activity at some distance from the occurrences we regard as the actual movement of goods from state to state. But how far removed can the activity be?

The litigation which thrust this question most sharply before the courts arose under national statutes forbidding business combinations and practices which effect a restraint on interstate commerce and national statutes which, by regulating business enterprise, attempt to ensure that commodities in nation-wide demand will continue to be produced and moved in interstate commerce.

The first significant decision of the Supreme Court concerning this area of national regulatory effort was *U.S.* v. *E.C. Knight Co.* (156 U.S. 1, 1895). The American Sugar Refining Company purchased the stock and properties of Knight and three other sugar-refining companies, by these purchases completing a consolidation program that set American Sugar up as producer of at least 90 per cent and possibly 98 per cent of all the refined sugar on the U. S. market. The attorney general brought suit to force the restoration of the four purchased companies to their former independent status on the grounds that the consolidation was a combination in restraint of trade or commerce among the states and that the agreement to purchase and sell was a conspiracy to restrain trade or commerce among the states and therefore in violation of the Sherman Anti-Trust Act of 1890. The Sherman Act opened with this sentence (elaborated in later sections of the act): "Every contract, combination in the form of trust or otherwise, or conspiracy, in restraint of trade or commerce among the several States, or with foreign nations, is hereby declared to be illegal."

Before deciding whether the Sherman Act forbade the transaction and resultant corporate structure presented in the case, the Court felt obliged to determine whether the national government had been vested with authority to forbid such a transaction and combination. The Court, by vote of eight to one, ruled that the power of the national government did not extend that far. It then decided that the lawmakers had not intended the statute to apply to such a case, thus saving the Sherman Act for application in other situations which might, in the Court's judgment, fall within the range of authority given the national government.

The Court's opinion, by Chief Justice Melville W. Fuller, presents special difficulties for the reader, but, allowing for this, I think we can identify three important positions in the opinion.

A. Authority is given to government in chunks, in segments that can be separated in the mind. "The power to regulate commerce," said Fuller, "is the power to prescribe the rule by which commerce shall be governed, and is a power independent of the power to suppress monopoly." The power to suppress monopoly and acts that restrain trade among the citizens of a state was retained by the states and is "essentially exclusive." The national government's commerce power "may operate in repression of monopoly whenever that [effort to repress] comes within the rules by which commerce is governed or whenever the transaction [i.e., what the national government is repressing] is itself a monopoly of commerce" (p. 12).

B. In addition to authority to regulate carriers and the activities that constitute transportation, the commerce power (as respects commerce among the states) restricts the national government to regulation of things and activities that are actually in transit or directly involved in movement from one state to another. The manufacturer's disposition of his product "may result in bringing the operation of commerce into play," said Fuller, but his disposition of his product "does not control it [commerce], and affects it only incidentally and indirectly. Commerce succeeds to manufacture, and is not a part of it. . . . Contracts to buy, sell, or exchange goods to be transported among the several states, the transportation and its instrumentalities, and articles bought, sold, or exchanged for the purpose of such transit among the states, or put in the way of transit, may be regulated, but this is because they form part of interstate trade or commerce. The fact that an article is manufactured for export to another state does not of itself make it an article of interstate commerce, and the intent of the manufacturer does not determine the time when the article or product passes from the control of the state and belongs to commerce" (pp. 12–13).

C. Whether a thing or activity is involved in movement and therefore within the reach of the national government's commerce power may be determined by the ends sought by those who control the thing or perform the activity. "Contracts, combinations, or conspiracies to control domestic enterprise in manufacture . . . might unquestionably tend to restrain external as well as domestic trade, but the restraint would be an indirect result, however inevitable and whatever its extent, and such result would not necessarily determine the object of the contract, combination, or conspiracy. . . . [I]t does not follow that an attempt to monopolize, or the actual monopoly of, the manufacture [of refined sugar by American Sugar Refining Company] was an attempt . . . to monopolize commerce, even though, in order to dispose of the product, the instrumentality of commerce was necessarily invoked" (pp. 16–17).

The view of national power taken by Fuller and his colleagues denied the national government authority to break up a merger of properties by which one firm removed the last of its effective competition and obtained control of 90 per cent or more of the nation's refined sugar, and that in spite of the fact that most of the nation's population could not buy a pound of refined sugar unless it came to them as interstate or foreign commerce. As a majority of the Court saw it, the refining operations preceded movement in interstate commerce and so were not actually in or a part of such commerce, and nothing was shown to indicate that it was the purpose of the surviving refiners to reduce the movement of sugar from state to state. It might be that the managers of the monopoly would raise prices and that the movement of sugar in interstate commerce would actually diminish; but it was equally likely that they would make a fair effort to cause more sugar than ever before to move across the country.

The conditions for national action implied by the doctrines of the Knight case were presented to the national government by the meat-packing industry a decade later. In *Swift & Company* v. *U.S.* (196 U.S. 375, 1905), the Supreme Court unanimously affirmed an injunction restraining a group of packing companies from proceeding under several agreements they had entered into which the Court found in violation of the Sherman Act. This victory for the government was followed by a later defeat in litigation under that statute, so Congress and the president supplemented it with the Packers and Stockyards Act of 1921. This act forbids practices on the part of stockyard owners and those doing business in stockyards which result in restraint of interstate commerce and gives the secretary of agriculture considerable authority to issue general rules and individual orders which make the statutory prohibitions effective. The year following its enactment, the new statute was held valid and was applied to the dealers and commission men operating in the Chicago stockyards. The conditions which prevailed in the packing industry and the reasoning by which the Supreme Court justified national intervention are sufficiently presented for our purposes in the later case, *Stafford* v. *Wallace* (258 U.S. 495, 1922).

During the first twenty years of this century, five packing companies (Swift, Armour, Cudahy, Wilson, and Morris) maintained, according to a report of the Federal Trade Commission, "complete control of the trade from the producer to the consumer." One of the essential means by which they had eliminated other firms and terminated competition among themselves, according to this report, was by creating a special corporation to control the facilities and activities in the stockyards of each packing center. The Union Stockyards & Transit Company of Chicago, owned by the five big packers, in turn owned everything connected with the Chicago stockyards except the sunshine and the weather, and it was charged that this company imposed its will on everything that moved within its precincts except the contrariest steer. The consequences of this tight control for stock-raisers and shippers were alleged abuses of three types: unreasonable charges and objectionable practices in handling animals within the yards; suppression of competition among the packers by various kinds of collusion in bidding for livestock; and, by "wiring ahead," making sure that the shipper who was not satisfied with the price at one center would not be offered a better price in any other.

The suit in *Stafford* v. *Wallace* was brought by commission men and dealers operating in the Chicago stockyards. Commission men receive the incoming livestock and sell it for the shippers, either to packers or to dealers. Dealers purchase animals for their own profit-making enterprise, reselling some of them to packers but mainly to feeders, who remove the animals to farms for further growth and fattening. The commission men and dealers, in this suit, did not deny that interstate commerce was going on about them; they argued that their operations were at an interlude in interstate commerce and that the federal statute was therefore invalid if applied to them. One interstate movement, they contended, is from the farms and ranches to the stockyards. There the first movement comes to an end. Later, a new movement begins, perhaps an intrastate movement to the feed lots in Illinois or an interstate movement to the feed lots of other states. For a half or more of the animals passing through the commission men, the termination of the first interstate movement is even more decisive. Sold to a packer, the soul is freed from the body, and the body is reassembled for a new shipment, mainly interstate, to jobbers who move the meat on toward the family and the restaurant trade.

Is the movement of meat from the farms and ranches to the nation's tables a single connected flow of goods, every phase of which may be regulated by the national government? Or is it a number of separate flows—one from the farm or ranch to the stockyards, another from the stockyards to the packing house, still another from the packing house to the warehouse of the jobber or wholesaler, and a final one which carries the meat on to retailer and consumer? Seven members of the Supreme Court agreed that it was one continuous flow of goods; one justice dissented without saying why, and another justice did not sit in the case. Said Chief Justice William Howard Taft, writing for the majority:

> The stockyards are not a place of rest or final destination. . . . The stockyards are but a throat through which the current flows, and the transactions which occur therein are only incident to this current from the West to the East, and from one state to another. Such transactions cannot be separated from the movement to which they contribute, and necessarily take on its character. [From here I compact several sentences.] The commission men are essential in making the sales, and the dealers are essential to the sales to farmers and feeders. The sales create a change of title, but they do not stop the flow, not interfering with, but, on the contrary, being indispensable to, its continuity. This is the definite and well-understood course of business. The stockyards and the sales are necessary factors in the middle of this current of commerce. Whatever amounts to more or less constant practice and threatens to obstruct or unduly to burden the freedom of interstate commerce is within the regulatory power of Congress under the commerce clause, and it is primarily for Congress to consider and decide the fact of the danger and meet it. (Pp. 515–516, 521.)

The Court accordingly stated that the Packers and Stockyards Act is "clearly within Congressional power and valid," and they held it fully applicable to the practices of commission men and dealers in the stockyards. It should be added that Taft's opinion expressed approval of a declaration in the earlier Swift case that the national government may break up a combination which "embraces restraint and monopoly of trade within a single state [if] its effect upon commerce among the states is not accidental, secondary, remote, or merely probable."

The reasoning in *Stafford* v. *Wallace* gave Pres. Franklin Roosevelt and his supporters ground for hope, a decade later, that they could use the language of the commerce clause to justify a vast program of legislation designed to restore the vigor of American business which had been lost in the Depression. If the national government may regulate transactions which obstruct commerce at the throat, through which commodities move in interstate transit, does it not follow that it may also regulate transactions at the mouth, where entry to interstate transit may be obstructed? And, continuing the biological analogy, if the national government may remove obstructions in the throat, may it not also remove obstructions at the point where commodities fulfill the objectives of all previous movement by entering the digestive process—the point where interstate transport delivers commodities to the nation's productive plant and commercial trade?

The first half of this dual issue was presented to the Supreme Court in *Carter* v. *Carter Coal Company* (298 U.S. 238, 1936); the second half, in *Schechter Poultry Corp.* v. *U.S.* (295 U.S. 495, 1935). The lawmakers were rebuffed at both ends. A comprehensive program for regulation of the bituminous-coal-mining industry went down in the Carter case. A special code for regulation of the live-poultry trade in metropolitan New York went down in the Schechter case. In these two cases and *U.S.* v. *Butler* (297 U.S. 1, 1936) went down a good one-half of the innovation in public policy which the nation called the New Deal. The reverberation shook out of the White House a proposal to put new judges on the Supreme Court.

In the Schechter case, which came to the Court before the Carter case, all judges agreed that the national government had gone beyond the confines of its commerce power in regulating wages, working hours, and other conditions of employment and in forbidding certain practices branded as unfair and discriminatory in the sale and slaughtering of poultry in the New York area. More than 95 per cent of the live poultry came into the area by crossing state lines; the report does not disclose how much of the dressed meat moved from one state to another. Chief Justice Charles Evans Hughes said for the whole bench that "neither the slaughtering nor the sales [by the slaughtering companies] were transactions in interstate commerce. . . . [T]he flow in interstate commerce had ceased. The poultry had come to a permanent rest in the State." Furthermore, he said, the code provisions regulating the terms and conditions of employment in the slaughter houses and the provisions regulating sale of live and dressed poultry by the slaughtering companies could not be saved on the ground that they had their impact on matters affecting interstate commerce. The power of Congress, he said, extends to the protection of interstate commerce from injury, and "it matters not that the injury may be due to the conduct of those engaged in intrastate operations." But, if the impact does not fall on interstate commerce itself, it must be found that what it falls on has a direct effect on interstate commerce. "But where the effect of intrastate transactions upon interstate commerce is merely indirect, such transactions remain within the domain of State power. . . . [T]he distinction between direct and indirect effects of intrastate transactions upon interstate commerce must be recognized as a fundamental one, essential to the maintenance of our constitutional system."

In the Carter Coal case, six justices agreed that the provisions of a New Deal statute which guaranteed collective bargaining and fixed other requirements for employment in the soft-coal-mining industry exceeded the authority of the national government to regulate interstate commerce and were also invalid on other grounds. Five of the six judges thought the labor provisions inseparable from another main part of the statute relating to prices and marketing of coal, so the validity of the latter part of the statute was not discussed in the Court's majority opinion. Hughes was one of the six justices who thought the labor provisions invalid, but he contended that they were separable from other parts of the statute and, further, that the price and marketing section of the law was within the power of Congress. The remaining three judges held that the main parts of the statute were separable and that the price and marketing section was valid, but they considered a suit protesting the labor provisions premature and for that reason did not express themselves on the validity of that part of the act.

In a case which I have not discussed (*Railroad Retirement Board* v. *Alton Railroad Company*, 295 U.S. 330, decided in 1935), the Supreme Court held that the federal government's retirement and pension system for railroad employees was invalid because it was not intended to be a rule or regulation of commerce and transportation, but rather was intended to protect employees from dependency in their old age. The drafters of the Bituminous Coal Conservation Act sought to protect that statute from vulnerability on the same ground by expressly stating that the production and distribution of coal bears upon and directly affects interstate commerce, that various practices which the statute seeks to correct have led to disorganization of interstate commerce in coal and burdened and obstructed such commerce, that conditions in the coal business which affect interstate commerce make necessary national regulation for the protection of that commerce, and so on.

Justice George Sutherland, writing for the five judges who stood together, rejected this effort to weld the statute's provisions to the commerce clause. The impact of the statute's provisions relating to employment conditions, he said, "primarily falls upon production and not upon commerce." But the preamble of the statute declares that the production and distribution of coal "bear upon and directly affect its interstate commerce." Therefore, he continued, the Court is forced, as its final and decisive inquiry, to determine "whether here that effect is direct, as the 'preamble' recites, or indirect." The point to be determined is not whether interstate commerce is greatly or only slightly disturbed by strikes, inefficiency, and other actualities of employment in the mines; the point to be determined is whether these actualities are directly or only indirectly related to interstate commerce.

There is the prime gift of the Carter Coal case to judicial doctrine elaborating the commerce clause. Conviction that a regulatory act will effectively remove colossal obstructions to interstate commerce does not establish the right of national lawmakers to enact that regulation; the right of the national government to act is determined by a decision whether the matter it proposes to regulate is directly or only indirectly related to interstate commerce. Here are the more relevant sentences in Sutherland's opinion:

> The word "direct" implies that the activity or condition invoked or blamed shall operate proximately—not mediately, remotely, or collaterally—to produce the effect. It connotes the absence of an efficient intervening agency or condition. And the extent of the effect bears no logical relation to its character. The distinction between a direct and an indirect effect turns not upon the magnitude of either the cause or the effect, but entirely upon the manner in which the effect has been brought about. (Pp. 307–308.)

Concerning the contention of the national government that strikes, curtailment of production, and other matters which the statute attempts to deal with do in fact greatly affect interstate commerce, Sutherland said:

> The conclusive answer is that the evils are all local evils over which the federal government has no legislative control. The relation of employer and employee is a local relation. . . . Such effect as they may have upon commerce, however extensive it may be, is secondary and indirect. An increase in the greatness of the effect adds to its importance. It does not alter its character. (Pp. 308–309.)

2. SHUFFLE AND NEW DEAL

The foregoing reports on the Schechter and Carter Coal cases scan the reasoning by which the Supreme Court brought down some main pillars of President Roosevelt's New Deal program. Thwarted by the Court, the President struck back with his proposal to reorganize the federal judiciary, one feature of which would enable the president, with Senate consent, to appoint additional judges to the Supreme Court. The plan was laid before Congress on February 5, 1937. During that week, the Supreme Court heard argument on the constitutionality of another vital New Deal statute, the National Labor Relations Act of 1935. On April 12, 1937, the Supreme Court, by vote of five to four, held the act valid as applied to three business firms involved in the suits before it. The change in position, observed by comparing the orders and the opinion in the later case with those in the Schechter and Carter cases, is the dramatic event that many writers have called the somersault of 1937 and a federal judge referred to as the timely consent that kept an aggression against the judicial branch from becoming a rape.

Chief Justice Hughes and Justice Owen J. Roberts were among the six members of the Court who thought the commerce clause did not empower the national government to regulate the terms of employment in coal mines (Carter Coal case). In 1935, Hughes took the position that the national government could impose a pension and retirement system on railroad companies engaged in interstate commerce, but Roberts was on the other side and wrote the opinion which argued that the commerce clause did not confer that authority (Railroad Retirement Board case). When the National Labor Relations Act was considered, both these judges found it within the scope of national authority and so created the majority of five which declared the act valid and made it enforceable. The decision which held the act valid is reported as *National Labor Relations Board* v. *Jones & Laughlin Steel Corp.* (301 U.S. 1, 1937); it will be referred to as the NLRB case.

The purpose of the National Labor Relations Act, as stated in its first section, is to "eliminate the causes of certain substantial obstructions to the free flow of commerce and to mitigate and eliminate these obstructions when they have occurred." This result is to be achieved by (1) guaranteeing workers the right to bargain with employers through representatives of their own choosing; (2)

specifying and branding as unfair certain practices which obstruct the efforts of workers to bargain through representatives of their own choosing; and (3) creating a National Labor Relations Board and empowering it to prevent persons from "engaging in any unfair labor practice affecting commerce." The statute defined commerce as "trade, traffic, commerce, transportation, or communication among the several States" and stated that "affecting commerce" means "in commerce, or burdening or obstructing commerce or the free flow of commerce, or having led or tending to lead to a labor dispute burdening or obstructing commerce or the free flow of commerce."

The three business firms over which the National Labor Relations Board had asserted authority were: (1) The nation's fourth-largest manufacturer of iron and steel products, a concern which owned and operated as an integrated industrial empire iron-ore deposits, coal mines, limestone quarries, land and water transportation facilities, smelting facilities, rolling mills, and fabricating plants. Its plants, offices, and other facilities were located in many states, and more than half its supplies and product moved across state lines. (2) The nation's leading manufacturer of trailers used in automobile trucking. Manufacture was located exclusively in one state, but more than half the finished product moved across state lines. The trailers were marketed through branch offices in twelve states and through local dealers scattered throughout the nation. (3) A small manufacturer of men's clothing. Almost all of the raw materials used came to the manufacturing plant from other states, and more than 80 per cent of the finished product was shipped into other states.

Opinions differ as to how far Hughes and Roberts had to travel in order to get from their positions denying national authority in the earlier cases to their stand in favor of national authority in the NLRB case. It seems to me that Hughes did not reject any of his own earlier statements or even notably twist their meaning in writing the majority opinion which held the NLRB statute valid. In one or another prior majority opinion of the Court, he could find a statement on which he could rest every main point of his argument. In most instances where the prior language seemed to run contrary to his needs, the key words were so vague or general in their meaning that he could deny them a controlling effect if he could not construe them to support his position. Where the previous language would help his argument, he embraced it; where previous language would embarrass him, he skirted it. If this is a proper way for judges to fit previous statements to new situations, Hughes gave us a masterly demonstration of opinion-writing.

Here is the heart of his contention, in his words. For every phrase or clause he put in quotation marks, he cited its origin in a previous decision.

> The fundamental principle is that the power to regulate commerce is the power to enact "all appropriate legislation" for "its protection and advancement"; to adopt measures "to promote its growth and insure its safety"; "to foster, protect, control and restrain." That power is plenary and may be exerted to protect interstate commerce "no matter what the source of the dangers which threaten it." (Pp. 36–37.)

Justice Sutherland had said in the Carter Coal case that the regulations relating to employment in the coal mines fell on production and not on commerce and, falling as they did on production, did not have their impact on anything that directly affected interstate commerce. Further, said Sutherland, it is irrelevant whether the matters regulated have a small or a great effect on interstate commerce; the relevant question is the directness of their relation to interstate commerce and not the magnitude of their effect on it. In writing his NLRB opinion, Hughes did not say: "I was wrong in going along with Justice Sutherland and four other judges in this view of the commerce clause." What he said was: The Carter Coal decision is not controlling here, and "the fact that the employees here [in the three firms involved in the NLRB case] were engaged in production is not determinative." The key question, he said, is "as to the effect upon interstate commerce of the labor practice involved." Having committed ourselves to a federal system which allocates authority between nation and states, he held, the scope of national power "may not be so extended as to embrace effects upon interstate commerce so indirect and remote that to embrace them . . . would effectually obliterate the distinction between what is national and what is local and create a completely centralized national government." But, allowing this limiting principle, where activities which may be intrastate when separately considered "have such a close and substantial relation to interstate commerce that their control is essential or appropriate to protect that commerce from burdens and obstructions, Congress cannot be denied the power to exercise that control." The activities of each of these three firms—great steel empire, leading manufacturer of trailers, small manufacturer of men's clothing—is so far-flung that the stoppage of its operations by industrial strife "would have a most serious effect upon interstate commerce. . . . [I]t is idle to say that the effect would be indirect or remote. . . . [I]t would be immediate and might be catastrophic." The National Labor Relations Act being a studied effort to forestall the strife that stops the operations of such enterprises, it follows that Congress and president had authority under the commerce clause to enact that statute.

Only the future can fix the significance of the NLRB decision. Certainly, the decision permitted the enforcement of legislation which, tested by certain judicial doctrines of the preceding decades, would not have been within the scope of national authority. Certainly, also, the language which Hughes employed was sufficiently flexible to allow Congress and the president to regulate acts that occur long before or long after the journey that crosses a state line in their effort to ensure that goods will continue to move from one part of the country to another. Some writers on constitutional law have stretched these facts into a conclusion that the Supreme Court will never again hold a national statute invalid on the ground that it is not necessary and proper to an enumerated power or encroaches on a power reserved to the states. I see little warrant for this conclusion, either in the record of judicial action to date or in the argument developed in the NLRB decision. Indeed, I think it possible that the Court, at any future time, may find that the language employed by Hughes gives judges a greater invitation to enthrone their own judgments as to what is sound public policy than they can find in earlier opinions which were more concerned to formulate rules designed to instruct the political and judicial branches alike as to where the limits to national authority are to be found. Further inquiry along these lines comes better, however, after we have examined some other lines of constitutional development.

3. REGULATION EMBRACES EXCLUSION

Quoting from previous statements of the Supreme Court in his opinion in the NLRB case, Hughes said that the power to regulate commerce is a power to promote the growth and ensure the safety of commerce—to advance, foster, control, and restrain commerce. The number and order of the verbs may suggest that the grant of authority to the national government mainly confers power to cause commerce to flourish and in much less degree confers power to restrain commerce and cause it to decrease or terminate. No doubt the men who wrote the Constitution expected that the whole body of national law on the subject would encourage and develop a nation-wide trade, but they may well have thought that this general result would be in part accomplished by removing some objects from the channels of trade. A tariff which wholly prevents certain foreign goods from entering the country comes to mind. Quarantines, temporary or permanent, might have been contemplated. Some men who shared in writing or adopting the Constitution must have looked forward to national legislation forbidding the shipment of slaves from one state to another.

The authority of the national government to exclude from interstate commerce has several times been questioned in the Supreme Court—what commodities, persons, messages may be excluded under what circumstances? These cases present lines of reasoning quite as interesting as those we have already examined, but we shall not go into them at equal length. It will be enough to summarize the positions taken by the Supreme Court, rather than the reasoning by which those positions were justified.

The United States declared embargoes on the import and and export of commodities from and to other countries before the Constitution was twenty years old, but authority for these acts could be found in a joinder of the commerce clause with the inherent power of the national government to control relations with foreign peoples. National authority over commercial intercourse between two or more states stands on the commerce clause alone and therefore may be thought not sufficient for absolute embargo on shipments from state to state. The question of national authority to exclude from interstate movement came squarely before the Supreme Court for the first time in 1903, in *Champion* v. *Ames* (188 U.S. 321). The things barred from shipment across a state line were lottery tickets.

The act of Congress was held valid by a Court that divided five to four. The opinion for the majority stood on a series of previous general statements in which Supreme Court judges had repeated and elaborated the point that, as respects commerce that is interstate in character, all the power that governments possess for controlling commerce had been given to the national government. John Marshall had said, in *Gibbons* v. *Ogden,* that what may be regulated is commercial intercourse, that the power to regulate is the power to prescribe the rule by which commercial intercourse is to be governed, and that the power to govern may be exercised to its utmost extent and knows no limitations except such as are prescribed by the Constitution. Although the Lottery opinion quoted from many other cases, when it came to stating conclusions all that was offered could be found in Marshall's propositions. Compacted here for easy comprehension, the final sentence in the opinion reads:

> We decide nothing more in the present case than that lottery tickets are subjects of traffic; that the carriage of such tickets from one state to another is interstate commerce; that under its power to regulate commerce among the several states Congress has plenary authority over such commerce and may prohibit the carriage of such tickets from state to state; and that legislation to that end is not inconsistent with any limitation imposed upon the exercise of powers granted to Congress.

The four dissenting judges, holding that the national government could not prohibit the carriage of lottery tickets across state lines, also started with Marshall, but drew their main support from another line of previous cases. Marshall said that the regulatory power conferred by the commerce clause is power to regulate *commercial* intercourse. It has been held for many kinds of contractual relations that the paper which states a contract is not an article of commerce, and a lottery ticket is a contract. The lottery ticket not being an article of commerce, the attempt of the national government to exclude it from shipment is, therefore, not a regulation of commercial intercourse. What the act of Congress is can be seen in the objectives of the enactment. It is an effort to make lotteries unprofitable and so put an end to their operation in the United States, and the reason for doing this is solely to protect the morals of the population. The statute is, therefore, an effort to exercise a police power which was not granted to the national government by the Constitution, but was instead reserved to the states.

Within a quarter-century after the Lottery decision, the Supreme Court was confronted with federal statutes forbidding interstate shipment of impure foods and drugs and diseased livestock, transport or escort of women from one state to another with a view to illicit sexual relations, carriage of intoxicating liquor into states which made the sale of intoxicating liquor unlawful, movement of stolen goods and of kidnapped persons across state lines, and shipment in interstate commerce of commodities produced by child labor. The precedent in the Lottery decision and extensions of the reasoning presented by the majority in that case were sufficient to sustain the validity of all these statutes except the last cited. In *Hammer* v. *Dagenhart* (247 U.S. 251, 1918), the Federal Child Labor Law of 1916 went down by vote of five to four.

In proper style, the majority opinion in the Child Labor case opened with reference to Marshall in *Gibbons* v. *Ogden.* Marshall said that the power to regulate commerce is the power "to prescribe the rule by which commerce is to be governed." "In other words," said Justice William R. Day for the majority in the Child Labor case, "the power is one to control the means by which commerce is carried on, which [in turn] is directly the contrary of the assumed right to forbid commerce from moving and thus destroy it as to particular commodities." The statutes relating to impure food and drugs, immoral use of women, and stolen goods had come before the Supreme Court prior to the child labor statute, and all had been found to be lawful exclusions from interstate commerce. They presented issues significantly different from the issue now before the Court, Day said. The right to exclude which was acknowledged in the earlier cases rested on "the character of the particular subjects dealt with" and on the fact that "the authority to prohibit is, as to them, but the exertion of the power to regulate." In each of the earlier cases, "the use of interstate transportation was necessary to the accomplishment of harmful results." As respects the persons and commodities excluded, regulation of interstate transportation "could only be accomplished by prohibiting the use of the facilities of interstate commerce to effect the evil intended. This element is wanting in the present case. . . . The goods shipped are of themselves harmless. . . . When offered for shipment, and before transportation begins, the labor of their production is over. . . ." The necessary effect of this act, he said later in the opinion, "is, by means of a prohibition against the movement in interstate commerce of ordinary commercial commodities, to regulate the hours of labor of children in factories and mines within the states, . . . a purely state authority." Elsewhere, Day said: "The grant of power to Congress over the subject of interstate commerce was to enable it to regulate such commerce, and not to give it authority to control the states in their exercise of the police power over local trade and manufacture."

Four judges could not find any significant elements in the earlier cases that were wanting in the Child Labor case. Writing for them, Justice Oliver Wendell Holmes made the following argument: (1) It is well established that the power to regulate commerce includes the power to prohibit carriage of commodities. (2) If carriage of the goods at issue in this case cannot be prohibited, it is because of the consequences the prohibition has for state governmental authority. (3) Previous cases establish that the powers of the national government cannot be reduced or qualified because of the fact that their exercise may interfere with the carrying out of the domestic policy of any state. (4) If the power to prohibit carriage is limited to things evil in character, "It does not matter whether the supposed evil preceded or follows the transportation. It is enough that, in the opinion of Congress, the transportation encourages the evil." (5) If civilized countries are agreed that any one matter is evil, it is that premature and excessive child labor is evil. (6) The national lawmakers may well see as inimical to national welfare something which the lawmakers of a state may not think inimical to the welfare of its population, and the national lawmakers may enforce their understanding of the national welfare by all the means at their command.

Holmes's reasoning came to triumph in 1941. The federal Fair Labor Standards Act forbade shipment in interstate commerce of goods produced under circumstances not in keeping with the minimum wage and maximum working hours specified by that statute. The constitutionality of the act was settled in *U.S.* v. *Darby* (312 U.S. 100, 1941). Speaking for all eight judges then on the Court, Justice Harlan F. Stone said:

> The conclusion is inescapable that *Hammer* v. *Dagenhart* was a departure from the principles which have prevailed in the interpretation of the commerce clause both before and since the decision and that such vitality, as a precedent, as it then had has long since been exhausted. It should be and now is overruled. (Pp. 116–117.)

I find nothing else in Stone's opinion likely to clarify one's understanding as to what that Court considered the outward limits of national power to regulate interstate commerce.

Corwin wrote in 1953 that debate over the right of the national government to exclude things from interstate commerce came to an end with *U.S.* v. *Darby*. Pessimists may be pardoned for their doubt that any issue in constitutional law is ever finally laid to rest. It may be noted, however, that hope of upsetting restrictive legislation has been greatly reduced in recent years by a relatively new venture in cooperative state-national relations. Several acts of Congress now provide that specified commodities may not be taken out of a state contrary to the laws of that state or may not be brought into a state which has laws forbidding their entry or disposition. Under such legislation, the hunter who kills game illegally cannot escape prosecution by scooting for a state border; the joinder of national commerce power and state police power removes all question of conflict between jurisdictions, and either national or state authorities may prosecute. The validity of federal legislation of this type has been upheld in several suits before the Supreme Court.

CHAPTER FOURTEEN

Due Process of Law

1. THE COMPLETE CONSTITUTIONAL GUARANTEE
2. FROM MODE OF PROCEEDING TO CAUSE AND OBJECT
3. NO DEFINITE MEANING

In the preceding chapter we examined fewer than a dozen of the many hundreds of cases in which the Supreme Court has given meaning to the constitutional language allocating authority to regulate commerce. One who comes new to the study of constitutional law must see, in the few cases we have examined, a recurring reluctance of the Supreme Court to settle important issues about constitutional authority, to restate constitutional language in ways that will clarify the limits of governmental authority, to formulate the supplementary rules that will instruct lawmakers as to what they may and may not do, and inform the governed as to when they can count on the courts to rescue them from unlawful exercise of governmental power.

It is true that the judges have offered guiding propositions—rules in embryo—in many of their opinions, as when Sutherland (in the Carter Coal case) said that, to be valid, the regulation must fall directly on commerce, not make its impact through an intervening agency, and that the magnitude or seriousness of a disturbance of commerce has no relevance for establishing the existence or want of power to remove the cause of that disturbance. But it is equally true that in many other cases the opinion of the Court seems carefully designed to give as few hints as possible as to what will be treated as boundaries of authority in subsequent cases. Note, for instance, the statement of Hughes in the NLRB case that Congress has power to regulate activities which have such a close and substantial relation to interstate commerce that their control is essential or appropriate to protect that commerce—or shall we say, Congress has power to regulate what it is essential or appropriate to have regulated? This does not seem to add much to the Constitution's statement that Congress shall have power to regulate commerce among the several states.

We shall note later some of the consequences of these alternatives in method, elaborating the Constitution's language with supplemental rules or consciously avoiding the proposal of rules which would control subsequent actions. It is sufficient here to point out that the absence of rules with which they would feel obliged to comply enlarges the freedom of judges to decide each later case according to the values and convictions pre-eminent in their minds when the case comes before them. This observation is especially pertinent now, when we are to examine the sector of constitutional law in which our judges have been least hampered by rules and have therefore enjoyed the greatest freedom to enthrone their personal views as to what constitutes sound public policy.

1. THE COMPLETE CONSTITUTIONAL GUARANTEE

The United States Constitution refers twice to "due process of law." The Fifth Amendment, which imposes limitations on the national government, states that "no person shall be . . . deprived of life, liberty, or property, without due process of law"; and the Fourteenth Amendment, which imposes limitations on state and local governments, states: ". . . nor shall any State deprive any person of life, liberty, or property, without due process of law."

One will not go far wrong if he thinks of the due-process requirement as the complete constitutional limitation on government, making all other constitutional restraints unnecessary. Justice John Marshall Harlan expressed such a view in these words: "In my judgment the words 'life, liberty, or property' in the 14th Amendment should be interpreted as embracing every right that may be brought within judicial cognizance, and therefore no right of that kind can be taken in violation of 'due process of law' " (dissent in *Taylor* v. *Beckham,* 178 U.S. 548, at 603–604, decided in 1900). If asked, he probably would have said that the Fifth and the Fourteenth amendments combine to forbid any branch or arm of government to deprive any person of any right recognized in law, unless the deprivation is made in accord with due process of law.

The justification for this sweeping statement becomes apparent when one studies the meaning which judges have put into the several words and phrases that make up the two due-process requirements. (1) They limit national, state, and local government; and they apply to the acts of every department of government, every officer, and every agent who acts for a government. (2) Everyone is given the protection of the limitation—citizens, aliens lawfully within the country, every kind of profit and nonprofit corporation, and partnerships and other forms of business enterprise. (3) "Life," "liberty," "property," and "deprivation" are interpreted most broadly. If a man is subjected by government to any restraint or frustration which seriously hinders him in the enjoyment of what the law treats as a right, he can properly plead that the act to which he objects is a deprivation of his life, his liberty, his property, or some combination of these. (4) "Due process of law"—here is the bone of contention. Every act of government which seriously interferes with the enjoyment of a right by anyone must accord with a due process of law. But what is due process? This is the subject of inquiry throughout this chapter.

The Supreme Court decisions which interpret and apply the due-process clauses run into the hundreds. It is impossible to explore the whole range of their significance in one chapter. Because we are interested in how the Supreme Court has used its power, we will confine our attention to cases in which the manifestations of its power have been most striking, that is, some cases in which the Court enforced or nullified legislation regulating business and industrial life.

2. FROM MODE OF PROCEEDING TO CAUSE AND OBJECT

It will be remembered that the Supreme Court invalidated only two acts of Congress prior to the Civil War on grounds of conflict with the Constitution. *Marbury* v. *Madison* made inoperative a minor provision in the Judiciary Act of 1789, and the Dred Scott decision invalidated the statute popularly known as the Missouri Compromise. Prior to the latter decision, the Supreme Court more than once discussed the relationship of particular legislative provisions to restrictive language in the Constitution and overruled pleas that it refuse to enforce the statute. In a very few cases, it inquired into the meaning of the due-process requirement of the Fifth Amendment, in each instance treating it only as a limitation on the way in which the objective of the statute was to be achieved.

In the Dred Scott case (1857), however, the due-process clause was given a substantive effect. In the leading opinion, Chief Justice Taney assumed that the act of Congress (the Missouri Compromise), which declared slavery "forever prohibited" in certain territory west of the Mississippi River, deprived the slave-owner of his property if and when he took a slave into that territory, and he asserted that such a deprivation "could hardly be dignified with the name of due process of law." This does not seem a forceful way of announcing the meaning of a constitutional provision or of settling a political issue which is recognized to have in it the seeds of secession, if not civil war. The strength of Taney's holding as precedent is further weakened by the fact that five of the six judges who agreed with him in the disposition of the litigation wrote separate opinions, and it is not clear that four of these men (enough to make a majority of five) believed the statute invalid on the due-process ground.

The period before the Civil War produced another line of judicial doctrine which could be appealed to in fixing the scope of the due-process clauses in the national Constitution. There were, from the beginning of the federation, provisions in state constitutions which in various kinds of language indicated that state and local governments were to proceed according to "due process of law" or in keeping with "the law of the land." From time to time, state laws and local ordinances were challenged in state courts on the ground that they violated such a provision in the state constitution. For several decades, state judges consistently showed great reluctance to hold acts of the legislature unenforceable on any ground, and they made it clear that such phrases in the state constitution as "due process of law" and "law of the land" were not intended to limit the goals which the legislators might seek to achieve.

The general agreement among state judges was abruptly upset in 1856, however. In *Wynehamer* v. *State of New York* (13 N.Y. 378), the highest court of New York held invalid a prohibition law of that state which destroyed the value of liquor already in the hands of manufacturers and dealers. The judges found nothing objectionable in the procedure by which the law was to be enforced —the arrangements for seizing and destroying liquor or for arresting, indicting, trying, and punishing offenders. The fault in the law was that it attempted to do a wrongful thing in destroying the value of liquor which had been lawfully acquired. To destroy the value of the liquor already on hand, said one of the judges, would be a violation of the constitution, even though done "by the forms which belong to due process of law."

The United States Supreme Court was asked to make the due-process requirement a limitation on the substantive content of legislation in three cases that came before it less than ten years after the Fourteenth Amendment was ratified. In one case, the Court (two justices dissenting) held that the statute did not violate the due-process requirement, but neither the majority nor the dissenting opinions made any differentiation between a procedural and a substantive limitation. In the other two cases, a majority of the judges clung to the traditional position that due process was a limitation on procedure only; in each of these cases, one or more judges argued that the post-Civil War amendments were being given too narrow an application. The issue in interpretation is best revealed in the latest of the three cases, *Davidson* v. *New Orleans* (96 U.S. 97, 1878).

A Louisiana statute, providing for the drainage of swamp-lands adjacent to New Orleans, named the business firm which should make the drains and levees, fixed terms of the contract with that firm, required owners of land in the improved area to bear the costs, and specified how costs should be allocated among individual landowners. A Mrs. Davidson, a principal landowner, thought the Legislature had no authority to designate the firm and fix the terms of the contract and that the amounts allocated to her in the assessment procedure were excessive. She therefore fought the assessment in court and, losing in the highest court of Louisiana, carried her cause to the United States Supreme Court on appeal. She contended that the state law deprived her of her property (her assessment) without due process of law, thus violating the Fourteenth Amendment to the Constitution.

The judges of the Supreme Court agreed unanimously that the Louisiana statute had made adequate provision for due process of law in taking Mrs. Henrietta Davidson's property, but they did not agree on the basic issue as to scope of the due-process requirements. Justice Samuel F. Miller said in the main opinion:

> But however this may be, or under whatever other clause of the Federal Constitution we may review the case, it is not possible to hold that where by the laws of the State the party aggrieved has, as regards the issues affecting his property, a fair trial in a court of justice, according to the modes of proceeding applicable to such case that he has been deprived of that property without due process of law.

The justice then described the safeguards which the Louisiana law specified for the protection of the landowners' interests, including provisions for complaint, hearing, and judicial review of the assessment. "If this be not due processs of law," he said, "then the words can have no definite meaning as used in the Constitution."

Justice Joseph P. Bradley agreed that due process of law had been observed in the case before the court, but he thought "the conclusion and general tenor of the opinion" narrowed the scope of inquiry as to what due process of law is "more than it should do."

> It seems to me [he said], that private property may be taken by a State without due process of law in other ways than by mere direct enactment, or the want of a judicial proceeding. . . . I think, therefore, we are entitled, under the XIVth Amendment, not only to see that there is some process of law, but "due process of law," provided by the state law when a citizen is deprived of his property; and that, in judging what is "due process of law," respect must be had to the cause and object of the taking, whether under the taxing power, the power of eminent domain, or the power of assessment for local improvements, or none of these; and if found to be suitable or admissible in the special case, it will be adjudged to be "due process of law"; but if found to be arbitrary, oppressive and unjust, it may be declared to be not "due process of law." (P. 107.)

Davidson v. *New Orleans* may be viewed as the last stand of that conservative position which viewed the two due-process clauses as guarantees only of a rightful procedure in the achievement of public policies. Bradley's plea that "respect must be had to the cause and object of the taking" was fully honored before he left the Supreme Court in 1892. In 1887, not a single one of his associates recorded an objection or a caution when Justice Harlan asserted:

> They [the courts] are at liberty—indeed, are under a solemn duty—to look at the substance of things, whenever they enter upon the inquiry whether the Legislature has transcended the limits of its authority. If, therefore, a statute purporting to have been enacted to protect the public health, the public morals, or the public safety, has no real or substantial relation to those objects, or is a palpable invasion of rights secured by the fundamental law, it is the duty of the courts to so adjudge, and thereby give effect to the Constitution. (*Mugler* v. *Kansas,* 123 U.S. 562, at 661.)

The doctrine announced in the Mugler case did not necessitate the invalidation of the statute at issue, a Kansas prohibition law. The Court was unable "to perceive any ground for the judiciary to declare that [the Kansas prohibition law] is not fairly adapted to the end of protecting the community against the evils which confessedly result from the excessive use of ardent spirits."

Even though the Supreme Court's new view of the limiting effect of the due-process requirement was not used in this case, it was nonetheless firm doctrine. In 1894, the Court held invalid an order of a state regulatory commission, and in 1898 it invalidated a state statute, both of which fixed maximum rates to be charged by railroads carrying passengers and freight in intrastate commerce.

It can be argued that a moderate stretching of the concept of procedure would bring railroad rate cases within the earlier view of the scope of the due-process requirement. The invalidation, in 1905, of a New York law regulating hours of labor cannot be accounted for in that way. In this case, *Lochner* v. *New York* (198 U.S. 45), the Court gave no hint of displeasure with the procedure of enactment or enforcement. The statute went down because five of the nine judges thought the New York lawmakers had regulated a matter that ought to be left to individual choice and bargaining among employers and their workers. Probably no other decision of the Supreme Court is so frequently cited as proof that judges, by making the due-process requirement a limitation on the goals or purposes of legislation, have transgressed the boundaries of the judicial function and invaded a realm assigned exclusively to the elected branches of government.

We shall see that it is not feasible to summarize the reasoning which the Supreme Court has offered in support of its conclusions that the substantive content of legislation does or does not meet the constitutional requirement of due process. The range of choice which is available to the judges may be sensed, however, by reading key portions of a few decisions.

Jacobson v. *Massachusetts* (197 U.S. 11, 1905). A Massachusetts law authorized boards of health in cities and towns to require all inhabitants to be immunized from smallpox by vaccination, free of charge, and specified that persons above twenty-one years of age who did not comply should forfeit $5. The act was held valid by vote of seven to two. Justice John Marshall Harlan wrote the majority opinion:

> The authority of the state to enact this statute is to be referred to what is commonly called the police power,—a power which the state did not surrender when becoming a member of the Union under the Constitution. Although this court has refrained from any attempt to define the limits of that power, yet it has distinctly recognized the authority of a State to enact quarantine laws and "health laws of every description"; indeed, all laws that relate to matters completely within its territory and which do not by their necessary operation affect the people of other states. According to settled

principles, the police power of a state must be held to embrace, at least, such reasonable regulations established directly by legislative enactment as will protect the public health and the public safety. . . . The defendant insists that his liberty is invaded when the state subjects him to fine or imprisonment for neglecting or refusing to submit to vaccination; that a compulsory vaccination law is unreasonable, arbitrary, and oppressive, and, therefore, hostile to the inherent right of every freeman to care for his own body and health in such way as to him seems best; and that the execution of such a law against one who objects to vaccination, no matter for what reason, is nothing short of an assault upon his person. [To this contention, the Justice responded that society could not exist without imposing many restraints on the individual. He also asserted that it was not unusual, unreasonable, or arbitrary for the legislature to invest a local board of health with authority to decide when threat of epidemic justified resort to vaccination. Then, speaking to a point that medical authorities disagree as to the effectiveness of vaccination, he continued:] We must assume that, when the statute in question was passed, the legislature of Massachusetts was not unaware of these opposing theories, and was compelled, of necessity, to choose between them. It was not compelled to commit a matter involving the public health and safety to the final decision of a court or jury. It is no part of the function of a court or a jury to determine which one of two modes was likely to be the most effective for the protection of the public against disease. That was for the legislative department to determine in the light of all the information it had or could obtain. It could not properly abdicate its function to guard the public health and safety. . . . If there is any such power in the judiciary to review legislative action in respect of a matter affecting the general welfare, it can only be when that which the legislature has done comes within the rule that, if a statute purporting to have been enacted to protect the public health, the public morals, or the public safety, has no real or substantial relation to those objects, or is, beyond all question, a plain, palpable invasion of rights secured by the fundamental law, it is the duty of the courts to so adjudge, and thereby give effect to the Constitution. (Pp. 25–26, 30–31.)

Lochner v. *New York* (198 U.S. 45, decided two months after *Jacobson* v. *Massachusetts*). A New York statute forbidding persons employed in bakeries or confectioneries to work more than ten hours in a day or sixty hours in a week was held invalid by vote of five to four. Justice Rufus W. Peckham spoke for the majority. Peckham had thought the Massachusetts vaccination law invalid. Harlan, who wrote the opinion sustaining that law, again disagreed with Peckham; he thought the New York bakery law valid also. Peckham said the following in the bakery case:

In every case that comes before this court, therefore, where legislation of this character is concerned, and where the protection of the Federal Constitution is sought, the question necessarily arises: Is this

> a fair, reasonable, and appropriate exercise of the police power of the state, or is it an unreasonable, unnecessary, and arbitrary interference with the right of the individual to his personal liberty, or to enter into those contracts in relation to labor which may seem to him appropriate or necessary for the support of himself and his family? [The act is not valid as a labor law, pure and simple, for there is no reasonable ground for differentiating bakers from other occupations for regulation of the labor contract.] The law must be upheld, if at all, as a law pertaining to the health of the individual engaged in the occupation of a baker. . . . We think the limit of the police power has been reached and passed in this case. There is, in our judgment, no reasonable foundation for holding this to be necessary or appropriate as a health law to safeguard the public health, or the health of the individuals who are following the trade of a baker. . . . In our judgment it is not possible in fact to discover the connection between the number of hours a baker may work in the bakery and the healthful quality of the bread made by the workman. The connection, if any exists, is too shadowy and thin to build any argument for the interference of the legislature. . . . It is manifest to us that the limitation of the hours of labor as provided for in this section of the statute . . . has no such direct relation to, and no such substantial effect upon, the health of the employee, as to justify us in regarding the section as really a health law. (Pp. 56–58, 62, 64.)

Adkins v. *Children's Hospital* (261 U.S. 565, 1923). An act of Congress provided for appointment of a Minimum Wage Board for the District of Columbia, authorized the board to study working conditions and to set standards of minimum wages for women and minors, and, in the case of women, to ascertain and declare what wages are inadequate to maintain them in good health and protect their morals. The provisions of the act applying to women were held invalid by vote of five to three, one justice not participating in the decision. Justice Sutherland delivered the opinion of the Court. He said, in part:

> The statute now under consideration is attacked upon the ground that it authorizes an unconstitutional interference with the freedom of contract included within the guaranties of the due process clause of the Fifth Amendment. . . . There is, of course, no such thing as absolute freedom of contract. It is subject to a great variety of restraints. But freedom of contract is, nevertheless, the general rule and restraint the exception; and the exercise of legislative authority to abridge it can be justified only by the existence of exceptional circumstances. [On the point that an adequate minimum income is conducive to better moral conduct on the part of women, he said:] The relation between earnings and morals is not capable of standardization. It cannot be shown that well-paid women safeguard their morals more carefully than those who are poorly paid. Morality rests on other considerations than wages; and there is, certainly, no such prevalent connection between the two as to justify a broad attempt

> to adjust the latter with reference to the former. As a means of safeguarding the morals the attempted classification, in our opinion, is without reasonable basis. No distinction can be made between women who work for others and those who do not; nor is there ground for distinction between women and men; for, certainly, if women require a minimum wage to preserve their morals, men require it to preserve their honesty. For these reasons, and others which might be stated, the inquiry in respect of the necessary cost of living and of the income necessary to preserve health and morals presents an individual, and not a composite, question, and must be answered for each individual, considered by herself and not by a general formula prescribed by a statutory bureau. . . . The feature of this statute which, perhaps more than any other, puts upon it the stamp of invalidity is that it exacts from the employer an arbitrary payment for a purpose and upon a basis having no causal connection with his business, or the contract, or the work the employee engages to do. The declared basis, as already pointed out, is not the value of the service rendered, but the extraneous circumstances that the employee needs to get a prescribed sum of money to insure her subsistence, health and morals. . . . A statute requiring an employer to pay in money, to pay at prescribed and regular intervals, to pay the value of the services rendered, even to pay with fair relation to the extent of the benefit obtained from the service, would be understandable. But a statute which prescribes payment without regard to any of these things, and solely with relation to circumstances apart from the contract of employment, the business affected by it, and the work done under it, is so clearly the product of a naked, arbitrary exercise of power, that it cannot be allowed to stand under the Constitution of the United States. (Pp. 545–546, 556, 558–559.)

West Coast Hotel Company v. *Parrish* (300 U.S. 379, 1937). A statute of the State of Washington entitled "Minimum Wages for Women" declared it unlawful to employ women or minors under conditions of labor detrimental to their health or morals and created a commission which was authorized to establish such standards of wages and conditions of labor "as shall be held hereunder to be reasonable and not detrimental to health and morals, and which shall be sufficient for the decent maintenance of women." The statute was upheld by vote of five to four. Hughes wrote the opinion sustaining the validity of the law. Sutherland, who wrote the opinion in the preceding case holding a similar law invalid, wrote a dissenting opinion in this case, arguing that the Washington law should also be held invalid.

Hughes wrote the following:

> The constitutional provision invoked is the due process clause of the Fourteenth Amendment governing the States, as the due process clause invoked in the Adkins Case governed Congress. In each case the

violation alleged by those attacking minimum wage regulation for women is deprivation of freedom of contract. [After quoting from dissenting opinions written for the Adkins case by Taft and Holmes (neither on the Court in 1937), Hughes said:] We think that the views thus expressed are sound and that the decision in the Adkins Case was a departure from the true application of the principles governing the regulation by the State of the relation of the employer and employed. . . . The legislature of the State was clearly entitled to consider the situation of women in employment, the fact that they are in the class receiving the least pay, that their bargaining power is relatively weak, and that they are the ready victims of those who would take advantage of their necessitous circumstances. The legislature was entitled to adopt measures to reduce the evils of the "sweating system," the exploiting of workers at wages so low as to be insufficient to meet the bare cost of living, thus making their very helplessness the occasion of a most injurious competition. The legislature had a right to consider that its minimum wage requirements would be an important aid in carrying out its policy of protection. The adoption of similar requirements by many States evidences a deep-seated conviction both as to the presence of the evil and as to the means adapted [*sic*] to check it. Legislative response to that conviction cannot be regarded as arbitrary or capricious and that is all we have to decide. Even if the wisdom of the policy be regarded as debatable and its effects uncertain, still the legislature is entitled to its judgment. . . . Our conclusion is that the case of Adkins v. Children's Hospital should be, and it is, overruled. (Pp. 391, 397–400.)

3. NO DEFINITE MEANING

I noted above that the statements of the Supreme Court about national power to regulate commerce which were examined in Chapter XIII had not established and adhered to rules or, instructive formulations which reliably inform lawmakers as to the bounds of their authority and commit the judges to consistent application of constitutional language. The four examples we have just examined indicate that the Supreme Court judges have been even less friendly to decision by rule when the due-process clauses of the Constitution were invoked. These four examples are in no way unusual or extraordinary. I selected them out of many that would have served my purpose because they present the thinking of the judges in most direct and unmistakable language.

Justice Samuel Miller died in 1900. If he had lived another ten years, he would surely have been entitled to say, "I told you so in *Davidson* v. *New Orleans*; if a time-honored mode of proceeding culminating in right to a full and fair hearing before a judicial tribunal is not what the due-process clauses mean, then the words 'due process of law' can have no definite meaning." Holmes filed a short but subsequently famous dissent in the New York bakery case, *Lochner* v. *New York*. Rejecting the reasoning by which the majority denied the state's lawmakers authority to regulate hours of labor, Holmes said:

> This case is decided upon an economic theory which a large part of this country does not entertain. . . . But a Constitution is not intended to embody a particular economic theory, whether of paternalism and the organic relation of the citizen to the state or of *laissez faire*. It is made for people of fundamentally differing views, and the accident of our [we Supreme Court judges] finding certain opinions natural and familiar, or novel, and even shocking, ought not to conclude our judgment upon the question whether statutes embodying them conflict with the Constitution of the United States. (Pp. 75–76.)

These words were spoken in 1905. Twenty-five years later, still dissenting, Holmes was able to add:

> I have not yet adequately expressed the more than anxiety that I feel at the ever increasing scope given to the 14th Amendment in cutting down what I believe to be the constitutional rights of the States. As the decisions now stand I see hardly any limit but the sky to the invalidating of those rights if they happen to strike a majority of this Court as for any reason undesirable. I cannot believe that the Amendment was intended to give us carte blanche to embody our economic or moral beliefs in its prohibitions. (*Baldwin* v. *Missouri,* 281 U.S. 586, at 595, decided in 1930.)

Holmes put his thumb down on a basic issue in constitutional theory: whose judgment on the wisdom and practicability of legislative programs ought to prevail? Granted that his language was too inclusive when he said that judges nullify legislation which they think "for any reason" undesirable, still the language from four majority opinions quoted above makes it clear that, in every case, the voting of the judges turned on their conclusions as to whether the legislation before them was "reasonable" in its purpose and its method. Note the use, in the key sentences quoted, of the words "reasonable," "unreasonable," "appropriate," "fair," "unnecessary," "arbitrary," "capricious," "oppressive." The word "arbitrary" appears in the quoted language of every case.

Holmes put his thumb down on the issue, but he did not move to one side of the issue and stand there. In quoting what he said in the Lochner case, I omitted some of his remarks in order to fix emphasis on a main point. He said that a constitution was not intended to embody a particular economic theory and that judges should not allow or nullify statutes on the basis of what seemed to them natural, familiar, novel, or shocking. But he also said that he thought the language in the Fourteenth Amendment was perverted when used to nullify legislation "unless it can be said that a rational and fair man necessarily would admit that the statute proposed would infringe fundamental principles as they have been understood by the traditions of our people and our law." My reading of their language in many cases convinces me that Peckham, Sutherland, and several other judges, when they justified the nullification of an act on due-process grounds, wished their remarks to embrace the following proposition: "This statute is invalid because a rational and fair man will admit that it does infringe fundamental principles as they have been understood by the traditions of our people and our law."

Furthermore, Holmes on a few occasions voted for invalidity of a statute where his position must have rested on a conviction that the lawmakers had simply gone too far. For instance, he wrote the majority opinion rejecting a Pennsylvania statute which forbade the mining of anthracite coal in such a way as to cause the subsidence of dwellings, factories, mercantile establishments, or places of public resort (*Pennsylvania Coal Co.* v. *Mahon*, 260 U.S. 393, decided in 1922). He said that the protection of property which is afforded by the Fifth and Fourteenth amendments is qualified by the police power and that the natural tendency of human nature is to extend the qualification until, at last, private property disappears. "The general rule at least is, that while property may be regulated to a certain extent, if regulation goes too far it will be recognized as a taking." The decisive sentence stated that "the act cannot be sustained as an exercise of the police power, so far as it affects the mining of coal under streets or cities in places where the right to mine such coal has been reserved [in the contract giving title to the surface]." It should be noted that Holmes did not brand the Pennsylvania law unreasonable, arbitrary, oppressive, or capricious. But it should be equally noted that his associate, Justice Louis D. Brandeis, justifying the enactment in a dissenting opinion, did say that the statute was "an appropriate means" for preventing subsidence of the surface and that he had been confronted by no evidence that the restriction which it imposed on mining operations was "an unreasonable exercise of the police power."

Harlan, Holmes, Hughes, Peckham, Sutherland, and all the

other judges who participated in the due-process cases we have examined are long departed from the Supreme Court. The quick readiness to nullify legislation because it seemed to move the nation from free enterprise to the welfare state departed with them. Justice William O. Douglas, on the Court since 1939, wrote in 1955: "The day is gone when this Court uses the Due Process Clause of the Fourteenth Amendment to strike down state laws regulatory of business and industrial conditions, because they may be unwise, improvident, or out of harmony with a particular school of thought."

Douglas did not say that the judges will tolerate and enforce legislation that regulates *personal conduct* if the most they can say against it is that it is unwise and improvident and is out of harmony with a school of thought to which a majority of the judges adhere. Indeed, Douglas very recently condemned his colleagues, in language more caustic than that of Holmes, for allowing their various philosophies to control their voting in cases where denial of personal rights is involved. The incident is worth brief quotation.

In *Hannah* v. *Larche* (363 U.S. 420, decided in 1960), the Supreme Court by vote of seven to two held that certain procedures of the U.S. Commission on Civil Rights were not in violation of the due-process-of-law requirement (for example, persons called to testify concerning registration of voters and administration of elections were not told the nature of the alleged violations of law which were being investigated). Justice Felix Frankfurter, writing a separate opinion to support the majority's decision, stated that the prime issue was whether there had been a departure from due process of law and on that point wrote these two sentences:

> Inquiry must be directed to the validity of the adjustment between these clashing interests—that of Government and of the individual, respectively—in the procedural scheme devised by the Congress and the Commission. Whether the scheme satisfies those strivings for justice which due process guarantees, must be judged in the light of reason drawn from the considerations of fairness that reflect our traditions of legal and political thought, duly related to the public interest Congress sought to meet by this legislation as against the hazards or hardship to the individual that the Commission procedure would entail. (P. 487.)

Douglas thought that the "light of reason" which his colleague mentioned had too often blinded the judges to the firm teachings of law and history. Frankfurter's formulation, he said in a dissenting opinion,

> makes due process reflect the subjective or even whimsical notions of a majority of this Court as from time to time constituted. Due process under the prevailing doctrine [as characterized by Frankfurter] is what the judges say it is; and it differs from judge to judge, from court to court. This notion of due process makes it a tool of the activists who respond to their own visceral reactions in deciding what is fair, decent, or reasonable. . . .
>
> When we turn to the cases, personal preference, not reason, seems, however, to be controlling. (Pp. 505–506.)

It may be that Justice Douglas could safety predict, in 1955, that the day will never return when the Supreme Court will use the due-process clauses to strike down laws that regulate business when the most that can be said against them is that the judges think them unwise, improvident, or out of harmony with a school of thought which the judges find attractive. My own interpretation of the history of our great tribunal and the doctrines it has espoused makes me unwilling to risk such a prophecy.

IV • A NEW CONSTITUTIONAL REGIME?

We now turn to the recent actions of the Supreme Court relating to racial segregation. Chapter XV examines the contention that the Supreme Court at least overstepped the bounds of judicial power, if, indeed, it did not in effect amend the Constitution, and records my own conviction that, in its decisions relating to segregation, the Supreme Court has raised itself to a new peak of judicial power. Dislike for the Supreme Court's actions in relation to segregation is not due solely to the consequences of its decisions. The method pursued by the Court in these cases has also excited reproach. This is the subject of Chapter XVI. In Chapter XVII, I give a hearing to a school of thought which supports the Supreme Court in these, its boldest expressions of power.

CHAPTER FIFTEEN

The Outlawing of Segregation

1. CHARGE: JUDICIAL VIOLATION OF THE CONSTITUTION
2. CHARGE: NOT A JOB FOR JUDGES
3. A NEW PEAK OF JUDICIAL POWER
4. A NEW CONSTITUTIONAL REGIME?

The fury and the stubbornness excited by judicial orders to terminate racial segregation are not a product of constitutional theory. They are a response to the prospect that a way of life may have to be changed. The struggle to escape the change is waged on many fronts, and one of them is the polemics of constitutional obligations and judicial power.

Two lines of argument have been mainly relied on to support the contention that the Supreme Court did not have the authority to order termination of segregation: (1) that the Constitution acknowledged the lawfulness of the "separate-but-equal" rule and that, in voiding it, the Supreme Court either violated the Constitution or amended it; and (2) that, if the Constitution permitted the national government to terminate segregation, the authority to do so was not vested in the judicial branch. We shall see how each of these arguments has been developed, then turn to a contention that the Supreme Court's decisions relating to segregation are without equal as examples of judicial ventures into policy-making.

1. CHARGE: JUDICIAL VIOLATION OF THE CONSTITUTION

This is the argument: (1) Prior to adoption of the Fourteenth Amendment (1868), the right of the states to separate the races in schools and other public places was established and uncontested, and the right to separate the races remains with the states today unless it be proven that the Fourteenth Amendment terminated that right. (2) Insofar as the intent of those persons who participated in writing, submitting, and ratifying the Fourteenth Amendment can be ascertained, the evidence strongly supports a conclusion that they intended separation of the races to remain lawful. (3) Subsequent decisions of highest state courts, inferior federal courts, and the United States Supreme Court confirmed this conclusion and settled the question by ruling that segregation in public schools and other places was lawful. (4) When the intentions of the men who adopted the constitutional language and the interpretations given that language by the Supreme Court are in agreement, the meaning so fixed becomes the supreme law of the land, and action in conflict with it either violates the Constitution or amends it.

I believe no informed and thoughtful person denies the first point, so we may dismiss it from further consideration.

On the question of what the men who added the Fourteenth Amendment intended it to accomplish, here is what Warren said in the Brown case:

> [Argument by attorneys in the case] covered exhaustively consideration of the Amendment in Congress, ratification by the states, then existing practices in racial segregation, and the views of proponents and opponents of the Amendment. This discussion and our own investigation convince us that, although these sources cast some light, it is not enough to resolve the problem with which we are faced. At best, they are inconclusive. The most avid proponents of the post-War Amendments undoubtedly intended them to remove all legal distinctions among "all persons born or naturalized in the United States." Their opponents, just as certainly, were antagonistic to both the letter and the spirit of the Amendments and wished them to have the most limited effect. What others in Congress and the state legislatures had in mind cannot be determined with any degree of certainty. (P. 489.)

The evidence as to intent seems not at all inconclusive to many people who have given it some study. The Virginia Commission on Constitutional Government has published a pamphlet concerned with the probable understandings and intentions of the congressmen who submitted and the state legislators who ratified the Fourteenth Amendment.[1] The report cites two acts of Congress,

[1] Virginia Commission on Constitutional Government, *A Question of Intent*, "The States, Their Schools, and the 14th Amendment" (Richmond). The report is a reprint of testimony before a committee of the United States Senate, May 14, 1959, by David J. Mays, an attorney.

adopted in the same session that submitted the amendment, which specifically recognized and made provision for schools in the District of Columbia admitting Negroes only. The report gives a paragraph to each of the thirty-six state legislatures that had the proposed amendment before it. It was submitted by Congress on June 16, 1866, and was declared in force on July 28, 1868. During this period or within two years at either end of the period, according to this pamphlet, fourteen of the thirty-six states made enactments giving official sanction to racial segregation in public schools. In these fourteen states, separation of the races was required, made optional for local school authorities, or declared in keeping with public policy.

Speaking of the Supreme Court's rejection of just such evidence, Dean Ribble of the University of Virginia Law School said:

> I think this unfortunate. It seems to me that Mr. Bickel is quite right in his survey of the evidence. It is also quite inconceivable to me that Congress could have submitted an amendment which would eliminate segregation in the public schools of the states at the very time it was providing for segregation in the public schools of the District of Columbia.[2]

Ribble referred to an article by Alexander Bickel, whose analysis of the evidence seems to be widely regarded as the best provided from the academic side. Professor Bickel's main conclusions about the intentions of those who added the Fourteenth Amendment to the Constitution appear in these sentences:

> The obvious conclusion to which the evidence, thus summarized, easily leads is that Section 1 of the fourteenth amendment, like Section 1 of the Civil Rights Act of 1866, carried out the relatively narrow objectives of the Moderates, and hence, as originally understood, was meant to apply neither to jury service, nor suffrage, nor antimiscegenation statutes, nor segregation. . . . Nothing in the election campaign of 1866 or in the ratification proceedings negatives it. Section 1 received in both about the attention it had received in Congress, and in about the same terms. One or two "reconstructed" Southern legislatures took what turned out, of course, [to be] temporary measures to abolish segregation. There is little if any indication of an impression prevailing elsewhere that the amendment required such action.[3]

[2] F.D.G. Ribble, "The Development of the Supreme Court as a Center of Controversy in the United States," *South Texas Law Journal*, 4 (1959), 158.

[3] Alexander M. Bickel, "The Original Understanding and the Segregation Decision," *Harvard Law Review*, 69 (1955), 58–59.

We may reserve for a later point Bickel's position on the significance of the evidence he so carefully arrayed and so sharply summarized.

So much for the intention of the men who added the amendment to the Constitution. The contention that the Supreme Court either violated or amended the Constitution in the Segregation cases continues with the argument that decisions of state and federal courts, including the Supreme Court of the United States, had definitively interpreted the Constitution as not forbidding racial segregation. This line of reasoning is carefully developed in another publication of the Virginia Commission on Constitutional Government:

> Within fifteen years after adoption of the Fourteenth Amendment, while the understandings and intentions and circumstances of the instrument were fresh in everyone's mind, seven cases were decided on this specific question of right and power. Five of these decisions were written by the highest courts of Ohio, Indiana, Nevada, California, and New York. Two of them were written by Federal courts, one in Ohio, the other in Louisiana. These cases so clearly established the meaning of the Fourteenth Amendment in regard to racially separate public schools that the Supreme Court could dismiss the question as settled beyond further argument.[4]

The Supreme Court decision referred to is one I mentioned in the first chapter of this book, *Gong Lum* v. *Rice* (275 U.S. 78, decided in 1927). This case involved the right of a state to require an American citizen of Chinese extraction to attend a segregated school which had been assigned to Negroes. Taft asserted for a unanimous Court:

> The question here is whether a Chinese citizen of the United States is denied equal protection of the laws when he is classed among the colored races and furnished facilities for education equal to that offered to all, whether white, brown, yellow, or black. Were this a new question, it would call for very full argument and consideration, but we think that it is the same question which has been many times decided to be within the constitutional power of the state legislature to settle without intervention of the federal courts under the Federal Constitution. (Pp. 85–86.)

The Chief Justice then cited a number of decisions by state and federal judges and added:

[4] Virginia Commission on Constitutional Government, *Did the Court Interpret or Amend?* (Richmond, 1960), pp. 6–7, 42–43.

> Most of the cases cited arose, it is true, over the establishment of separate schools as between white pupils and black pupils, but we cannot think that the question is any different or that any different result can be reached, assuming the cases above cited to be rightly decided, where the issue is as between white pupils and the pupils of the yellow races. The decision is within the discretion of the state in regulating its public schools and does not conflict with the Fourteenth Amendment. (P. 87.)

Looking back on its analysis and ample quotations from the several court decisions and opinions, the Virginia commission summarized:

> The judiciary thus performed its interpretive function. In the field of public education, the Constitution stood clearly defined and, so far as education is concerned, the people have changed it not one iota.
>
> Did the Supreme Court have the right to issue the opinion it did in *Brown*? The answer is found by adverting again to the argument advanced in the beginning of this exposition, the truth of which the members of the Supreme Court apparently recognize, albeit only when it suits them.

The Virginia commission did not answer its question with a categorical yes or no, but the reasoning it presented would admit of only one answer—that the Supreme Court did not have a right to outlaw racial segregation because in doing so it either violated the Constitution or amended it. The commission had found that original intention and judicial interpretation combined to fix a meaning for the Constitution which made segregation lawful. The argument opening its pamphlet, referred to in the above quotation, held that, when meaning was fixed in this way, that meaning was the supreme law of the land and that only a constitutional amendment could take that meaning out of the Constitution. Whether this is a rightful view of the nature of constitutional prescriptions is at the heart of debate about the lawfulness of the Supreme Court's action, so the commission is entitled to be heard in its own words.

> But words, it is said, often have different meanings, and it may be necessary to have them construed or interpreted by resort to the judicial function. Where, then, does "interpretation" of the Constitution end, and where does "amendment" begin? Granted that courts have power to interpret; how is one to know when the necessary power to interpret has been corrupted into a usurped power to amend?
>
> The question answers itself if we return to the point of beginning: Words have meanings. And the words of a contractual instrument, as

applied to particular events or conditions in the minds of the parties at the time the instrument is agreed to, have a permanent meaning. Such a meaning is necessarily fixed. It becomes, in fact, the instrument itself; to alter it would be to alter the instrument itself. This is true even if some disagreement among the parties themselves led or forced them to have the courts interpret the instrument and judicially establish this meaning for them. If that original meaning, however determined, is to be abandoned, then it must be by consent of the parties and the instrument must be formally amended.

2. CHARGE: NOT A JOB FOR JUDGES

Bickel was in agreement with the Virginia commission that the men who proposed and adopted the Fourteenth Amendment did not understand that it made forced separation of races unlawful. But he disagreed with the premise of the commission that the meaning of a constitutional provision is fixed by the original understanding, even if that understanding is later declared the right one by the highest court of the land. He said:

> If the fourteenth amendment were a statute, a court might very well hold, on the basis of what has been said so far, that it was foreclosed from applying it to segregation in public schools. The evidence of congressional purpose is as clear as such evidence is likely to be, and no language barrier stands in the way of construing the section in conformity with it. But we are dealing with a constitutional amendment, not a statute. (P. 59.)

Dealing, as Warren and his colleagues were, with a constitutional provision instead of a statute, the judges, according to Bickel, had to ask two questions about the intentions that accompanied the new constitutional amendment. First, the Supreme Court needed to know how the men who added the amendment expected it to be applied in the immediate future. Second, they needed to know what vision those men had about application of the amendment at later times when the nation's social problems would have changed. It was this second question, Bickel suggests, "that the Chief Justice must have had in mind when [in the Brown case] he termed the materials 'inconclusive.' For up to this point they tell a clear story and are anything but inconclusive" (p. 63).

It is Bickel's view that the prohibitions which are written into a constitution ought to be given flexibility—that their application, the things they are made to prohibit, ought to change over time. It appears to be his view also that the vision of the men who put the prohibition into the constitution ought to impose some restraint on the flexibility that is later allowed; that is, men of later time, when they are challenged to adapt the prohibition, should consult the original understandings and be restrained by them in fitting the constitutional language to the new social situation.

The first of these propositions, that a constitution must adjust to changing needs, has been endorsed with varying limitations by thoughtful men ever since the Constitution was a few years of age. I suspect that many who take that position today would not have the later generation pay much attention to the vision of the originators of the language. I think this may be a fair statement of a position widely held in our day: Many provisions in the United States Constitution, and not all of them are prohibitions, incorporate an ideal, and all who give effect to constitutional provisions are charged to achieve the ideal even if that require an action which the constitution-makers would not have condoned.

This may be called a bottom-level issue about the fundamental character of the American Constitution. At one extreme is the position of the Virginia commission quoted above. In this view, using the words of a prominent Southern lawyer and law teacher, the Constitution "was adopted to provide a continuing framework of government and not to serve only as a basis for its beginning." [5] Opposed to this conception is the view that the Constitution is an oracle and a monitor, a repository of ideals and an array of instructions which enjoin our officials to make government conform to the highest ideals of the nation. If the first view determines official behavior, the Constitution exerts a stern restraint on the acts of officials; if the second view prevails, the Constitution is an instrument to be invoked by officials when its words confirm their acts.

I called this question about the fundamental character of the Constitution a bottom-level issue. A companion issue, and one only a shade less basic, is this: If a constitutional provision embodies an ideal which men in all generations must try to achieve, who is the decisive authority in deciding what that ideal is? Stated another way: If the Constitution, as positive requirement, changes as social conditions present new challenges to the ideal, who shall say finally what action will fulfill the demand which the ideal imposes? All may agree that the Constitution charged the national government to promote and protect a nation-wide interchange of goods and services, but also

[5] A. A. White, "The Supreme Court's Avenues of Escape from the Constitution," *South Texas Law Journal,* 4 (1958–1959), 129.

imposed a barrier to consolidated power by constructing a federal system. If Congress and the president conclude that the ideal of a vigorous nation-wide economy makes national regulation of employment in coal mines lawful and five Supreme Court judges conclude that the ideal of a sturdy federal relationship makes such a national regulation unlawful, which set of officials should win? If the Supreme Court judges are allowed final authority to formulate the ideal which is to come out of the Constitution's words and final authority to say what positive requirement this ideal now imposes on the nation's lawmakers, should one conclude with Senator Hatch that the Supreme Court is making public policy and has invaded a realm which the nation assigned to the political branches? Or should one adopt a view which dominates the leading law reviews today—that the Supreme Court is chief custodian of the nation's conscience and must be supreme in saying what that conscience requires?

I quoted the Virginia Commission on Constitutional Government in support of a restrained judicial authority. As witness for the other side, I offer the following statement, quoted at length to disclose the authors' rationale.

> The role, then, of the Supreme Court in an age of positive government must be that of an active participant in government, assisting in furthering the democratic ideal. Acting at least in part as a "national conscience," the Court should help articulate in broad principle the goals of American society. . . . Historically, the Court has espoused such goals as the free market, political democracy, and fairness in governmental activities affecting individuals. Today there is an equal need for more conscious normation on the part of the members of the Court. . . .
>
> Hence we suggest that judicial decisions should be gauged by their results and not by either their coincidence with a set of allegedly consistent doctrinal principles or by an impossible reference to neutrality of principle. The effects, that is to say, of a decision should be weighed and the consequences assessed in terms of their social adequacy. Alternatives of choice are to be considered, not so much in terms of who the litigants are or what the issue is, but rather in terms of the realization or non-realization of stated societal values. What those values might be, we do not now set forth. Rather we contend that judges have always done this, in greater or lesser degree, overtly or covertly, consciously or unconsciously; and that now it should become a matter of conscious choice. . . .
>
> In the attainment of these goals [personal freedom and individual liberty], the judiciary has as important a role to play as any other organ of government. Perhaps it is even more important than the legislature or the executive. For while it is true of course, as we are often told by Mr. Justice Frankfurter, that the other branches of

government also have the capacity to govern, it is the courts that can best protect the rights of minorities which tend to become submerged in the political processes of government. The other branches of government, precisely because they are more political and thus more susceptible to the prevailing winds, may and do find it difficult at times to withstand the pressure of majority opinion. A majority, as DeTocqueville and John Stuart Mill have indicated, can be despotic. It is, accordingly, the quintessence of democracy for an appointive judiciary to further the ends of the integrity of the individual.[6]

We are now back to the question about placement of authority in the constitutional system which has been the main point of attention throughout this book. I think I need not say more on that issue now. It does seem appropriate, however, to report the perplexity of one man who served in both parts of our institutional structure—as attorney general during the New Deal and as a member of the Supreme Court after 1941. Writing while on the Supreme Court, Justice Robert H. Jackson said:

> The question that the present times put into the minds of thoughtful people is to what extent Supreme Court interpretations of the Constitution will or can preserve the free government of which the Court is a part. A cult of libertarian judicial activists now assails the Court almost as bitterly for renouncing power as the earlier "liberals" once did for assuming too much power. This cult appears to believe that the Court can find in a 4,000-word eighteenth-century document or its nineteenth-century Amendments, or can plausibly supply, some clear bulwark against all dangers and evils that today beset us internally. This assumes that the Court will be the dominant factor in shaping the constitutional practice of the future and can and will maintain, not only equality with the elective branches, but a large measure of supremacy and control over them. I may be biased against this attitude because it is so contrary to the doctrines of the critics of the Court, of whom I was one, at the time of the Roosevelt proposal to reorganize the judiciary. But it seems to me a doctrine wholly incompatible with faith in democracy, and in so far as it encourages a belief that the judges may be left to correct the result of public indifference to issues of liberty in choosing Presidents, Senators, and Representatives, it is a vicious teaching.[7]

[6] Arthur S. Miller and Ronald F. Howell, "The Myth of Neutrality in Constitutional Adjudication," *University of Chicago Law Review*, 27 (1960), 689–694. © 1960 The University of Chicago.

[7] Robert H. Jackson, *The Supreme Court in the American System of Government* (Cambridge: Harvard University Press, 1955), pp. 57–58.

3. A NEW PEAK OF JUDICIAL POWER

Two charges against the Supreme Court, both elaborated in recent literature, have been examined. A third complaint, less fully developed in writing, has contributed importantly to discussion of judicial power since the Segregation cases. I shall set forth in my own way the reasons for believing that the Supreme Court, in its recent decisions relating to racial segregation, lifted itself to a new peak of judicial power. It ought to be said, now and frankly, that I am persuaded that this is a correct reading of the evidence and that the prospect that the Court may continue to operate on a new and higher plateau of power motivates much of what I say in the remainder of this book.

When John Marshall and his colleagues declared a provision of the Judiciary Act of 1789 of no effect, the immediate legal consequences of their order were limited. Marbury and his associated litigants lost their case, and all were notified that henceforth all but two classes of lawsuits subject to federal jurisdiction would have to start in a lower court and come to the Supreme Court on appeal. The decision had enormous social consequences—more properly called political than legal—and they would be realized only in later decisions when the judiciary might refuse to enforce other legislative acts.

The Supreme Court next held an act of Congress invalid in 1857 (Dred Scott). This case also had enormous political consequences, but the immediate legal effect was to say that the law relating to ownership and disposition of slaves would be the same from then on as it was before the Missouri Compromise Act was put on the statute books. The decision infuriated a large part of the population, but it did not require any notable alteration of political or social institutions, and it did not order the abandonment of deeply rooted attitudes and practices of the population. The statute was intended to force highly significant social changes; the Court's decision delayed the necessity of making those changes.

Such, I think it must be admitted, is the essential effect of all judicial nullifications of legislation down to the Segregation decisions. When five justices voted that the New York bakery law was invalid, they decreed that employment in bakeries in New York should continue under the law that ruled before this particular statute was enacted. The same is true of the orders invalidating the NRA codes, the Bituminous Coal Act, and the minimum wage law for the District of Columbia. In each case, the judicial order had the effect of reinstating the regime of law that existed prior to the particular enactment; or, if some of the previous law had been repealed because of the new statute, Congress and the president were notified to patch up the now-incomplete coverage of the law.

The Segregation decisions had a social consequence of a vastly different order. They called for a rewriting of state and federal legislation relating to public education. When to the Segregation decisions are added the later judicial acts extending the new constitutional regime to other places of public assembly, one must acknowledge that judicial orders have required a basic revision of social structure and a root change in human relationships. The Supreme Court did not order Alabama and Mississippi and South Carolina to forget about an innovation in public policy and continue life as they had lived it before the promulgation of that innovation; the Court ordered people in those and other states to fashion legislation of a kind they had never had on their statute books and to institute some social relationships that had never prevailed in those places.

The judicial order in abatement of a nuisance, in bankruptcy and corporate reorganization proceedings, and in some other actions in equity have, as respects style, a great deal in common with the nonsegregation orders. But the point stands that the nonsegregation orders are without precedent for comprehensive and deep-cutting social consequences and for application of judicial method to issues of obligation arising directly out of constitutional language.

This is my view of the significance of the Supreme Court's recent decisions and orders relating to racial segregation. It is a view shared by many students of constitutional law and interested observers of the American social scene, but not by all such students and observers. I have been told—patiently, gently, vehemently, and harshly—that the Brown and Bolling cases have no such significance as I see in them, indeed, that they only gave formal pronouncement to a constitutional requirement which had been made apparent to all thoughtful students of law in previous decisions and fixed procedures for scheduling compliance with a moral standard with which the nation was going to comply anyway.

4. A NEW CONSTITUTIONAL REGIME?

There will be general agreement on these points. If one believes the decisions on segregation have the significance I have assigned to them, he must reorder his thinking about the relation of the judicial branch to our other instruments for making public policy. And, if a man who had previously acquired dislike for judicial intrusion into public policy is persuaded that the Supreme Court has lifted itself to a new plateau of power, he is bound to be apprehensive as to how the judges will use their power in the future.

What the thoughtful man, distrustful of judicial ventures into policy-making, may see in the new constitutional regime is suggested by these two questions.

(1) Will the new constitutional regime be confined to separation of the races? As of the time I write, the Supreme Court has not ordered termination of all racial discrimination which has its foundation in law and acts of government. The orders issued in 1955, in the Segregation cases proper, applied only to separate schools for whites and Negroes. One may argue whether the opinions in these cases applied only to whites and Negroes or whether that language also announced the unlawfulness of separation on racial lines generally, making, for example, separate schools for the American Indian unlawful. In several actions after these decisions, the nonseparation rule has been extended to other facilities and places where whites and Negroes would mingle if the law permitted.

But forced separation of the races is not the only form in which governmentally supported racial discrimination is manifested. Let us assume, as a *first* illustration, that the governing authorities of a city have not, for a period of years, allocated public funds with a show of equal treatment for all parts of the population. Streets that cross the Negro residential areas do not get repaired at public expense; streets that lie among the residences of the white population, rich and poor alike, are maintained in notably better condition than those in the Negro sections of town. May the Supreme Court order municipal governments to make a more equitable distribution of the public money and instruct judges in the district courts to approve and disapprove municipal budgets as they were instructed to supervise the effectuation of desegregation in public schools? *Second* illustration: Suppose the Court is shown that a state's public health laws effectively combat all major industrial diseases except one or two that plague certain industries which draw their working force, in that state, almost wholly from the Negro population. Let it be shown to the satisfaction of the judges that failure to extend protection to these Negro-dominated occupations stems from an anti-Negro bias in the state legislature. If their sense of judicial propriety will not let them correct the situation by statutory construction, may the judges order the state lawmakers to extend the substantive provisions of the statute to the neglected diseases and to adapt the administrative machinery and allocate resources in a manner calculated to terminate the discrimination?

(2) Will the new constitutional regime be confined to discrimination on the basis of race? If one thinks it likely that the new regime will be extended beyond separation of the races to other manifestations of racial discrimination, should he also expect it to extend to discrimination which is not keyed to race? If he sees such a prospect for judicial control of public policy as that suggested in the preceding paragraph, should he allow that judges may order revisions of legislation and governmental practice which effect a notable disadvantage for particular religious groups or other differentiable segments of the population? Indeed, should he contemplate a judicial order terminating the death penalty for any crime if statistics show conclusively that many rich men have been prosecuted but none has gone to the electric chair in a state where the chair has many times been made hot for poor men?

It is no answer for the man who foresees events he dreads to be told that these events may not come about. He is entitled to ask for evidence or analysis which will show that they have small chance of coming about. I have not been able to find the evidence or develop an analysis which forces a conclusion that the Supreme Court judges will refuse to make further extensions of the new constitutional regime comparable to those made since the Brown and Bolling decisions and comparable to those I suggest. Law review articles have appeared which proffer one rationale or another to the judges if they decide not to extend the new regime further than it has now been carried. I see nothing in such reasoning or in any reasoning I have been able to develop to induce a judge to forego further extension if his personal bent is in that direction. If the evidence as to understandings and intentions when the Fourteenth Amendment was adopted were "not enough to resolve the problems" before the Court in the Segregation cases, I do not see how the judges can possibly find in that evidence persuasive instruction for the issues I pose here.

Bickel said that, as respects the separation of races in schools, the evidence as to congressional purpose "is as clear as such evidence is likely to be," and the evidence, he found, is that the Fourteenth Amendment was "meant to apply neither to jury service, nor suffrage, nor antimiscegenation statutes, nor segregation." Others who have examined the origins are in agreement that the men who gave us the Fourteenth Amendment were much more disposed to outlaw the kind of discrimination I have mentioned than they were to outlaw separate facilities for the two races in places of public assemblage.

From all this it follows that the hard tasks of reconciling the Fourteenth Amendment, as an addition to the fundamental document and as a product of history, to current standards of fair treatment have been accomplished. If the intentions and understandings of the generation that gave us that amendment are at all relevant, they should impose no obstacle to the efforts of judges to correct and prevent such differential impacts of public policy as cited in my hypothetical queries above. To forestall any notion that such further extensions of judge-decreed restrictions on public policy will have occurred only to me, I offer the following judgment of a law school dean who sees a prospect that the new constitutional regime will be carried to discriminatory behavior far beyond the points to which my imagination took it.

> Deserving of examination in this connection is the proposition that the failure by the state to bar discrimination is state action denying the equal protection of the laws. . . . We are here concerned with something more than failure to protect against violence to person or property. But the concept of equal protection of the laws involves more. It may be thought to involve the right to be protected against arbitrary restrictions, like those based on color, wherever the power of the state reaches. This would mean that a state denied equal protection to the extent that, in the face of actual discrimination, it failed to exercise available legislative power to correct it. The Fourteenth Amendment would then be flouted by a state's failure to pass laws prohibiting discrimination in private employment, private schools, perhaps private rental housing, and all places of public accommodation. The measure of the state's obligation would simply be the limits of its power under due process to prohibit discrimination. Presumably under this limitation it would still be permissible for a home-owner to exclude all of his Negro acquaintances from a garden party. But it would not be permissible to exclude Negroes as such from private rental housing and employment.[8]

If one harbors the thought that, no matter how far it may reach to types of discriminatory behavior, the new constitutional regime will surely be confined to differentiations keyed to race, color, or other ethnic condition, he should reconcile his thinking with the

[8] J. D. Hyman, "Segregation and the Fourteenth Amendment," *Vanderbilt Law Review,* 4 (1951), 569–570.

Bolling case. This is the second half of the Segregation cases, outlawing segregation in schools controlled by national law. This decision and opinion made the due-process-of-law requirement a barrier to separation in schools equally with the equal-protection clause. The due-process-of-law clauses have a long history of elaborate interpretation, and nothing is more prominent in this body of constitutional doctrine than that the guarantee of due process in the acts of government applies to all men regardless of race, color, social condition, or other characteristic differentiating one man from another.

CHAPTER SIXTEEN

Justification of Judgments

Corwin wrote that, for cases involving the commerce clause, the Supreme Court keeps two horses ready to go and mounts the one which will take it directly to the place the judges are determined to get. This is one of the milder charges that have been directed against the Court's methods in deciding issues and explaining decisions. The offenses charged, roughly classified, are of two kinds. They relate either to the way judges explain how they arrive at the meaning of a constitutional provision or to the reasoning employed when the judges fit the constitutional requirement to the statute they are asked to enforce or set aside.

1. FIXING MEANING FOR THE CONSTITUTION

What basic considerations might guide the judge when he seeks the meaning of language in the Constitution? Three main alternatives are obvious, and why a choice may have to be made among them can be seen by examining one two-sentence paragraph in the Constitution (Article III, Section 3).

> Treason against the United States shall consist only in levying war against them, or in adhering to their enemies, giving them aid and comfort. No person shall be convicted of treason, unless on the testimony of two witnesses to the same overt act, or on confession in open court.

(1) The judge can confine his attention to the words in the document itself. He has no trouble with the word "two." He can say that the requirement that two "witnesses" testify to the same overt act is met when a court controls the taking of testimony from two persons in a way that was contemplated by the law prevailing in the thirteen states at the time the Constitution went into effect. The same method of inquiry ought to serve equally well for "confession in open court." But the method may not serve at all well for either if the inquiry forces a conclusion that law in the thirteen original states varied widely as to who might be a "witness," what constitutes acceptable "testimony," and so on.

When the judge is unable to find a clearly indicated meaning in the words themselves, he may turn to another alternative: (2) the intent of the men who gave us the Constitution. This is a happy solution if it turns out that several members of the convention of 1787 made compatible statements about the result they wanted to get by the words they adopted, if nothing was said in the state ratifying conventions to challenge the men at Philadelphia, and if no one who ought to be listened to offered an alternative explanation of what framers and ratifiers had in mind. Unhappily, a high congruence of testimony is rarely disclosed by research.

Even if the judge can find a clearly indicated meaning in the words themselves or in expressons of intent, he may be convinced that that meaning must be rejected. In that case he may adopt alternative (3)—the enthronement of an ideal which each generation of Americans must try to make effective. Note the sentence defining treason. "Treason against the United States shall consist only in levying war against them, or in adhering to their enemies, giving them aid and comfort." Let us suppose that the evidence is undeniable that the framers wanted the sentence as a whole and each word in it interpreted and applied in accordance with the law of England as of the date of the latest authoritative statement prior to ratification of the Constitution. Let us suppose, also, that the Supreme Court judges in 1963 have no doubt what the English law was in 1787. What shall the judges say about the number of witnesses required to convict a person charged with giving aid and comfort to a foreign government which is not levying war against the United States but which has declared itself an implacable enemy of the American people and given abundant evidence that it will strike at the earliest moment it is confident of success? Perhaps the constitution-makers of 1787 and the English law they referred to did not contemplate "latent hostility." If so, should the judges say that making provision for war is not a case of levying war and that giving aid and comfort to a government that plots war is not a case of giving aid and comfort to enemies of the United States? If the answer is yes, then the testimony of one person may secure a conviction for any crime relating to the plotting of war. But why did the framers write the rule of English law into the Constitution? Could their more general purpose have been to declare that, in times of great national danger, when the population is panicky, a second witness to each overt act is a necessary safeguard against injustice? If that was the deeper intent underlying the declared intent, should the judges ignore the statements of the framers that they expected an application of the English law as it had been authoritatively expressed in 1787? Should judges hold that men who would require two witnesses to convict of treason in 1787 would certainly require two witnesses to convict of giving aid and comfort to potential enemies in 1963?

The Supreme Court judges, in fixing meaning for constitutional language, have utilized each of these three methods and some others not mentioned. Many of their opinions offer rules to govern selection among the alternatives. But the judges have not lived up to the rules. One group of opinions states that, if the Constitution's language is clear and unambiguous, the Court must enforce that meaning and not seek evidence that another meaning might have been intended or be preferable for other reasons. But critics of the Court cite cases in which a majority of the judges rejected the obvious meaning of plain language to enforce a meaning which they derived from statements of the framers or from experience prior to adoption of the constitutional language. They also point out that the same judge who announced a rule governing choice among alternatives later violated the rule he had expounded. There is especially objection to the readiness with which judges have rejected both the plain meaning of constitutional language and evidence of original intent in order to announce an ideal which is declared more binding than either language or intent. Instead of the Constitution being a form to which government shall be molded, say some of the critics, the Constitution becomes a series of hints which invite the Supreme Court to write a new constitution.

Behind discontent with the Court's selection of alternatives to guide its search for meaning is a more fundamental objection—that the judges are not guided by these methods at all, but use them to bolster explanation of decisions which may have been reached for very different reasons. The findings of a careful student published in 1938 include the following:

> In fact, it seems clear that while the high tribunal frequently utilizes convention debates and proceedings to rationalize and buttress a stand taken, the intention of the framers thus disclosed will not control the decision rendered. There are instances in which the holding of the Court has directly conflicted with the undeniable will of the Constitution makers determined on this basis. . . . We must conclude, therefore, that while the United States Supreme Court will use convention debates and proceedings to show that the intention of the framers thus revealed affirms or does not contradict the position of the Court, such intent so discovered will be disregarded when in conflict with the interpretation of the Constitution announced by the Court.[1]

2. FITTING THE CONSTITUTION TO THE SITUATION

When the judges have determined what the Constitution requires, they must still apply it to the facts presented in the suit. The Supreme Court judges are frequently accused of inconsistency in fitting the Constitution's requirements to the situation before them. Two illustrations of inconsistency in judicial opinions will reveal the cause of complaint.

(1) "Give an inch, take a mile." Should the Court, in deciding whether a statute conflicts with the Constitution, confine its attention to the particular statute that has been challenged? That is, should the Court restrict its decision to the question: Is this particular statute, considering its content and its probable effect, a violation of the Constitution? Or may the Court anticipate that this statute, if held valid, will be extended and supplemented by later statutes which will overrun the limits fixed by the Constitution? May the judges forbid the lawmakers to move an inch because they fear the lawmakers will later move an unconstitutional mile?

The Supreme Court judges have been highly inconsistent on this question of method. There are many opinions for the majority which firmly declare that the Court will not guess at later legislative enactments. But there are also many other opinions in which fear of future enactments is offered as a main reason for holding the present enactment invalid. It seems undeniable that, in many

[1] Jacobus tenBroek, "Admissibility and Use by the United States Supreme Court of Extrinsic Aids in Constitutional Construction," *California Law Review*, 26 (1938), 448, 451.

instances, the judge adopted one of the two positions according to which would support a decision he had reached on other grounds. If he had concluded that the statute did not violate the Constitution and ought to be enforced, he refused to consider a contention that this statute might invite further legislation which would have to be held invalid. If, in another case, the judge had concluded that the statute should not be enforced, he made much of the fact that it was likely to prove just a first step in a legislative program that would later be found unconstitutional.

(2) "One step at a time." Conceding that the lawmakers have authority to devise a legislative program to solve a complicated social problem, may they deal with it piecemeal?

Some attempts at piecemeal legislation are bound to be resisted by the judges. If the lawmakers, in order to experiment, required grocery stores at odd-numbered addresses to close on Sundays while competing stores stayed open, any judge would feel obliged to rule that the regulated merchants were denied equal protection of the law or deprived of property without due process of law. But it is equally true that the lawmakers cannot devise a statute that perfectly fits all the contours of a social problem, and there is promise of great social gain if they are permitted to start with an effort to correct the most glaring manifestations of the evil. Holmes addressed himself to this conflict in a case involving the validity of a state law that authorized sterilization of persons suffering certain hereditary afflictions, but made sterilization compulsory only for persons confined in institutions named in the statute. After rejecting other grounds for holding the statute invalid, Holmes noted a contention that the act was faulty because it applied only to the small number being treated in the designated institutions and made no provision for the far greater number of persons who suffered the same affliction but were not under institutional care. "It is the usual last resort of constitutional arguments to point out shortcomings of this sort," he said. "But the answer is that the law does all that is needed when it does all that it can, indicates a policy, applies it to all within the lines, and seeks to bring within the lines all similarly situated so far and so fast as its means allow" (*Buck* v. *Bell,* 274 U.S. 200, at 208, decided in 1927).

We must expect judges to disagree as to when a first-step enactment inaugurates an intolerably discriminatory regime. The reasoning of the judge becomes offensive if one is convinced that he trumps up a charge of unequal application of a statute in order to bolster an argument that the law is invalid on other grounds. Just such offensive trumping-up was seen by many political leaders and students of law in Sutherland's reasoning in the District of Columbia minimum wage case cited above. Sutherland examined the statute as an effort to safeguard the morals of the population. He found deficiency in the fact that the act applied only to women who worked for wages. Conceding that a guarantee of minimum wages safeguarded the morals of employed women (a concession which Sutherland did not make), it had to be admitted that the statute did nothing to safeguard the morals of women who did not work for wages and nothing to protect the morals of men, whether employed or not. Such a differentiation of the population whose morals could stand improvement seemed to the justice and four of his colleagues a classification without reasonable basis.

Lawyers who are willing enough to criticize the Supreme Court for particular decisions and opinions are likely to make a general defense of the Court's methods of reasoning. They say that the ways of the Supreme Court are those of all judges and that these ways are essential to the development of any important body of law. Anglo-American law, they claim, is a truly great system of law because it develops by adjusting to and making provision for the emerging social problem. The flexibility and growth of the law are products of the judges' open choice. For the Constitution to develop as the nation's needs develop, the judge must at one time see the language of the Constitution as an anchor put down in 1787 to keep the ship of state from drifting onto dangerous reefs. But another time the judge must view a constitutional provision as a polestar by which he must steer the ship of state toward those placid waters given to the nation as a goal in the preamble to the Constitution.

The lawyer is better equipped than the intelligent nonlawyer to evaluate many of the Supreme Court's decisions. But any informed and thoughtful citizen may confidently declare his position on those decisions which have the most striking political consequences. If one agrees with Alexander Hamilton (in No. 78 of *The Federalist*) that the Constitution embodies the will of the people, that the power of judicial review is given to the judges so that they may confine the lawmakers to what the people have authorized, and that "the power of the people" is superior to both the lawmakers and the judges—if one takes this view of our constitutional system, surely he may demand that the Supreme Court explain its great interpretations of the Constitution in language that the informed and thoughtful citizen can readily understand regardless of whether he finds it convincing. The dean of one of our most respected law schools put it this way in a recent address:

> Beyond that function [justification of the decision to litigants and lawyers], the opinion is a piece of rhetoric and of literature, intended to educate and persuade. In the clearest possible way, it represents the conception of the judges speaking directly to the people, as participants in an endless public conversation on the nature and purposes of law, in all its applications. It recognizes the special responsibility of judges, appointed for a time as delegates of the people, charged with the duty of doing justice to the men before them, as spokesmen for the people of their common or customary conception of law.[2]

In an endless conversation between judges and the people, one might expect the judge to structure his exposition in accordance with the norms of straightforward and ingenuous discourse. Some of the methods of reasoning noted in this chapter have been decried as departures from these norms and cited as evidence that the Supreme Court judges have abused the power with which they were entrusted.

3. A PAUSE IN CONVERSATION

If the judges do in fact conceive themselves to be engaged in endless public conversation, they have interrupted an important part of the story the public wants to hear. The pause began in 1954.

Only the Chief Justice spoke to the nation in explanation of the original Segregation decisions. There is a widespread conviction among lawyers and other close observers of the Court that the Supreme Court judges were far less in agreement than Warren's explanatory essays would indicate. Review again his reasoning, summarized with substantial quotation at the beginning of this book. He asked whether segregation of children in public schools solely on the basis of race deprived the children in the minority group of equal educational opportunity and answered that these children were in fact denied equal educational opportunity. The proof that they were denied equal educational opportunity lay in the facts that forced separation because of race generates a feeling of inferiority and that the feeling of inferiority may affect their hearts and minds

2 Eugene V. Rostow, "The Court and Its Critics," *South Texas Law Journal*, 4 (1959), 163.

in a way unlikely ever to be undone. Corroboration of these conclusions was found in arrays of evidence to which the Chief Justice referred in footnotes not quoted in this book.

The two opinions, Brown and Bolling, are notable for what they did not say. They did not say that it is unlawful for a state to separate Negro children from white children because Negroes are human beings and, as human beings, are entitled to be incorporated fully into American society. They did not say that the Negro has a right inherent in the human being, an inalienable right which had previously been unlawfully alienated, to mix with other people without being restrained by law or governmental act, to mix with other people regardless of whether he may be kept from doing so without ascertainable injury, or to mix with other people regardless of age and of other disposition or occasion to be sensitive about differentiation.

Lawyers and other students of constitutional law create images of each judge, drawing the materials from his voting record, the opinions he writes, and what he says on other occasions. The explanations of the Brown and Bolling cases do not jibe with the predominating images of some of the judges. Some of the judges, it is widely believed, must have argued against a rationale which made the personal and social consequences of segregation the test of compliance with the ideals incorporated in the equal-protection and due-process requirements of the Constitution. At the least, it is believed, some of the judges would have preferred an opinion which declared that segregation of Negro children in school is unlawful because it is unlawful for national, state, or local governments to segregate Negroes of any age in any place of common assembly. Perhaps one or more of the judges argued for language going beyond a concept of segregation to an opinion which would forewarn the American people that the Court would strike down laws and other governmental acts subjecting the Negro to offensive discrimination in any form.

If belief that the judges differed significantly in their preferences was warranted, it was reasonable to expect that separate opinions would be written by those judges who were most disappointed with the grounds on which a majority decided to stand. Separate opinions when the judges differ on best grounds for decision have long been customary practice, and especially so since World War II. There must have been special reason for refraining from debate in the Segregation cases.

The presentation of one opinion for all nine judges was certainly surprising, and it may have been disappointing to many people. It could hardly be condemned as a failure to meet judicial obligations, however, for Supreme Court judges have passed up myriad opportunities to express disagreement with a decision or dissatisfaction with an explanation.

But subsequent behavior of the judges has been condemned as failure to do what the nation has a right to expect. Decisions of lower federal courts, justified in formal opinions, have outlawed separation of the races in public buildings, parks and playgrounds, swimming pools and beaches, transportation—in every kind of meeting place and every kind of facility where a properly instituted lawsuit has shown to the satisfaction of a court that separation was the result of legal provision or governmental action. The Supreme Court has approved these extensions of the nonsegregation rule, but to date has offered no explanation of why the judges believe that governmentally induced segregation outside the public school and affecting adults rather than children is a denial of equal protection of the laws or a deprivation of liberty without due process of law. The judges can hardly have believed that Warren's reasoning in the Brown and Bolling cases was all-embracing, rendering superfluous any further explanation of the spreading ban on segregation. A federal district judge said enough to forestall that conclusion. "The whole basis of the decision in the Brown and Bolling cases," said Judge George Bell Timmerman of the South Carolina district, "is the claimed adverse affect which segregation has on the educational and mental development of Negro children, or as otherwise stated, 'the children of the minority group.' Certainly, no such effect can be legitimately claimed in the field of bus transportation. One's education and personality is not developed on a city bus." [3]

A hypothesis widely accepted among lawyers and students of constitutional law offers a neat explanation of why the judges agreed on a single opinion for each of the original Segregation cases and have thus far refused to supply any opinions supporting the decisions which extend the ban on segregation beyond the public schools. The judges, according to the hypothesis, were not of one mind as to how the equal-protection and due-process requirements should be applied to the wide range of situations where discrimination is practiced. If opinions were to be written, unanimity in explaining decisions would not be possible. If separate opinions appeared, it

[3] *Flemming* v. *South Carolina Gas & Electric Co.* (128 F. Supp. 469, 1955; reversed by Circuit Court in 224 F. 2d 752, 1955).

would come out that there is disagreement at the top as to what the Constitution permits, requires, and forbids. And disagreement among the voices that speak will not only encourage doubt that the pronouncements of the judges are as binding, legally and morally, as the words of the Constitution itself, but it will impair the influence of those who strive for compliance with the Supreme Court's orders and weaken an important deterrent to vigorous resistance. Such is the widely accepted explanation, resting on speculation rather than confident knowledge, of why the judges have interrupted the conversation which Rostow described as endlessly progressive.

Great emphasis has been put on dissatisfaction with, protest against, and defiance of the Supreme Court. But the Court always has friends who defend it most stoutly when its enemies press hardest. We shall now give a hearing to a contemporary school of thought known as the "judicial activists." They insist that the Supreme Court must henceforth apply even more severe tests of constitutionality than it has at any time in the past. I shall refer to the judicial behavior which activists recommend as "aggressive judicial review."

No injustice will be done any adherent of this school, I believe, if we describe their common and general position as follows. Judicial activists put highest in the array of values to which the Constitution has relevance those generally in mind when one speaks of human rights and democratic government. They contend that imposition of these values on all arms and branches of government is a main reason for having a constitution and that our judges are required to fashion out of these prime values realizable ideals which will control the meaning of the fundamental document. To make ideals effective in day-to-day government, they are for more rigorous judicial scrutiny of legislation, and to get that result they urge judges to enlarge the scope of their attention, to press more vigorously their search for error, to treat more sympathetically evidence that error has occurred, and perhaps to prescribe more drastic remedies for error than they have in the past.

The relation of human rights to national ideals and interpretation of constitutional language requires no elaboration. A paragraph from an article by a leading law school dean will indicate how activists relate aggressive judicial review to the democratic process.

> One of the central responsibilities of the judiciary in exercising its constitutional power is to help keep the other arms of government democratic in their procedures. The Constitution should guarantee the democratic legitimacy of political decisions by establishing essential rules for the political process. It provides that each state should have a republican form of government. And it gives each citizen the political as well as the personal protection of the Bill of Rights and other fundamental constitutional guarantees. The enforcement of these rights would assure Americans that legislative and executive policy would be formed out of free debate, democratic suffrage, untrammeled political effort, and full inquiry.[1]

The strategy which activists endorse for achieving their goal of more vigorous judicial review requires fuller explanation. We may be able to catch the main implications of their recommendations by looking briefy at two general proposals which they advance: (1) that the Supreme Court extend its reach for issues of constitutionality and (2) that the Supreme Court apply stricter tests when it examines legislation for compliance with the Constitution.

1. A WIDER REACH OF JUDICIAL POWER

There are several courses by which an activist Supreme Court might extend the reach of judicial power. Two courses which appear especially promising will be noted here. The Court might enlarge the scope of activity which is forbidden by constitutional guarantees, and it might recede from its doctrine of political questions.

A. *A broader scope of forbidden activity.* The provisions of the Constitution which can be immediately related to the status of individuals contain nearly forty separable guarantees. All but two of them (Article IV, Section 2, mentioning privileges and immunities, and the Thirteenth Amendment, outlawing slavery) are expressed as restraints on exercise of governmental authority. Except for these two provisions, which are addressed to private citizens as well as

[1] Eugene V. Rostow, "The Democratic Character of Judicial Review," *Harvard Law Review,* 66 (1952), 210.

CHAPTER SEVENTEEN

A Plea for Boldness in Judges

1. A WIDER REACH OF JUDICIAL POWER
2. A BOLDER GRASP OF ISSUES
3. A REACTION AGAINST JUDICIAL RESTRAINT

public officials, only the national, state, and local governments are forbidden to work specified injustices on the American people.

What constitutes an act of government? This becomes a prime issue in litigation arising out of constitutional guarantees. We noticed, in considering the relation of the Constitution to racial discrimination, that opinions differ as to what discriminatory practices may properly be cited as default by government. Hyman, writing on this point, asked whether "the failure by the state to bar discrimination [by private citizens, organizations, and business firms] is state action denying the equal protection of the laws" and suggested that a state has "denied equal protection to the extent that, in the face of actual discrimination, it failed to exercise available legislative power to correct it." It is a good guess that this view of constitutional obligation is shared by virtually all students of constitutional law who think of themselves as judicial activists.

The Supreme Court fifteen years ago pointed out a route which need be traveled only a few steps further to bring the Court to the enlarged conception of "act of government" which Hyman suggests. The crucial step was announced by Chief Justice Fred M. Vinson in *Shelley* v. *Kraemer* (334 U.S. 1, decided in 1948). This is the famous restrictive covenant case. Suits originating in the state courts of Michigan and Missouri were joined for hearing by the Supreme Court of the United States. The events that led to litigation in Missouri tell us all we need for understanding the constitutional issue and the contribution to constitutional law which resulted.

An agreement put into writing by persons owning real estate in a particular section of St. Louis restricted the use and occupancy of that land to persons of the white race for fifty years. Shelley, a Negro, purchased a residence with intent to live in it. Kraemer and others, owners of property covered by the restrictive agreement, brought suit to restrain Shelley from occuping the property and won it on appeal to the highest Missouri court. Shelley, who had moved in during the period of appeal, was ordered by the Missouri court to vacate the place he had bought, but he went on to the Supreme Court of the United States, offering among other grounds for relief that he was being denied equal protection of the laws.

Six judges heard the case, and they ruled unanimously for Shelley. Vinson's opinion elaborated three main points. (1) The Fourteenth Amendment inhibits "only such action as may fairly be said to be that of the States." The restrictive agreements, standing alone, do not conflict with the Fourteenth Amendment. "So long as the purposes of those agreements are effectuated by voluntary adherence to their terms, it would appear clear that there has been no action by the State and the provisions of the Amendment have not been violated." (2) The action of the Missouri courts in this case was an action by the state within the meaning of the Fourteenth Amendment. ". . . [F]rom the time of the adoption of the Fourteenth Amendment until the present, it has been the consistent ruling of this Court that the action of the States to which the Amendment has reference, includes action of State courts and State judicial officials." (3) The state of Missouri, through the action of its courts, denied Shelley the equal protection of the laws.

> These are not cases, as has been suggested, in which the States have merely abstained from action, leaving private individuals free to impose such discriminations as they see fit. Rather, these are cases in which the States have made available to such individuals the full coercive power of government to deny to petitioners, on the grounds of race or color, the enjoyment of property rights in premises which petitioners are willing and financially able to acquire and which the grantors are willing to sell. The difference between judicial enforcement and non-enforcement of the restrictive covenants is the difference to petitioners between being denied rights of property available to other members of the community and being accorded full enjoyment of those rights on an equal footing. (P. 19.)

Undoubtedly, individuals can find many ways of mistreating people of another race without any help from public officials. Still, allowing for the extent to which law and governmental authority pervade our lives today, it seems likely that nearly every one of the most oppressive shackles fastened on minority groups depends in one way or another on a provision of law or act of government. Consider my problems in running a business establishment, not "affected by a public interest," for the patronage of white people only. If I operate under license, an activist court may rule that the state or local government cannot issue a license for a place that maintains a discriminatory policy. If no license is required, when Negroes press into my place uninvited I will be able to maintain an action in trespass only if I cite grounds that would be applicable to people of all races. Police officers, too, will be able to give me little assistance. I can alert the policeman to a disturbance likely to become a breach of the peace, but I cannot call in a policeman to evict Negroes simply because I do not want them in my place of business. It would seem no great step beyond the Shelley case for a court, committed to the termination of discrimination as an ideal embodied in the Constitution, to declare me the aggressive party and rule that the policeman shall patrol my behavior rather than that of the group which entered my place uninvited.

B. *Recede from the doctrine of political questions.* The concept "political question" has provided judges with an easy escape from many difficult issues. Judicial activists urge the Supreme Court to grapple with many questions which it has heretofore sidestepped by resort to this concept.

The Supreme Court, with other courts, refuses to decide a suit if the judges conclude that any point essential to a rightful disposition of the litigation has a "political involvement" in which the judiciary should not get tangled. The case which is political in this sense is declared nonjusticiable.

Writing on this subject reveals a notable lack of agreement as to what considerations and conditions make an issue so politically involved that the judges ought to keep their hands off it. The following statement in a recent opinion by Justice William J. Brennan, Jr., presumably is the nearest to authoritative at this time. He lists a series of tests for determining the political character of an issue before a court. (I have inserted the numbers which precede the items.)

> Prominent on the surface of any case held to involve a political question is found (1) a textually demonstrable constitutional commitment of the issue to a coordinate political department; or (2) a lack of judicially discoverable and manageable standards for resolving it; or (3) the impossibility of deciding [the issue] without an initial policy determination of a kind clearly for nonjudicial discretion; or (4) the impossibility of a court's undertaking independent resolution [of the issue] without expressing lack of the respect due coordinate branches of government; or (5) an unusual need for unquestioning adherence to a political decision already made; or (6) the potentiality of embrassassment from multifarious pronouncements by various departments on one question. (*Baker* v. *Carr,* 369 U.S. 186, at 217, decided in 1962.)

One need not be a constitutional lawyer to see instantly that nearly every condition set forth in Brennan's list is expressed in vague rather than precise, or defining, terms. If judges will disagree on anything, they are bound to disagree as to what is denied them by Brennan's language. What standards for resolving an issue can judges discover and adequately manage? What kind of an issue cannot be decided without an initial policy determination, and what kind of a policy determination is unsuitable for determination by judges? What kind of judicial act resolving an issue would display too little respect for the legislative or the executive branch? And so on.

The list of suits which the Supreme Court has dismissed on the sole ground that a political question was presented is a short one. But these few decisions, augmented by the explanations which accompanied the decisions have, until very recently at least, effectively discouraged litigation of several categories of questions which Rostow must have had in mind when he said: "The Constitution should guarantee the democratic legitimacy of political decisions by establishing essential rules for the political process." The courts have generally entertained suits which charge violation of the laws regulating admission to the polls, conduct of polling, counting and reporting of votes, and certification of nomination or election to office. Statutory provisions regulating these matters may also be tested for compliance with constitutional requirements. The conduct of investigations by legislative bodies have been scrutinized in the courts, but the rules and practices governing debate and voting in lawmaking assemblies have generally been treated as political questions. The leniency which allows the filibuster and the severity which expresses itself in gag rule—both have, in the main, escaped judicial test. Whether lawmakers or judges are to be final as to the obligations of a presidential elector, torn between his own preference and that of a party nominating convention, is now uncertain. A widely held opinion that courts would not force legislative bodies to reallocate their seats or take on the task of reallocation themselves was roughly shaken, if not destroyed, in March, 1962. In *Baker* v. *Carr,* the case supplying Brennan's statement quoted above, the Supreme Court held by vote of seven to two that a justiciable question was presented in a complaint that the distribution of seats in the Tennessee legislature resulted in a denial of equal protection of the laws to people living in certain underrepresented districts. This ruling governed the decisions in suits from other states which followed close on the heels of the Tennessee suit.

Earnest supporters of aggressive judicial review may see a place for the concept of political questions. Their writings to date do not tell us how far toward the background they would push it. Certain to be eviscerated in time by an activist Court, it seems to me, is the rule announced in *Luther* v. *Borden* (7 Howard 1, decided in 1849) and followed in some later cases: that the Supreme Court will not issue orders designed to enforce the Constitution's provision that "The United States shall guarantee to every State in this Union a republican form of government." Surely everything which Rostow conceives to be relevant to "free debate, democratic suffrage, untrammeled political effort, and full inquiry" can readily be subsumed under the idea "republican form of government."

An important first act in the removal of questions of this character from the "political" category occurred in *Baker* v. *Carr*. Brennan, speaking at least for himself and two other justices, asserted that the nonjusticiability of claims arising under this guarantee "has nothing to do with their touching upon matters of state governmental organization." A suit charging departure from a republican form will be held nonjusticiable, Brennan appears to say, only if it goes to a matter which necessarily involves another branch of the national government. Since each house of Congress is declared by the Constitution to be "the judge of the elections, returns, and qualifications of its own members," a lawsuit challenging a state's layout of seats for the national House of Representatives may be thought so politically involved as to be nonjusticiable; the layout of seats for the state lawmaking assembly which is identical in its departure from democratic ideals and its violation of constitutional guarantees may be held proper for approval, condemnation, or correction by judges.

2. A BOLDER GRASP OF ISSUES

The activist not only asks the Supreme Court to take hold of issues it previously ignored; he wants the Court to act more aggressively in the cases it accepts. There appear to be two main recommendations for judicial strategy.

A. *Translate the language of powers and prohibitions into a language of ideals.* I cited Alexander Bickel above for the view that the equal-protection clause had two significations at the time it was adopted. One might say that it was fused for two explosions, one instant, the other delayed. The judges of our day, Bickel said, are required to search the constitutional language and the environment of its birth for a vision of future needs, for a grander purpose behind the immediate purpose. I have called such a vision and conception of purpose an "ideal."

I suppose all thoughtful people will travel this road with Bickel for some distance. All may agree that the national government is given all the authority essential for managing our relations with other peoples, even though the Constitution mentions only the appointment of persons to represent us with other nations, punishment of piracy and offenses against the law of nations, and the power to declare and carry on war. But there will be violent dissent if anyone finds a grander purpose behind the Seventh Amendment which allows the national government to abandon jury trials.

No doubt the cutting edge of argument, on this as on so many matters of great public concern, will be the practical application of tests of reasonableness. One man will say that the ideal which the Supreme Court honored in the Segregation cases was inherent in the phrase "equal protection of the laws" as that phrase is illuminated by the circumstances of its adoption at the close of the Civil War. Another will say that the Supreme Court found the ideal in a public philosophy that came to flower in the decade after World War II and simply hooked that ideal onto the phrase in the Constitution that offered the best semantic attraction.

I do not see how fact and logic can prove either disputant right. Fruitful argument will be directed toward choice among ideals, whether and when and by what means particular ideals are realizable, and what repositories of conferred authority can best be trusted to make the nation's choice among ideals and fit them into the whole structure of values that we call the American way of life. Today's judicial activists announce a high confidence that today's Supreme Court will select wisely and fit securely.

The task for the activist is to persuade the judges to adopt his ideals and his judgment about effecting ideals, to persuade judges that they have a constitutional obligation to act boldly, and to persuade enough of the population that the judges act in fulfillment of that obligation to make a regime of aggressive judicial review a continuing reality.

Judges who are persuaded of obligation to act will have no difficulty in finding justification for their acts in the Constitution's language. The Constitution abounds in invitations to search for ideals and in phrases onto which ideals may be hooked. Judges possessed of a moderate amount of imagination can find in the Constitution words, phrases, or sentences so rich in potential meanings that a moderate amount of courageous squeezing will wring from them a justification for anything the judges think best for the country. Marshall and his colleagues in 1819 were able to secure the charter of Dartmouth College against modification by the state of New Hampshire though the Court thought it "more than possible" that such a conferral of rights and powers "was not particularly in the view of the framers" when the framers wrote into the Constitution the provision that no state shall pass any law impairing the obligation of contracts. The provision that no state may deprive a person of life, liberty, or property without due process of law gave Justice Joseph P. Bradley and later judges all the authorization they needed to save the country from any laws which, in Holmes's extreme language, "happen to strike a majority of this Court as for any reason undesirable." I find it difficult to believe that the future promises any dangers from which the judicial act can save us that cannot be subdued by an imaginative and courageous wielding of the due-process-of-law clause, the equal-protection clause, the privileges-and-immunity clauses, the first eight amendments, and the provision that the United States shall guarantee to every state a republican form of government.

B. *Reverse the presumptions about constitutionality.* I use the word "presumption" here to embrace a good deal more than the lawyer would put into that word. I refer to certain self-imposed restraints, which, when fully observed by the judges, gave the traditional practice of judicial review its passive or conservative character and which the contemporary activists would have the Supreme Court justices moderate drastically, if not abandon altogether. We shall note two of them here.

First, the rule that constitutional language should be interpreted in a manner favorable to legislative power. Judges reach a conclusion about the validity of a statute by fitting together what they believe to be the requirements of the Constitution and what they believe to be the meaning of the statute and its probable effects. The outcome of their effort to test the statute against the Constitution is strongly affected by the rules which the judges apply to the process of making a decision. The validity or invalidity of a statute is not susceptible to proof. Evidence and logic do not force one conclusion. When everything thought relevant has been examined, men may reasonably disagree as to whether the statute should be enforced or declared unenforceable because of conflict with the Constitution. In such a case, the outcome of the judge's deliberations will be greatly affected by the state of mind he brings to the issue. If he starts with a presumption that the Constitution authorizes what the lawmakers have done and is determined to decide that way unless evidence and reasoning move him to the other side, he enlarges the likelihood that his final decision will be for validity. If another judge brings to the case a presumption that the law violates the Constitution and stands there until shown why he should move, he may well end up where he started.

Supreme Court judges at times find it useful to make an express statement about the rules governing the process of decision. I believe that, without exception, up to the abrupt change in judicial policy in 1937, all statements about presumption were firm declarations that the statute was presumed valid, that the burden of pulling the Court over the hard places falls on the parties who contend that the statute is forbidden by the Constitution. It was a common occurrence, of course, for critics of the Court to say that the judges had approached the case with firm intention to put a statute to death if they could make the Constitution support their goal. But there appears to be no record of public admission by any Supreme Court judge prior to 1937 that he entered on the consideration of any constitutional issue in that frame of mind.

Since 1937, the Supreme Court judges have not been consistent on this point. The present bench is lenient toward legislation regulating business activity; it examines each such case with a presumption that the statute is valid and requires the parties opposing the statute to bring the Court to a different conclusion. But, if the statute is attacked on the ground that it endangers personal rights and liberties, some, perhaps a majority, of the judges now on the Court start their examination of the case in a state of mind more friendly to those who attack than to those who defend the statute's validity. I think it would exaggerate the evidence to say that, in the latter class of cases, the Supreme Court makes a presumption that the statute is invalid and requires those who defend the statute to bear the burden of convincing. Perhaps most students of constitutional law will accept this formulation: that, when the Court is confronted by legislation involving personal rights and liberties, the relevant constitutional guarantees enjoy a preferred position. Or, if that is thought too inclusive, then: that the judges will put in a preferred position the First Amendment guarantees (freedom of religion, freedom of speech and press, right of assembly) when they become the test that determines the validity of legislation.

The term "preferred position" originated with the Supreme Court judges. In a famous footnote to one of his opinions, Chief Justice Stone suggested: "There may be narrower scope for operation of the presumption of constitutionality when legislation appears on its face to be within [i.e., protected by] a specific prohibition of the Constitution, such as those of the first ten amendments, which are deemed equally specific when held to be embraced within the Fourteenth." A few years later, Justice Wiley Rutledge said:

> The case confronts us again with the duty which our system places on this Court to say where the individual's freedom ends and the State's power begins. Choice on that border, now as always delicate, is perhaps more so where the usual presumption supporting legislation is balanced by the preferred place given in our scheme to the great, the indispensable freedoms secured by the First Amendment.

It will be noted that Stone spoke of narrowing the presumption of constitutionality and that he would resort to the narrower presumption in cases involving specific prohibitions "such as" those in the first ten amendments. Rutledge, on the other hand, spoke of a preferred place, and he put in that preferred place only the freedoms secured by the First Amendment. The judges who are most concerned to advance personal rights and freedoms have not yet agreed on a precise formulation which would give assurance as to where they stand as a group, and there is enough variance in the statements of each to cause one to suspect that none has fully made up his mind as to what the rule governing decision should be. It should also be noted that some judges will apparently have little or nothing to do with a preferred position for any part of the Constitution. In a case involving freedom of speech, Frankfurter said: "I deem it ['preferred position'] a mischievous phrase, if it carries the thought, which it may subtly imply, that any law touching communication is infected with presumptive invalidity." [2]

The disagreement among judges about preferred position is paralleled by differences among lawyers and teachers of law. Perhaps most men who think of themselves as activists would endorse some style or shade of preferential treatment for the constitutional guarantees most essential to preservation of personal rights and liberties. Without suggesting that he speaks for anyone but himself, I will quote one lawyer and former law teacher.

> I suggest that the following proposals would bring us a little closer to the plan of the fathers. . . . [T]he doctrine of presumption should be completely eradicated in cases involving basic liberties. In that area, a presumption of unconstitutionality should prevail. In free speech cases, in particular, the Supreme Court has no business paying "great deference," or indeed any deference to the judgment of the legislature. It should do the exact opposite.[3]

[2] Stone in *U.S.* v. *Carolene Products Co.* (304 U.S. 144, at 152, 1938); Rutledge in *Thomas* v. *Collins* (323 U.S. 516, at 529–530, 1946); Frankfurter in *Kovacs* v. *Cooper* (336 U.S. 77, at 90, 1949).

[3] John P. Frank, in Edmond Cahn, ed., *Supreme Court and Supreme Law* (Bloomington: Indiana University Press, 1954), pp. 132 f.

Second, in order to achieve an aggressive judicial review, certain rules that control the scope of the decision and the opinion in constitutional cases ought to be relaxed or abandoned. The following rules, especially, have combined to give the practice of judicial review the passive character it has heretofore maintained: (*a*) that the Court will decide no question of conflict with the Constitution unless it is presented to the Court in a manner proper for that suit; (*b*) that the Court will decide only those questions which, when properly presented, must be decided in order to dispose of the litigation; (*c*) that the opinion explaining the decision will not announce positions on any constitutional issues which are not decided in that case.

The rules are by no means inflexible. The Supreme Court has made a number of notable departures from them. Nevertheless, they describe approximately the conditions under which the constitutionality of statutes has traditionally been determined.

It is readily seen that the development of constitutional doctrines will be greatly affected by the manner in which issues are formulated and presented to the Court. Attorneys for the government, intent on a decision upholding the statute if they can get it, watch for that particular set of circumstances which will permit them to make the best case for validity of the statute. They will relax enforcement of the statute in order to avoid coming to suit when the circumstances are not right. When they have found a litigable situation that involves only those aspects of the statute least likely to be offensive to the judges or one where the operation of the statute works least damage to legitimate and treasured interests—when they have found either set of circumstances or, happily, both combined, the time is right for public officials to enforce the law, encourage resistance, and bring the case to trial.

As government officials jockey for advantage in litigation, so other persons and business firms that have the resources necessary for a waiting game will pass up opportunities to assert their rights and then force a suit when they see good reason to think they will win it and so conduct a statute to its grave. Occasionally both parties to a suit would like to see the statute fall. In that case they may agree on a formulation and presentation of the issues thought most likely to bring the statute down.

The fact that a statute survives the charge of invalidity in one appearance before the Supreme Court does not preclude a later suit which also charges invalidity. But the second suit must stand on some point which creates a new issue clearly differentiable from the one tried before. It is a rare occurrence, however, for a statute to survive one round before the Supreme Court and then come up for the constitutional test again after an interval of time. As a practical matter of constitutional law, therefore, the fate of a statute is likely to be determined in the first suit that gets to the Supreme Court.

It is easily seen that these ways of doing things do not ensure an aggressive judicial enforcement of the Constitution. They are undeniable proof that judicial restraint reigns precisely where many of our contemporaries would enthrone, in one law teacher's words, "vigorous, vigilant, courageous activism on the part of the Court."

If the judges resolve to enlarge their grasp of constitutional issues, they will have a wide range of alternatives from which to choose in devising new rules to replace those that govern them now. We cannot explore here the possibilities and probabilities. We may be sure that the activists generally, perhaps without exception, would retain the rule that the Supreme Court will declare a law invalid only when the opportunity to do so is presented in a lawsuit. What they recommend is that the judges make the most of every opportunity. If the parties to a suit have formulated the issue so as to bring only certain parts of the statute into question, some activists would allow the judges to extend the inquiry to other parts of the statute and to test those parts for compliance with the Constitution. Instead of testing compliance solely on the basis of facts presented in the case before them, the judges should, according to the activists, look outward for probable effects of the statute when applied to other situations.

Rule *c,* above, restricting the scope of the opinion is certainly doomed if the activist program is adopted by the Court. The objective of the activist is to force compliance with the Constitution, not merely to prevent the consummation of violations already launched. The judicial opinion is the means by which the judges tell the lawmakers what they may expect the judges to do if statutes akin to this one are brought before the Court in the future. The endless conversation of which Rostow spoke is with all the nation, but in it are lectures and warnings addressed directly to the men and women who make our laws. Activists would have Supreme Court judges make bold use of their opportunities to settle doubts and remove erroneous suppositions about constitutional obligations before those doubts and suppositions can precipitate litigation.

C. *Relax the rule of* stare decisis. The traditional passive doctrine of judicial review honors a rule that a previous decision of the Supreme Court will not be overruled if a way can be found to save it. The chief justices of thirty-six states, it will be remembered, thought that there was considerable doubt that we are still a government of laws and not of men. One of the two reasons they gave for doubting was the readiness with which the Supreme Court departs from its own previous rulings. "We concede that a slavish adherence to *stare decisis* could at times have unfortunate consequences; but it seems strange that under a constitutional doctrine which requires all others to recognize the Supreme Court's rulings on constitutional questions as binding adjudications of the meaning and application of the Constitution, the Court itself has so frequently overturned its own decisions thereon. . . ."

The rule that previous decisions will be allowed to stand advances two great values. It gives you and me and the lawyers who advise us confidence that we can foresee what the law will be in the future. And it gives judges and lawmakers assurance that there is an enduring structure of law to which they may attach additions with confidence that the growing structure will maintain the consistency and integration essential to a legal system.

No doubt most contemporary activists will insist that they value certainty in the law and rational legal structure as much as the next man. Most of them, I believe, contend that revision of interpretation is likely to affect only a small part of the Constitution's content and that even considerable uncertainty as to how these provisions will be interpreted and applied can have little effect on the planning of activities and enterprises that enjoy the nation's approval. As for the vision of a consistent, integrated, and continuously developing legal structure, virtually every member of the activist school will say that the vision cannot be realized if the pillars, main beams, or indeed any essential parts of the structure are rotten. The structure now standing, they will insist, must be made sound before sound growth can continue.

3. A REACTION AGAINST JUDICIAL RESTRAINT

There is no organization which identifies members of the activist school and no official statement of what they believe. Both the general position and the particular proposals which are ascribed to them above represent my understanding of their goals and their strategy. The following paragraphs should correct any error I may unwittingly have introduced.

Prof. Charles L. Black, Jr., of the Yale University Law School, produced a small book, written mainly, he tells us, "as a reaction against what I feel to be a prevailing overemphasis on this concept of judicial self-restraint, under whatever guise it may appear." The book contends that the power of judicial review is both necessary to our constitutional system and provided for in the Constitution itself and makes a forceful argument for a more aggresive practice of judicial review in the future.[4]

When we are confronted by the class of controversies, says Black, "in which the claim is that an act of Congress violates one of the *express prohibitions* [his italics] placed on Congress in the Constitution—then it seems to me that the case for 'judicial restraint' becomes very weak, and the case for creative and courageous activism very strong" (p. 94). Because the expressed prohibitions are set out in textual form and therefore provide an unimpeachably authoritative starting point, "the application of the concept of 'judicial restraint' to these guarantees cannot be justified on the ground that the judicial mind ought to check itself sharply against devising purely speculative limitations on Congress" (p. 95). ". . . [E]verything about the prohibitions in the Bill of Rights points to the propriety of their being construed with extreme breadth, . . . and the job of so construing them, and enforcing them as construed, is properly the job of the Court." "Everything points to the propriety of high judicial vigilance in these areas, and of unembarrassed judicial courage in acting where these considerations compel action" (pp. 96, 108).

In a half-dozen pages (pp. 110 ff.), Black seeks an answer to the question "whether there is a sound distinction between the judicial activism of the thirties and the kind of judicial activism which I am advocating." The judicial activism which the author identifies with the 1930's is the aggressive judicial review we encountered earlier in this book, exemplified by Peckham in *Lochner* v. *New York,* by Sutherland in the Carter Coal case, and by the latter justice in the case involving a minimum wage law for women in the District of Columbia. All those decisions were wrong, says Black. Decisions that invalidated a statute on the ground that the national government had reached beyond the authority granted it were wrong because the limits to power which were announced by the Court were "derived from mere political theory and not from any constitutional provision." This statement seems to account for the

[4] Charles L. Black, Jr., *The People and the Court* (New York: Macmillan, 1960).

Carter Coal case, though Black did not mention it specifically. Decisions that invalidated statutes for violation of the due-process-of-law clause—for example, the ten-hour law for bakers and the minimum wage for women—were wrong because they "grotesquely misread" the words "due process of law." In the due-process cases,

> [T]he construction was wild rather than merely liberal or broad. "Due process" came to mean "reasonable," and "reasonable" came to mean "economically sound and fair in the opinion of judges" which, in turn, meant that challenged governmental action regulating business had to conform to the laissez-faire philosophy of the bench. . . . That these words import some standard of substantive fairness is doubtless acceptable; that they import so narrow and restricted a standard is impossible to swallow.

I take it that Black means that the old interpretation of due process is more than a judicial activist can swallow, for it certainly was swallowed with manifestations of great pleasure by many lawyers and teachers of law during the period when the laissez-faire doctrines were being served at the Supreme Court's table. I am not clear how Black's disposition of those earlier decisions fits into the thinking of other activists who place great emphasis on the identification of ideals in constitutional language. I do not see how anyone can read the opinions of Peckham, Sutherland, and other judges of their persuasion without concluding that those judges had discovered in, or attached to, the due-process-of-law clauses an ideal which they cherished and believed the more thoughtful leaders of the nation also cherished—the maintenance of that free, private enterprise which they believed the crucial element in the nation's material welfare and a main contributor to the independence, self-reliance, and resourcefulness of the American people. If Black answers that language which requires compliance with due process of law in acts that effect deprivations is not truly an "expressed prohibition," he excludes deprivations of life and liberty from the case he makes for high judicial vigilance and unembarrassed judicial courage. And, further, if it be argued that the due-process-of-law clause is not an expressed prohibition, a regard for consistency might cause one to contend that the requirement of equal protection of the laws is not an expressed prohibition, either. I suspect that nearly all activists value aggressive judicial enforcement of that clause about as highly as they value such a policy for the First Amendment freedoms.

One more note should be made about the relation of Black's judicial activism to rights in property. The Constitution declares in one of its *express prohibitions* (Black's italics) that no state shall pass any law impairing the obligation of contracts. This guarantee, viewed as the embodiment of an ideal and interpreted and enforced by judges committed to a creative and courageous judicial activism, would enable a future Supreme Court majority to outlaw encroachments on freedom of contract, "right to work," and the maintenance of that state of free, private enterprise so urgently recommended by our contemporaries who see great danger in the welfare state. The obligation-of-contracts clause is made applicable to the states by the Constitution's express language. Judges of activist persuasion would readily make it a limitation on the national government, too, by adopting the method of *Bolling* v. *Sharpe*. It will be remembered that, in that case involving school segregation in the District of Columbia, Warren said: "In view of our decision that the Constitution prohibits the states from maintaining racially segregated public schools, it would be unthinkable that the same Constitution would impose a lesser duty on the Federal Government" (*Bolling* v. *Sharpe*, 347 U.S. 496, at 500).

V • JUDICIAL POWER AND DEMOCRATIC GOVERNMENT

We have explored the American experience with judicial review and examined the attitudes and beliefs which have made the Supreme Court a center of controversy. We turn now to the main alternative to decision by judges, the political process. A comparison of the most striking characteristics of the two processes may help us when choices must be made between regulation by court and regulation by law-making bodies. This is the concern of chapters XVIII and XIX. The final chapter of the book calls attention to some problems that lie along the frontier where judicial power comes into contact with the authority of elected officials.

CHAPTER EIGHTEEN
A Question of Democracy

1. A RESPONSIVE POLITICAL PROCESS
2. A NONPOLITICAL ORGAN OF GOVERNMENT

1. A RESPONSIVE POLITICAL PROCESS

Democratic government is government by the people. Constitutional requirements which fix bounds within which government must act do not breach its democratic character if the constitution, like ours, was ordained and established by the people and can be changed by a process responsive to the wishes of the people. The democratic character of a political system is measured by three tests: (a) How much of the population shares (b) in how much of the crucial decision-making (c) with how much impact?

The citizen of the United States can exert influence on his government in any of six ways. (1) Public officials respond to the overriding expectations of the population expressed in its culture and societal ways. Government is blanketed by compelling limitations which are the product of the whole population. This kind of impact will be given no further consideration here. (2) Government is established, regulated, and instructed by the content of written constitutions. In many states, the constitution and its amendments are submitted for approval or disapproval at the polls. (3) Several states make provision for initiation of governmental acts by popular petition and for approval or rejection of proposed acts by popular vote. In many states, this process is available for important issues in local government. In a few states, it is available for adoption of state legislation. In national government, we make some advances in this direction by providing for farmers to participate in decisions on agricultural programs. (4) We elect public officials by popular vote. (5) People have an opportunity to impress their wishes on public officials who make governmental decisions and put them into effect. (6) People influence what their governments do by the way in which they respond to governmental policies and efforts to carry them out. Lawmakers at national, state, and local levels modify what they would like to do by a healthy respect for what the people will tolerate.

A little thought about this list of opportunities for participation reveals that the political process in this country can be separated into two sectors: (1) the officially provided for or legally regulated sector and (2) the sector that is not officially provided for or legally regulated. In the sector of the political process where participation is officially provided for by legal regulations, equality among participants is enthroned, and decision in accordance with a majority rule can at least be approximated. Where such regulation is not imposed, advantage goes to those who have the will and resources to win.

Law and administration can secure a fair measure of equality and ascertain what a majority prefers only in situations where participation can be observed and policed. These conditions obtain most fully in voting. The time and place for voting can be fixed in advance, and the date announced. The issue to be decided can be precisely defined, and the definition made known. The qualifications entitling one to participate in the voting can be specified, and those not entitled can be excluded. Equality in impact can be ensured; for example, one man, one vote. And the terms for decision can be announced in advance and lived up to in practice; for example, the decision may be to act in accordance with the greatest number of expressed preferences (plurality), or to do whatever more than half the participants may prefer (majority rule), or to decide according to some other distribution of preferences such as agreement by two-thirds or three-fourths of the participants.

The ideals of equality and majority rule are in continuous conflict with the attractions of special advantage. In voting, where the two ideals are most nearly achieved, the drive for advantage prejudices the voter's understanding of the issues on which he is to express his own wishes, increases the turnout of those thought likely to vote the right way, and may even intimidate or bribe voters and corrupt the process of taking, counting, and reporting the vote.

Conversely, commitment to equality and majority rule accounts for some of the effort to bring the political process increasingly under regulation. Thus, proponents of the two ideals attempt to thwart special advantage by extending regulation to the administrative stage of government, stipulating that certain decisions be made only after formal hearings or establishing representative bodies to share in decisions or advise the decision-makers.

Both parts of the political process, the regulated and the nonregulated, appear essential to an effective democratic system. Equality among participants and decision on the basis of a count (plurality on some matters, majority on others) is all but universally defended as indispensable to democratic government. In a democratic system, everybody counts; government is run for the benefit of all the population. There is no way of knowing what is good for the people, what the people ought to have. The best we can do is find what the people want their government to do. To ensure that government does what the people want done, all of the mature population (less a few excluded for good reason) must share at crucial points in the political process. To assure that decisions made by counting participants will express plurality or majority demand, the participants must be accorded equal weight in the counting. Secondary advantages flow from compliance with this essential requirement. The process of sharing in decision-making under conditions of equality tends to make the population willing to compromise all but its most passionate demands and to make the population content to live peacefully under an order it had previously provided for or approved.

The unregulated political activity saves democratic government from a pallid mediocrity and rescues an outvoted minority from a decision that presses too hard. A government that acted only when a majority had agreed on the step to be taken would rarely, if ever, anticipate or deal imaginatively with a problem that forced itself into attention. Pressure by imaginative people seeking advantage alerts the public official to incipient crises, supplies him with ready-made solutions, and confronts him with prospects of discomfort that overcome a natural inclination to do nothing. Special advantage may be regarded as a fair price for injecting imagination, competence, and vigor into democratic government, provided that not too much advantage is dispensed. The stubborn refusal of a large part, but surely far less than a majority, of the adult population to acquiesce in Prohibition forced the abandonment of that "noble experiment." A supposition that the Supreme Court's desegregation orders can be successfully withstood by a broad front of stubborn resistance may explain why there has not been a greater resort to beatings, killings, and burnings of homes by violent opponents of integration in the South since 1954.

The regulated and unregulated sectors of politics are blended in varying proportions in the formulation, adoption, and administration of public policies at all levels of our complicated governmental system. Legislators and chief executives are elected by popular vote, and the principal administrative officials are appointed by the elected officials if they are not also elected at the polls. To enlarge the likelihood that major public policies will accord with a generalized public expectation, legislators are chosen by geographic districts, and these are laid out with some concern for uniformity in number of inhabitants.

The preceding paragraph identifies a goal rather than an accomplishment. We have a long way to go in the improvement of our electoral arrangements, including the acceptance of the Negro at the polls in a large part of the country and making honest the administration of balloting in virtually all parts of the country. We have not tried very hard to achieve a uniform allocation of legislative positions among the population. High administrative officials and the bureaucracies they head too frequently act as if their mission is to ignore the instructions given them by elected officials and to elude the accounting which our theory requires them to make. Nevertheless, granting that we fail by a considerable margin to achieve our goal, we may still congratulate ourselves for having created an officialdom that is remarkably sensitive to all clearly articulated demands emanating from groups which can significantly influence the nomination and election of officeholders.

We have, therefore, an authority structure which acquires its basic character from a firm commitment to principles of equality and rule by plurality or majority. Into this elaborate, octopuslike officialdom come the seekers of special advantage, bent on securing the enactment of policies favorable to themselves, determined to block action to their disadvantage, resourceful in negotiating a compromise when they cannot get all they want. The consequences are manifold—a ringing victory for one group and a stinging defeat for another group today, a reversal of fortunes tomorrow; a compromise that gives nobody everything he wants, but which resolves conflicting interests in a way that all find tolerable; a scheduling of solutions for social problems which allows sores to fester, but which applies a remedy when evidence piles up that the afflicted will respond to the treatment; and an accumulation of unsolved problems that culminates in a crisis whose disentanglement requires far greater sacrifice than would have been exacted if components of the mess had been dealt with as they appeared and pressed for attention.

This, as I see it, is the basic character of the political process in the United States. It stands in sharpest contrast to the judicial process.

2. A NONPOLITICAL ORGAN OF GOVERNMENT

Felix Frankfurter, speaking from the bench, called the Supreme Court "the non-democratic organ of our Government" and added that "the powers exercised by this Court are inherently oligarchic" (concurring opinion in *American Federation of Labor* v. *American Sash and Door Co.*, 335 U.S. 538, at 555, decided in 1949). Whether our highest tribunal is a democratic or a nondemocratic institution depends on the meaning which is given to "democracy," and what meaning that word ought to carry is hotly debated in the literature. I think no one will deny that the Supreme Court is a nonpolitical organ of government, if the word "political" is given the meaning I attach to it here.

"Political" can be given a meaning which makes everything connected with government a political fact or one which makes every decision that fixes policy a political decision whether related to government or not. In these uses of the word, every significant act of a judge is political. I have used the word both ways in earlier parts of this book, calling certain decisions of the Supreme Court political and calling the Supreme Court a political institution. But when I call an office, institution, or process "political" in this chapter, I refer to a relationship with a sizable population which makes it legitimate and customary for that population to control or influence that office, institution, or process. In this sense, the Supreme Court and its action on the cases that come before it are removed from politics. The judicial structure and the adjudicatory process are designed to insulate the judge from all influence except what is essential for intelligent decision, and intake of that influence is carefully regulated by law. If one prefers not to use the word "influence" as I do, he may contend that the goal is to insulate the judge from influence in all its manifestations.

All judges in the federal court system are appointed by the president with consent of the Senate. Ordinarily, considerations we label "political" figure in appointment, but we expect the attorney general (who recommends), the president, and senators to hold such considerations to a minimum. Once in office, the federal judge is not removable except for reasons stated in the Constitution, and these are rarely invoked. Most judges in most of the state systems are nominated in direct primary and finally chosen in a popular election. In many instances, the selection of state judges is political in the sense that choice of legislators and executive officials is political. The term of office is ordinarily limited, and public attitudes toward his conduct in the courtroom may contribute to the re-election or the replacement of a judge. But, allowing for all this, the selection of state judges is usually less responsive to public satisfaction and dissatisfaction with their discharge of official duties than is the case with the admittedly political offices. It may be added that there is always, some place or another in the land, an active campaign to remove the selection of judges from politics by one device or another.

In the performance of his duties, the judge is enveloped by precautions to remove him from every kind of appeal and pressure except what is proper for settlement of the case before him. Those who present evidence are limited to what the law recognizes to be evidence appropriate to the litigation, and it is offered in the presence of the parties in suit and under the supervision of lawyers. Argument by parties to the case and their attorneys is made in the presence of opposing litigants and attorneys, and everything said is subject to rebuttal. No one having an interest in the outcome of a suit may offer the judge advice or seek to persuade him except in accordance with the rules of procedure, and it is never permissible to threaten him. Disclosure of a violation of the rules leads to termination of the trial or reversal of the decision on appeal to a higher court.

The Supreme Court judges, it is true, are not so completely removed from politics as we could make them. In Chapter IV, I said that "the nominee's position on political issues of great importance has always been a major concern of presidents and senators in filling positions on the Supreme Court," and I mentioned several instances to illustrate my point. And a point of main attention throughout this book has been the successive barrages of criticism directed against the Court and the accompanying attempts to induce the judges to abandon a course of action or to erect some safeguards against objectionable judicial decisions in the future. Draw the greatest inferences you can from these controls and influences, and you must still readily admit that the Supreme Court judges are not entrapped in a political vortex in the way the president and congressmen are. We do not fight an election campaign in which Oliver Wendell Holmes seeks election to the Supreme Court by promising the people that the words "arbitrary," "capricious," and "oppressive" will be excised from all of the Supreme Court's opinions as long as he sits on the bench and has influence with his colleagues. Presidents do not ask Supreme Court judges to resign, and congressmen do not tell them that a change in the character of their decisions is the only way they can avoid a cut in appropriations. Pressure groups do not flood the judges with telegrams from constituents, lay down ultimatums in public hearings, or threaten reprisals if a decision goes against them. If they speak to the judges at all, they do it by appearance as *amicus curiae,* confining themselves to a dignified and respectful presentation, and they can do this much only if the judges give them permission.

To establish that the Supreme Court judges are not subject to popular control in the style we have adopted for legislative and executive officials does not answer either of two larger questions. (1) Do the Supreme Court judges in fact respond to the convictions and moods of the American people when they make decisions that give new meanings to the Constitution or which for other reasons have towering social significance? (2) Do we want decisions of this character—the kinds of decisions that have brought the Supreme Court under attack throughout our history—made by a group of men who are alert to the mind and conscience of the American people, or do we want those decisions made by men who stand apart from the nation and feel no obligation to fit their decisions to the expectations or preferences of a majority of the people, no matter how great the majority?

Ad 1. Only a research inquiry more elaborate than anyone has yet undertaken can produce an answer to the first question that will command agreement. One of the best minds in the academic study of American politics has given the problem an imaginative and incisive analysis. Here are some of his significant statements:

> If one wishes to be at all rigorous about the question, it is probably impossible to demonstrate that any particular Court decisions have or have not been at odds with the preferences of a "national majority."
>
> The fact is, then, that the policy views dominant on the Court are never for long out of line with the policy views dominant among the lawmaking majorities of the United States. Consequently

> it would be most unrealistic to suppose that the Court would, for more than a few years at most, stand against any major alternatives sought by a lawmaking majority.
>
> The two child labor cases represent the most effective battle ever waged by the Court against legislative policy-makers. The original legislation outlawing child labor, based on the commerce clause, was passed in 1916 as a part of Wilson's New Freedom. . . . In 1938, under a second reformist president, new legislation was passed, twenty-two years after the first; this a chastened Court accepted in 1941, and thereby brought to an end a battle that had lasted a full quarter-century.[1]

I doubt that Dahl's article will terminate argument as to whether the Supreme Court does or does not "follow the election returns." One may conclude, however, that there is unquestionably a sympathetic relationship between the main bent of judicial decision and the convictions and moods of the population. Most of the writing which contends that the Supreme Court judges regard themselves as instrumentalities of a democratic process, searching for a national will and seeking to make it effective, strikes me as long on argument and short on evidence. In my opinion, it succeeds only in showing that the judges are the product of their times and that judicial institutions, like all other institutions, make some response to the obdurate parts of their environment. The Supreme Court judges are shown to be subject to popular control in the sense that a stern father is subject to control by his children when he eases his punishment to win their love, in the sense that the preacher is controlled by the sinners when he ceases lecturing them on the street in hope that they will be attracted into the church to hear his sermons.

Ad 2. Most of the argument that the Supreme Court does respond to popular expectations and preferences comes from persons who think that that is the way it should be. They are committed to the democratic way in government, and their conception of the democratic way is that all great, enduring policies should be made by officials who feel an obligation to find out whether there is a dominant position among the population and, if there is, to act in accordance with its dictate. This commitment requires the thoughtful man either to conclude that the Supreme Court should reject its opportunities to make great policy pronouncements or to find that the Court does in fact inquire into a popular mind and

1 Robert A. Dahl, "Decision-making in a Democracy: The Supreme Court as a National Policy-maker," *Journal of Public Law,* 6 (1957), 283, 285, 290.

respond to it. Many students of constitutional law have announced a conviction that the Supreme Court judges do in fact manifest a sensitivity to popular expressions which fit them for making contributions to basic public policy.

There is another school of thought which denies the desirability of such a responsiveness on the part of judges. Adherents to this school believe that the Supreme Court judges should, in certain kinds of questions, maintain an indifference to popular expectations and preferences even when there is reason to believe that far more than a majority of the adult population are of a common mind. They believe not merely that the Supreme Court's decisions display wisdom, morality, or both superior to the wisdom and morality that mark the popular position, but that a governmental system which is enduringly just will create such an oracle and empower it to set the nation on courses of action which could not, for the time being at least, win preponderant public support. In consequence of these beliefs, they believe also that a wise and just people will, in their placid and contemplative moments, commit themselves to compliance with the pronouncements of the oracle they have created. In the most flamboyant of such writing, the Supreme Court appears as St. George, brandishing the Constitution as a sword, and the dragon is a tyrannical majority bent on destroying rights precious to a lesser part of the population. When the language is less florid, I get a picture of the Supreme Court as a wise father, admonishing his children to a higher morality by reading appropriate verses from Scripture.

This vision of judicial power, apart from the political struggle and indifferent to expectations of the people, is defended by those who share it as the final victory of men who strive for the democratic ideal. Note again some sentences in a piece I quoted at some length above.

> . . . [I]t is the courts that can best protect the rights of minorities which tend to become submerged in the political processes of government. The other branches of government, precisely because they are more political and thus more susceptible to the prevailing winds, may and do find it difficult to withstand the pressure of public opinion. A majority, as DeTocqueville and John Stuart Mill have indicated, can be despotic. It is, accordingly, the quintessence of democracy for an appointive judiciary to further the ends of the integrity of the individual.[2]

[2] Miller and Howell, "The Myth of Neutrality in Constitutional Adjudication," *op. cit.*, p. 694.

This is a vision, and a fitting of the vision to the democratic ideal, which has long had devoted adherence in this country. This is the conviction and the argument which gave Peckham, Sutherland, and other judges who agreed with them earnest support in their rulings that statutes "limiting the hours in which grown and intelligent men may labor to earn their living are mere meddlesome interferences with the rights of the individual" (Peckham in *Lochner* v. *New York*) and that a minimum wage law for employed women "is so clearly the product of a naked, arbitrary exercise of power that it cannot be allowed to stand under the Constitution of the United States" (Sutherland in *Adkins* v. *Children's Hospital*).

When one fixes his attention, not on the issues that come to the Supreme Court for settlement, but on the role which the nine judges play in American life, he is struck by the intellectual kinship of the contemporary judicial activists with the rugged individualists who applauded when the Court struck down social legislation. The conception of the Supreme Court as the nation's conscience and its bulwark against tyrannical majorities which today's activitists put at the center of their case for aggressive judicial review was developed for them by men who thought Peckham and Sutherland ideally suited to that role. We may close this chapter with the testimony of two adherents of that earlier school of judicial activism.

Witness No. 1: John Woodward. Writing in a leading law review a year before the Supreme Court invalidated the New York law limiting hours of work in bakeries, Woodward said this:

> Respecting the Anglo-Saxon respect for property, the courts have ever recognized that liberty and property are inseparable. Life, liberty and property are therefore equally protected by the law. Our whole social structure being founded on property there must be uniformity and freedom in the acquisition and transmission of wealth. There must be no special privilege, no confiscation. This has required eternal vigilance on the part of the courts. . . .
>
> It is the Legislature which, besieged by special interests, and often obsessed by enthusiasm for political nostrums and haphazard or academic panaceas, has ever manifested a growing tendency to overleap constitutional barriers.
>
> Upon the courts, which alone are placed above the ferment of political strife, hangs the safety of the people and the permanence of the nation; for if there were no power to intervene between unconstitutional enactment and inconsiderate execution, to curb the aggressions of the temporary depository of the public will and to prevent accumulations of privilege and accessions of class interest, the people would be enslaved, and this, too, while retaining the appearance of liberty or the form of republican government.

> When the Legislature virtually says, "We will make your constitution," it is for the courts, as the embodiment of the national conscience and of the incarnation of the true and universal law of the land, to say in behalf of the people: "The power to make a Constitution is too sacred to be given to any delegated authority. We and we only, the people of this State and Nation, possess this power and this we shall not cease to maintain."[3]

Witness No. 2: James M. Beck, solicitor general of the United States by appointment of Pres. Calvin Coolidge. I think it likely that any reader who was an adult during the 1920's would allow me to take judicial knowledge of Beck's high attachment to rights in property, but let him speak for himself.

> Property rights, as guaranteed by the Fifth and Fourteenth Amendments, have been impaired by many socialistic measures. . . . Above all, the taxing system has been perverted since the Sixteenth Amendment to redistribute property. The adequate defense of the Constitution against the spirit of Socialism ended with the progressive income tax, whose excessive graded taxes often effectually confiscate the wealth of the few for the benefit of the many. . . . No student of our institutions can question that the Constitution is in graver danger today than at any other time in the history of America.

And what is the relationship between the judicial courts and the lawmaking bodies in the realization of the guarantees embodied in the Constitution?

> "Due process of law" means that there are certain fundamental principles of liberty, not defined or even enumerated in the Constitution, but having their sanction in the free and enlightened conscience of just men, and that no man can be deprived of life, liberty, or property, except in conformity with these fundamental decencies of liberty. To protect these even against the will of a majority, however large, the judiciary was given unprecedented powers. It threw about the individual the solemn circle of the law. It made the judiciary the final conscience of the nation.

> The Supreme Court of the United States compels the living generation, too often swept by selfish interests and frenzied passions, to respect the immutable principles of liberty and justice. The Court is thus the trustee for the unborn, for it protects their heritage from spoliation in the mad excesses of party strife of living generations. Thus, the Court must often affront the pride of power of temporary majorities.[4]

[3] "The Courts and the People," *Columbia Law Review*, 7 (1907), 565, 561, 562.

[4] *The Constitution of the United States* (New York: George H. Doran Co., 1924), pp. 214–215, 272–273, 214, 230.

CHAPTER NINETEEN

A Choice of Forums

Frankfurter thought the Supreme Court a nondemocratic organ of government and its power oligarchic. Being nondemocratic and oligarchic, it is not a suitable organ for making public policy, he believed. The lawmaking authority is the proper organ for making public policy ("for mediating a clash of feelings and rendering a prophetic judgment"), he thought, and this is so because it is "the body chosen for these purposes by the people" (335 U.S. 538, at 557).

In the preceding chapter, we looked for the significance of the fact that legislators and chief executives are elected but the Supreme Court judges are not. We turn now to some consequences of the fact that the political and judicial branches were created with differing purposes in mind.

How do differences in resources, traditions, and methods affect the ability of the two organs of government to work out enduring solutions for issues that divide the population? We shall look at this question from four standpoints.

1. STRATEGY OF POLICY DEVELOPMENT

Rarely is a complicated social problem solved by one corrective measure. This is the case for two reasons. Those who are charged with the solution do not know how and cannot find out how to solve the problem when they first decide to deal with it. And, if confident they do know how to solve it, they are convinced that people who must cooperate in the solution are not ready to make the necessary sacrifices. So they delay attack on the problem and, when they do attack, proceed with a goal of partial solution and not a grand strategy of unconditional surrender.

This calls to attention a dilemma confronting members of legislative bodies and, indeed, all political leaders. The legislator must move ahead of his constituents, but he must enact public policies which accord with the expectations and preferences of the population. He must use his special opportunities for knowledge to develop proposals for action which, until he makes the proposal, have not been contemplated by most of the people to whom he answers. He must explain, appeal for support, and persuade people that what he proposes will work. Sometimes the bold legislator will push forward a measure against general public protest, taking a chance that success of the experiment will win post-factum approval.

But public policy must not run too far ahead of the public acceptance that is ultimately necessary for its successful execution. As the gap is enlarged, we incur increased risk that government is being forced on the people and that we no longer have government by the people. Furthermore, the gap between declared policy and popular acceptance may be so great that the determination of many to evade or violate the law and the unwillingness of many others to cooperate in enforcement combine to make the unpopular policy a dead item in the statute books, if not a fiasco that destroys confidence in government.

Lawmaking bodies are expected to proceed in this fashion of scheduled advance—step by step, do what you can, later but not now. They are made representative, elected by the people, and chosen by separate constituencies so that they will not only be concerned to have social problems solved but will also feel an obligation to move in conformity with public demand and will be in a favorable position for reading popular expectations and preferences. If the legislators are adequately representative and correctly read the minds of their constituents, we can tolerate a good deal of unevenness in the way public policies affect various parts of the population. We can regulate railroad transportation this year and let the competing carriers go unregulated for a while longer, and this is thought sufficiently proper if the regulatory measure seems a reasonably fair balancing of the pressures on the lawmakers.

Furthermore, nothing ordinarily compels the lawmakers to act except their own will to move forward and the demands and pressures on them. With relatively few exceptions, legislatures are not required by the constitution, national or state, to enact a law or try to solve a social problem; they are authorized or empowered to do so. Even the Thirteenth Amendment of the national Constitution, abolishing slavery, avoids a mandatory instruction to Congress; it says, "Congress shall have power to enforce this article by appropriate legislation." There are a few mandatory orders to Congress in the Constitution, but nearly all relate to its own organization and procedures; thus, "Each House shall keep a journal of its proceedings." If there is a positive requirement for action having its impact directly on the population, it is directed to all branches of the national government and not specifically to Congress. Article IV says, "The United States shall guarantee to every State in this Union a republican form of government, and shall protect each of them against invasion."

Judges do not have this amount of leeway in applying law to social problems. They act under a controlling assumption that courts do not make law but only give effect to law already in existence. When a judge announces a rule of law that other lawyers claim not to know about, they test the judge's judgment by looking for evidence that the rule was inherent in or implied by previous statements of the law; they are not satisfied with evidence that the new rule promises to fit a social need. When the judge perceives a need for adaptation or extension of a rule of law, he seeks a justification for such an act in previous decisions and explanatory statements. There is a strong presumption that previous authoritative statements of the law will be respected today, and previous decisions are overruled only with reluctance.

It follows from this controlling principle—that judges only announce existing law and do not make new law—that, when a new turn is given to a rule by bold and imaginative interpretation, the new meaning of the rule will have an ex post facto effect. The losing party in the suit that brought forth the new interpretation may feel that he has been subjected to a rule he could not have allowed for when he engaged in the conduct that involved him in litigation. When later suits arise, application of the new rule will not be limited to what men have done after the new interpretation was announced; it will be applied to affairs that were consummated when all parties thought they were operating under a very different legal regime.

There are many limitations on and exceptions to this brief account of the judicial process. Indeed, some students will say that everything said here is part of a grand fiction. They contend that judges do in fact make law and that a frank admission of the fact would enable everyone to make a more equitable adjustment to judicial power. Allowing for the limitations and exceptions and a good deal of fiction in the whole business, still it must be admitted that there is a great measure of viscosity and rigidity in the process, whether it is called judicial adaptation of law or lawmaking by judges. It does not lend itself conveniently to the scheduling of attack on social problems, to the adaptation of measures to fit a variety of emerging needs, or to total repeal and re-enactment when an experiment fails to realize the benefits expected.

2. PROTEST, RESISTANCE, AND NULLIFICATION

Legislation and law enforcement are separate processes. The statute is enacted today to become effective law tomorrow. On still other days it is invoked and applied. Different men, different organs of government, play crucial roles in the many steps from enactment to execution or enforcement. There is time to reconsider the wisdom and adequacy of the statute before men are required to fit their conduct to its provisions. So many men are involved that the law as effective regulator of conduct may be very different from the law as a series of words in the statute books.

The ability of legislatures to schedule attack on social problems and adapt corrective measures to a variety of special needs has been discussed. This process of scheduling and adjustment continues after the statute is enacted. Some statutes are general in their terms, and administrative officials are given a wide range of choice in applying them to practical situations. Even where the requirements of the act are precise and mandatory, officials may take their time about bringing people under the control which the statute clearly contemplated. It occasionally happens that administrative officials or affected parts of the public call the attention of congressmen to some feature of the new law or consequence of its vigorous enforcement which the congressmen did not allow for when they made the enactment. In such a case, the lawmakers may advise that the statute lie dormant until its provisions can be altered.

In the interim between enactment and enforcement and continuously during the period when enforcement is undertaken, there is opportunity for protest by people who find the law objectionable. When legislation is viewed as a series of enactments over time, it becomes apparent that protest by people who are affected by the law is an integral part of the lawmaking process. It is not a rarity for legislators to act before they consider themselves adequately informed because some necessity compels them to do something. In such a case, they may think of the statute as a tentative, experimental effort and look to public reaction as a guide to the improvement of the law in a later legislative session.

The regime of government under law developed in this country tolerates a substantial amount of resistance to enforcement efforts. Many provisions in the statute books were undoubtedly enacted with the expectation that they would lie dormant most of the time. The enactment of the provision gives the legislator relief from people who have been pressing for a law on the subject, and the provision is now a part of the law, available to be invoked in the unusual situation. Administrative officials, prosecuting attorneys, juries, and perhaps even judges take advantage of this lenient attitude toward law, and statutory requirements that are vigorously enforced in one part of the nation, or of a state, are allowed to slumber in another. What law enforcement officials can give, those subject to the law may take if they can. The most conscientious effort to enforce a law may fail because too much of the population is determined not to comply: Witness the failure of Prohibition in communities where officials were determined to make it effective. Witness speed limits on the highways. Witness laws against gambling.

No doubt all these things that happen to statutory law can happen to requirements which originate in the pronouncements of judges, but in smaller degree. Response to the segregation orders of the Supreme Court testifies that public officials will drag their feet on compliance and that public resistance can apply a brake, if not nullify the requirement, in communities where officials are committed to enforcement. But the time between enactment and enforcement of the statute is absent in the pronouncement and first enforcement of the judge-made rule. The judge does not announce a rule to become effective at some future time. The announcement is part of the act of enforcement. The judge, facing an issue for which the law as previously interpreted seems inappropriate, gives a new turn to the law and applies his restatement of the law in disposing of the suit. There is no opportunity for checking judgments and organizing opposition between the appearance of the new rule and its first application.

Criticism, protest, and resistance can appear between the judge's original announcement of the new rule and later opportunities to apply it. But they are not welcomed, as is so often the case with statute law, and generally they are not tolerated. There is a good reason for this. The judge-made rule, emerging in the act of law enforcement, is the judge's conclusion about the terms on which the law given to him can and should be enforced. When formulated or endorsed by a court of final appeal, it has been marked "approved for enforcement" by the highest authority in the law enforcement process. Public officials charged with putting the law into effect and lawyers advising their clients acknowledge their obligation to do anything the highest court tells them to do. For them, the law is *de facto* what the last judicial tribunal will order when they come before it in litigation. In order to foresee what that court might command, they are attentive to what the judges say the law is. To ignore the judge's restatement of the law, no matter how far it may have departed from the law that was given him, is to ask for defeat in the final steps of making the law effective.

3. ADEQUACY OF RESOURCES

In our governmental system, the legislative authority reaches to all public affairs. The representative assembly that enacts law to regulate the life and affairs of the population also creates the government offices not established by the constitution, describes the authority vested in those offices, raises money to meet the costs of government, and allocates that money in appropriations to the various offices. If Congress and the president undertake to force integration in public schools, they can mobilize a formidable array of forces under their power "to enforce, by appropriate legislation," the provisions of the Fourteenth Amendment. If they think financial assistance in constructing school buildings and training teachers will induce a reluctant white population to allow Negroes in their midst, they can make the money available. If they see a solution in a system of federal schools that give free education to children whose parents are willing to integrate, they can order the schools constructed, pay for them, and make it a crime for anyone to interfere with their operation. If they decide to force a stubborn white population to admit Negroes to all schools, they can write the needed law, create the appropriate crimes and specify penalties, and order the disposition of enforcement officials.

In this program of legislative effort, the lawmakers must depend on the judges for only one thing. The judges must order men to comply with the law when they come before a court in litigation. If the judges rule that the law is unconstitutional, they will not only refuse to enforce it, but, in a proper suit, they will order other officials not to enforce it either. Before a judge will issue an order of enforcement, he must decide what the statute requires, permits, or forbids. In the process of construing or interpreting the statute, he may throw away a good deal of what the legislators thought they had provided for. But, barring these two limitations on their cooperation, judges can be counted on to enforce the law which the legislators enact, whether they personally like the law or not. This is the purpose for which their office was created. When courts cease to make effective the law that is given them, it will be time to call a constitutional convention and start all over again.

If the Supreme Court judges decide that the two races must be mixed in public schools, they cannot do any of the things I cited above as a battery of powers available to Congress and president. All the judges can do, if they confine their action to the limits that have heretofore been respected, is tell other men what the law requires and order them to act as the law requires. And even this little they can do only as is appropriate for settlement of disputes brought to them in litigation. If the governor of Mississippi is enjoined in a suit, the judges can order him to comply with the law and in last resort order him to vacate his office or order another official to seize and hold the man or his property. But, if the official who is ordered to do so will not seize and hold the governor, the judges can only order another official to seize and hold. This is all they can do that we recognize as an act of power. Beyond that they can appeal for help. They can ask the president and Congress to invoke the powers vested in them in order to make a success of the new regime which the judges have ordered.

4. COMPATIBILITY OF FUNCTIONS

A legislature has nothing to do that is more important than the business of legislating. If the lawmakers hear a call to do something that is incompatible with their lawmaking function, they ought to withstand the call; we cannot allow them to withdraw from the main duty that was assigned them. It is currently argued that some Congressional investigations take on a character of prosecution and conviction and that prosecution and judgment of conviction should never be mixed with legislating. Every man who believes Congress to have offended in this respect asks that it recede from the investigatory activities; no one asks that it quit the business of lawmaking in order to administer a fairer investigation.

The same principle holds for the courts. The main business of the judicial branch of government is to settle disputes between litigants, including the dispute between the governmental official who claims to act under authority of law and one of the governed who contends that law does not authorize what the official proposes to do. We cannot allow our courts to be encumbered with any duties that significantly impair their ability to carry out their adjudicatory function.

It is a deeply held belief that the making of law and the adjudication of rights under the law should never be lodged in the same group of men. This is a tenet of the American doctrine of separation of powers, and it is a principle highly respected in most, if not all, Western nations that do not have a system of three branches of government to perform three kinds of activity.

No thoughtful student of law or government in this country would recommend that the Supreme Court or any other court become active in the enactment of law or in the performance of any of the other activities listed above as the main powers of a lawmaking assembly. There is a dispute, however, as to where the authority of the judge to fix the content of law should stop. The history of attack on the Supreme Court examined earlier is a story of protest that the Court has ventured further into the formation of public policy than is good for the nation. No doubt all who argue about the proper limits of judicial power agree that judges must be allowed some power to determine what the law shall be. A measure of power to fix the content of law is inherent in the process of adjudication. It is too much to expect that all men will find the same meaning in the words of a statute. The judge must come to a conclusion about the requirements embodied in the law before he can tell the parties in suit what the law commands them to do. The independence we have accorded the court makes it impossible for the judge to go elsewhere for an authoritative construction or interpretation of the law. He must decide for himself what the law is. He may be overruled and straightened out on appeal, but, pending the act of a court above, the judge who decides the case fixes the content of the law enforced in his court.

It follows that the Supreme Court, being the court of last resort for much of the nation's most important litigation, will constantly face the opportunity and necessity of giving meaning to the law that regulates the lives and affairs of the American people. This power is enlarged by our doctrine of judicial review. The Supreme Court is final not only as to the meaning and application of legislative enactments that come to it, but also as to the meaning of constitutional provisions that put limits on the power of executives and legislators. The Supreme Court thus fixes the content of law which becomes binding on the lawmakers themselves.

The power of judges to fix the content of law can be exercised willingly or reluctantly, boldly or timidly, arrogantly or in humility. The current controversy about the Supreme Court's use of its power is over whether the judges have been too willing to find new meanings in the Constitution and too bold in ordering elected officials to comply with their findings—whether they show appropriate humility in setting their judgment against the lawmakers who supposed that the Constitution permitted them to do what they did. It will be recalled that ninety-six Southern congressmen, speaking of the Segregation decisions, said that the Supreme Court judges "undertook to exercise their naked judicial power," and the chief justices of thirty-six states, thinking of several categories of decision, said that the Supreme Court "too often has adopted the role of policy maker without proper judicial restraint."

Conclusions about the compatibility of the Supreme Court's ventures into policy-making with its adjudicatory duties necessarily depend on the meaning that is given the word "compatible." Let us agree that there is incompatibility when there is an unwanted impairment of a valued thing. If the Supreme Court's ventures into policy-making seriously impair the quality of its adjudicatory acts, or vice versa, the two activities are incompatible. It is not necessary, in order to establish incompatibility, to show that the doing of one wholly destroys capacity for doing the other, though some of the debate about the Supreme Court's mixing of functions seems to stand on such an assumption. It is enough, it seems to me, to ascertain whether there is an unwanted impairment of one or both functions. The impairment is unwanted, it is too great to be tolerated, if the losses sustained by impairing one function outweigh the gains realized by having the other function performed by the same agency.

Two very different inquiries must be made before one can decide whether the two activities of the Supreme Court are incompatible. First, what is the impact, what is the effect, of performing one function on the capacity of the judges to perform the other? Does the performance of one function reduce effectiveness in performing the other, and, if it does, what is the measure of the loss? This is a complicated question, requiring search for evidence and evaluation of evidence. Nevertheless, we may think of it as a question of fact. The second inquiry is: When one has made his findings about the existence and the measure of impairment, how much impairment is too much to be tolerated? When does the loss in capacity to perform one kind of act outweigh the gain in having the Supreme Court perform the other kind? This we may call a question of value.

I am unable to report any research on the first question or any illuminating discussion of the second. There are statements of position on both issues, but they are either declarations of personal preference or first steps in analysis. We can only speculate as to what the full inquiry will involve, but surely the search for fact will have to answer these two questions:

First, does the knowledge that they can restate the language of the Constitution, that they can give the Constitution meaning not suggested in previous authoritative statements, invite the judges to avoid some of the most difficult problems encountered in the enforcement of law? A previous chapter commented on the concern of some judges that, if the lawmakers are conceded the right to take an inch, they may later move an unwarranted mile. It may well be the case that the first statutory attack on a social problem, if upheld, will be followed by additional enactments that press even closer to the edge of constitutional authorization. The judges may indeed foresee that, if they enforce the first statute, they will be hard-pressed to distinguish it from a second and to distinguish the second from a third. And they may correctly guess, when the first is before them, that the third will be more than they can allow. Surely there is a temptation to declare the first statute unconstitutional and so avoid the difficulties of distinction that would otherwise plague them in the future. A careful inquiry into the incompatibility of the Supreme Court's activities would have to ascertain what the judges have in fact done on this matter of anticipation and fix a measure to the social loss that their acts may entail.

Second, do the Supreme Court's ventures into policy-making lessen public confidence in the impartiality of the judges when they decide cases that dispose of the interests of litigants? Did the Court's boldness in *Marbury* v. *Madison* cause important segments of the population to doubt that the judges would strive for a strict fairness in enforcing legislation enacted under Jefferson's leadership? Did the fury and clamor that followed the Dred Scott decision justify a doubt that the rights of slave and slave-owner would be examined with equal care in cases involving the return of runaway slaves? Do present convictions that judges now on the bench are committed to an enlargement of the guarantees in the Bill of Rights and the Fourteenth Amendment cause men who have those convictions to believe that those judges will lean toward the accused when men are tried for violating a security act or inciting a crowd to riot? Questions like these are a part of the factual inquiry that must be made before we are ready to decide whether the performance of one of their functions impairs the ability of the Supreme Court judges to discharge another set of obligations.

On the broad problem of evaluation—how great an impairment of one or both functions we can tolerate—one comment will suffice. Until recently, it seems to have been the assumption of all parties to the debate that, if an incompatibility in its functions were found, the Supreme Court should withdraw from policy formation and realize its greatest potential in the adjudication of disputes that come to it in the course of litigation. There is no longer unanimity on this point. Some of the recent literature of the activist school of thought argues, more by implication than by express statement, that the Supreme Court's adjudicatory functions should give way to the need for judicial enlargement of constitutional guarantees if the two cannot thrive together.

CHAPTER TWENTY

Frontiers of Judicial Power

1. FOR THE CORRECTION OF POLITICAL FAILURES
2. TO SECURE A DEMOCRATIC PROCESS
3. JUDGES, IDEALS, AND CONFLICTING MORALITIES

This book comes to an end with a brief discussion of some problems that, in my judgment, are certain to confront the judges if they push further into the realm of affairs traditionally thought the special domain of the elected branches of government. I select for attention three possible avenues of aggrandizement which the Supreme Court might pursue. They are worthy of consideration because each is earnestly recommended to the Supreme Court today and because certain acts of the Court in recent years indicate that some of the judges may be ready to move in the directions proposed. The three recommendations for more aggressive judicial activity are (1) that the Supreme Court rescue the nation from major failures by the elected branches, (2) that the Supreme Court assume a special responsibility to make the democratic process secure, and (3) that the Court be bolder in identifying ideals and setting public officials in pursuit of those ideals.

1. FOR THE CORRECTION OF POLITICAL FAILURES

This proposal at its extreme has come to me in conversation. I have been told that the Supreme Court has a mandate from the Constitution to order termination of segregation in the schools and other places of assembly, but also that, even if the Constitution contained no such mandate, it would still have been the duty of the

Supreme Court to order termination of segregation in 1954. This would have been its duty because segregation was the key to incipient revolution; another year or two without hope of relief from segregation, and there would have been bloodshed and burnings extensive enough to be called revolution. When the price of failure to act is so high, all departments of government have an obligation to do the act which avoids the failure and averts the danger. If I interpret the argument correctly, Congress having failed to act, the president had as great an obligation to order the termination of segregation as did the Supreme Court.

The taproot that feeds this new growth of constitutional doctrine is the belief that the Constitution does more than grant authority to exercise governmental power; it requires the lawmaking authority to exploit the power granted to it. We encountered this position earlier in the proposition that the equal-protection clause requires state governments to protect the weaker part of the population from discriminatory treatment at the hands of the stronger.

If this new constitutional doctrine, as yet hardly noticed in the literature, persists, whole books will be necessary for its explication. I shall here limit myself to two very general comments.

A. *The doctrine of political obligation and judicial intervention in policy-making implies a deep devotion to the democratic ideal and a lack of confidence in the political process as a way of realizing that ideal.* The most aggressive judicial intervention may be justified on the ground that the political departments, by failure to enact and enforce law, are thwarting the expectations and preferences of the population. The judicial branch thus becomes a backstop for the legislature and Executive. When the latter fail to read the public mind correctly, the judges are authorized to come in with a correct reading. When the political departments read correctly but fail to respond to the instructions they read, the judges may order those departments to act, or may even formulate and announce the policies which they suspect they can never force from the elected officials.

The new doctrine does not necessarily imply a rejection of the basic political structure and main political processes of the United States. One may contend that the American electoral-representative system is more responsive to public expectations and preferences than any other yet constructed, but at the same time insist that all political systems suffer failures. To argue that the Supreme Court must take up where Congress and the president leave off is only to argue that the elective and nonelective branches of the government complement or supplement one another; it is not to argue that either should withdraw from the field of action or that the nation would be wise to give the whole of policy-making to the one institution and process which may be most trusted by most people.

B. *Adherents to the new doctrine must face the question: When is there a political failure?* We may differentiate four sets of circumstances that might account for the failure of the political departments to act when the judges think they should have done so.

First, there may be a lack of sensitiveness to, or a reluctance to respond to, popular expectations and preferences. Can we assume that judicial knowledge, pleadings, and the evidence and argument presented in the course of a trial will provide a better reading of the public mind than the lawmakers can obtain from their unrestrained contacts with their constituents and the forceful demands for attention put on them by people who favor and people who oppose any contemplated action? Can we assume that the appointed judges, when convinced that they know what the people want, will feel greater compulsion to respond to popular demands than an assembly made up of elected men who must soon win re-election or terminate their service?

Second, there may be a need for action when there is little public support for it. The statesman has a vision of public need that reaches far beyond that of the average man; otherwise he is no statesman. Statesmanship may lie in judges as surely as in elected officials. If they see no clear instruction in the Constitution and hear no clamor from an agitated population, how are the judges to explain their invasion of the policy-making area? Or is this an irrelevant question? It may be that the proponents of the new doctrine of positive obligation and judicial intervention do not recommend judicial action when there is no discernible will of the people.

Third, elected officials may fail to act when they are agreed that action is required. They fail to act because they cannot agree on the appropriate solution for the problem confronting them. This predicament raises all the questions discussed above in connection with scheduling solutions and adapting corrective measures. And it challenges one to review his confidence in the time-honored supposition that an assembly of men popularly elected and representative of all parts of the population is the best assurance that social problems will be dealt with when the emotional state of the nation is favorable to effective solution. If one undertakes a careful and thorough justification of judicial intervention to escape the political impasse, his inquiry will have much more to say about the distribution of popular expectations and demands and about experience with electoral-representative instruments than it will about the promise that judges will find solutions that bring tranquility to the population and free the society to realize its common ideals.

Fourth, elected officials may pursue policies which some people think tyrannical. This dilemma arises for any man when he concludes that the policy-makers are doing what most of the people want done, but he is at the same time certain that the majority of the people are demanding a wrong thing. How is one to know when the demands of any part of the population are tyrannous? The literature we call political theory has not developed tests on which scholars have agreed. If there are any trusted tests of tyranny in American law, they must be the tests which an earlier Court applied in due-process cases and which the present Court applies in cases arising under the First Amendment. I think the evidence shows that, in the application of these tests, differences of position among the judges are as great as the difference between a majority of the judges and the lawmakers who enacted the law.

Perhaps it is a doubt that suitable tests of political failure can be found that induces some contemporary judicial activists to propose a different primary objective for an aggressive judicial review. If one believes that judgments about political failure are too much an expression of undisciplined opinion, he may nevertheless be convinced that there are objective tests for deciding whether laws are the product of a healthy, functioning, efficacious democratic system. Such a belief is behind the second of the three recommendations cited at the beginning of this chapter.

2. TO SECURE A DEMOCRATIC PROCESS

The most pointed and positive proposal for the judiciary to undertake a general policing of the democratic process appears in an article by the same law school dean who supplied the figure of judges in endless conversation with the nation.

> The freedom of the legislatures to act within wide limits of constitutional construction is the wise rule of judicial policy only if the processes through which they act are reasonably democratic.
>
> One of the central responsibilities of the judiciary in exercising its constitutional power is to help keep the other arms of government

> democratic in their procedures. The Constitution should guarantee the democratic legitimacy of political decisions by establishing essential rules for the political process. It provides that each state should have a republican form of government. And it gives each citizen the political as well as the personal protection of the Bill of Rights and other fundamental constitutional guarantees. The enforcement of these rights would assure Americans that legislative and executive policy would be formed out of free debate, democratic suffrage, untrammeled political effort, and full inquiry.[1]

Rostow does not say whether he thinks all or nearly all the main tests of democratic character were written into the Constitution or whether the absence of some important ones will require the Supreme Court judges to identify a set of ideal institutions and behaviors and imbed them in the Constitution at points where its language most yields to impression—for instance, by making the Constitution's references to "republican form of government," "privileges and immunities of citizens," and "due process of law" requirements for the establishment of arrangements and practices that meet the judges' conceptions of a healthy democracy. The history of controversy over judicial power to date leaves no room to doubt that, for a great many people, the decision to accept or reject Rostow's proposal will turn on the answer to that question—whether the judges are to make effective the plain meaning of plain words in the Constitution or whether they are to impose idealizations which they are able to construct by drawing on our vast literature and experience.

If the judges, following the advice of contemporary judicial activists, strike boldly to realize Rostow's vision, they will have to construct an imposing body of constitutional law. They will have to adopt policy on points of great significance for which there is little guidance in law and little more in the literature of government and politics. The Supreme Court's contributions will of necessity be exploratory and creative in two sectors of democratic theory. The judges will have to go beyond the present reach of law and thoughtful literature in fixing the outer limits of mind and action thought relevant to the democratic process; and they will find sharp differences of position, at least in the general literature, if not in the law, relating to institutions and practices admitted to be at the center of the democratic way in government.

A. *The bounds of relevance.* Democratic government is more

[1] Eugene V. Rostow, "The Democratic Character of Judicial Review," *Harvard Law Review,* 66 (1952), 202, 210.

than formal organization and legal provision for an array of procedures. It is critically conditioned by the readiness and determination of the people to participate in their own government, to scrutinize what their officials do, to make clear their satisfactions and dissatisfactions with specific policies and the general character of public policy. Agreement is so nearly universal on this that argument would be superfluous.

The Constitution contains two provisions that are recognized to protect the democratic process at its outer bounds: the prohibition of laws abridging freedom of speech and press and the right to peaceably assemble and to petition the government for redress of grievances. The language chosen for the right to assemble was clearly not intended to cover all of the organization and interaction among men and women which James Madison deplored as a "dangerous vice" but which we today regard as essential to government by the people. Recent research creates a strong presumption that the men who adopted the free-speech and free-press guarantee did not intend that it should clear the way for that self-aggrandizing, irrational, and violent criticism of public policy and attack on public officials which today is generally defended as essential to popular self-government.[2] But forget these two facts. Assume that the nation will support the Supreme Court in pushing these two guarantees, free expression and free assembly, as far as the judges want to go. Still we are not at the bounds of relevance for the democratic process. Consider the distribution of wealth and the vigor of the nation's free-enterprise economy.

No thoughtful man will argue that freedom to speak, to write, to assemble, and to organize guarantees that adult citizens will be nearly equal in ability to influence the political process at the points of impact listed at the beginning of Chapter XVIII. The "untrammeled political effort" which Rostow appears to favor promises victory to those who move with greatest dispatch and the greatest array of force. The Constitution gives no assurance that every man shall have the resources necessary for influence or that resources shall be distributed in a fashion that gives all men an even break. Should we suppose that courageous judges, committed to an activist policy and having equality and majority rule as their ideals, will demand a further trammeling of political effort than we have put on the statute books of most of the states? Can we anticipate

2 See Leonard W. Levy, *Legacy of Suppression* (Cambridge: Harvard University Press, 1960).

that idealizations of equality and majority rule will always be adapted to the wealth structure that happens to exist at any time? Or must we allow for activist judges, bent on the high judicial vigilance and fortified by the unembarrassed courage which Professor Black envisages (see Section 3, Chapter XVII), insisting on provision for a minimum income which allows a little surplus for investment in the outcome of elections?

I shall not press a question about ownership and control of the main channels of communication. When the ideals of equality and majority rule are wedded to the Constitution's provision for a state of freedom in speech and press, attention is inevitably directed to the policies that fix the content and presentation of news and opinion that are distributed by great news services, radio networks, organizations that control television productions, and newspapers that escape the discipline of competition in a nation spotted with one-newspaper towns. The agenda of an activist Supreme Court might well include an inquiry as to whether America meets the specifications for a market place of ideas in which truth stands a fair chance to conquer error.

The nation's economic structure is related to the security of its democratic government in another and very different way. The point of contact is the prospect of a *coup d'état.* What do you do when the men who come to power in government make up their minds to use all the authority of office to keep themselves in power? The methods confirmed by success in other countries include: hold fast to the office after the term of office has expired; enact the new laws that make the usurpation appear lawful; revise the laws specifying who may vote; take over the machinery that administers the balloting, counts the votes, and announces the winners.

An assertion that we have a system that precludes the coup will not satisfy the thoughtful man. He asks: What is it in our system that discourages the bid for unrestrained power and makes failure certain if the bid is made? The answer seems to be that our security lies at two points. *First,* in the evidences that the population generally has a deep attachment to the elective principle, will not readily join the group that proposes a forcible take-over, and will stubbornly resist the effort when it is made. *Second,* in a social structure that maintains organizations which can collectively overpower the men who have a monopoly on public offices. Every viable organization is a nexus of loyalties, a structure of leadership, and a repository of resources. The society that evolved in this country raises economic organizations to primacy—the great industrial empire, the trade association, the labor union, the association of men sharing a common profession. Undoubtedly religious denominations combine loyalties, leadership, and resources. But I suppose most readers of this book would bet on the economic structure of the American people to furnish the first and main resistance to a political coup.

If my reasoning is approved, one must conclude that an activist Supreme Court committed to custody of the democratic process will be attentive to charges that the nation is being stripped of the muscle that might deliver it from those who reject the democratic way. If the Court again happens to be dominated by judges who believe that a competitive free-enterprise system is essential to a secure democratic government—it is a tenable thesis, honored in political theory—they may see steps toward a welfare state as steps away from the ideal they are pledged to realize and make secure. What they might do about it would depend on how fully they adopt the activists' recommendations for aggressive judicial review.

B. *The core of democratic method.* Difficulties encountered in fixing the outer limits of the democratic process are matched by problems relating to the main foundations. Any careful listing of points at which popular government may break down will give a high place to each of these: definition of the electorate; administration of voting, including the counting and reporting of results; assignment of seats in the legislature and district-making; procedure in lawmaking assemblies. These are only a few of many essential features of government by the people; they call up problems enough for our purposes here.

The men who compose the legislature at any time and the man who occupies the chair of the chief executive have a deep personal interest in each of these four matters. All stand to gain or lose by manipulation of the first three. These three items constitute a system which brought these men to their high places in government. Many of them have a vested interest in retaining the arrangements by which they were lifted up. Some, who fear they may go out by the same route they came in, will see personal advantages in changing the system. The fourth item, legislative procedure, may present less evidence of vested personal interest, but certainly one legislator gains in influence and another loses as the rules of the chamber are fitted to their respective statuses, roles, and policy objectives.

Perhaps no one can be trusted more than the elected lawmakers themselves to fix the rules that govern their deliberations and actions. An external group could possibly draw up rules that offer greatest promise of fulfilling an ideal of careful study, illuminating debate, above-board compromise, and an open outlet for every legislator's talents. Even if that be the case, the legislators will determine the actual effects of the rules by the way they respond to them, and, if enough of them refuse to comply, they will effectively nullify any code that others impose on them. This suggests the possibility that there is no way by which a legislative body may be policed while it is engaged in the business of making laws. Such a conclusion would, presumably, discourage intervention by even the boldest of judges, no matter how certain they might be that the filibuster or gag rule are major subversions of the democratic way.

The prospect for successful judicial intervention is quite different in the case of admission to the polls and conduct of elections. Legislatures and elected chief executives cannot control these matters by their personal acts in the way that legislators can determine the procedures of a legislative chamber. They can only make the rules by which these things are done, establish machinery and supervise its operation, fix penalties for violating the rules and obstructing the machinery, and appropriate the money that enables the machinery to work. Judges who are committed to an aggressive role, if convinced that the rules and their administration fall too far short of the democratic ideal, may believe that it lies within judicial power to improve them.

Allocating legislative positions among the population and fixing boundaries of the districts that choose them have always been frustrating experiences. The legislator is uniquely interested in the definition of his district. He faces no problem of altering boundaries if his district is frozen to the political map, as is the case for the United States senator. But, if the district is a special creation, made solely for the choice of one or more legislators, then the legislator will always be conscious that a change in boundaries will work to his gain or loss when he seeks re-election. The reluctance of American state legislators to reapportion their own seats is notorious.

The Supreme Court ruled in March, 1962 (*Baker* v. *Carr*, 369 U.S. 186), that a federal court may adjudicate a claim that the allocation of seats in a state legislature denies equal protection of the laws to citizens in certain parts of the state or deprives them of life, liberty, or property without due process of law. Frankfurter, speaking also for Harlan, protested. He thought federal judges were being catapulted into a mathematical quagmire. In this area of social conflict, he said, judges "do not have accepted legal standards or even reliable analogies to draw upon for making judicial judgments." He arrayed an impressive amount of evidence from American and British experience to buttress his argument that this is the case.

I am obliged to say that the judges will not find in the literature we call political theory any surer guide than Frankfurter was able to find in Anglo-American practice. No doubt this literature reveals a high agreement that legislative seats *ought* to be distributed in keeping with a constant ratio of constituent population to legislative member. This is the declaration of an ideal, not an assertion of what experience proves to be socially achievable, socially preferred, or socially acceptable. This literature does not refute Frankfurter's declaration that "representation proportioned to the geographic spread of population . . . has never been generally practiced, today or in the past."

Pleas for acceptance of the ideal—the rule of equal numbers—have not been supported by analysis worthy of the complicated lawmaking structure we have developed in this country. A statute is the product of three centers of authority—two legislative chambers and a chief executive. Surely our prime concern is to achieve an ideal representation in the combination of offices that makes the major public policies. If experience proves, in a given state, that the governor is traditionally especially responsive to an identifiable sector of the population, one might reasonably argue that the remaining parts of the population ought to be given a compensating advantage when seats in one or both of the legislative chambers are apportioned. This is only one of many unexplored or little-explored complications besetting the policy-making machinery of our national and state governments. Until they have received far more penetrating scrutiny than they have yet had, the literature of political science will offer little to the judge seeking a thoughtful presentation of realizable democratic ideals.

3. JUDGES, IDEALS, AND CONFLICTING MORALITIES

All contemporary recommendations for aggressive judicial review that I have seen confront the Supreme Court with two challenges. They urge the Court to identify and honor ideals—to go beyond the words of the Constitution in search of more fundamental purposes that lie behind the express language. And they urge the

Court to grasp new means for making ideals effective in the day-to-day conduct of government.

Consider, *first,* the point about new means for achieving the judges' ends. Throughout this chapter, in discussing possible judicial strategies, I have talked as if judges possessed lawmaking power. One may protest that judges, including Supreme Court judges, do not do things like this, that I have created a giant straw man for some hoped-for advantage in tearing him down. The fact is that contemporary writers about constitutional law are urging changes in judicial conduct in language which implies, if it does not expressly state, that judges should boldly order compliance with new standards of conduct. And, more significant, at least two recent experiences in judicial action suggest that the Supreme Court may be ready for some bold new ventures in policy formation.

I have said why I believe that the desegregation orders of 1955 were an innovation in display of authority by the Supreme Court. The more recent decisions relating to apportionment of state legislatures are a second demonstration of willingness to devise and order significant changes in public policy. In the first apportionment case, *Baker* v. *Carr,* the Supreme Court instructed a federal district court to hear a complaint that certain residents of Tennessee were denied equal protection of the laws because of improper allocation of seats in the Tennessee legislature. The leading opinion, written by Brennan, asserted that "we have no cause at this stage to doubt the District Court will be able to fashion relief if violations of constitutional rights are found." Clark, concurring, made clear that he thought it proper for the lower court to devise a more equitable assignment of legislative seats and put the judge-made apportionment into effect by order of the court. Orders since issued by a number of federal courts make it clear that federal judges are both ready to correct inequities in representation and ingenious in devising remedies.

These recent developments in use of judicial power cause me to think it is not premature to ponder the social consequences likely to follow upon judicial acceptance of the recommendations for more aggressive action outlined in this chapter.

The *second* challenge thrust on the Supreme Court by the recommended strategies for more aggressive judicial review urges the judges to strive for a finer vision of the good life.

The appeal for this finer vision, to which I have attached the terms "grander purpose" and "ideal," is advanced, characteristically, in language suffering from want of precision. Some of these appeals may have been credited with too refined an intent when I cited them as proposed strategies or recommendations for judicial action. It may be, in the case of most of these writings, that the thought supporting the appeal has advanced little beyond a sentiment that the country could stand a round of uplift. One may wonder, for instance, which of the rules worked out over time to regulate the activity that produces public policy would have to go down in order to establish the life of the forum that Rostow has in mind when he endorses "untrammeled political effort."

Want of precision is quickly corrected when serious students conclude that they are not understood as they wish to be. A more serious deficiency in contemporary appeals for a finer judicial vision, it seems to me, is failure to identify the several levels of a nation's morality and differentially relate the judicial role to them. A quick reminder of the tension between two of these levels should make my point clear.

We readily acknowledge that most white men in the United States have two moral positions vis-à-vis the Negro. I may call one position that of distant contemplation; the other, that of immediate confrontation.

Contemplating relations between the races as a problem enduring over time, as a challenge to one's sense of justice or commitment to Christian ideals, as a source of indignity and pain in places far away—contemplating racial discrimination in such a frame of mind, no doubt most white American citizens come out against it. They would feel better if it did not exist. They experience again the bitter taste of guilt, and they would like to be absolved. This is the morality of distant contemplation.

The responses are different when the facts are those of immediate confrontation. The man who is strong for justice at a distance may be among the first to resist Negro invasion of his residential area, among the first to shore up against admission of Negroes to his own employment status. It is possible for a man to say on Sunday that the Negro cannot rise esthetically, intellectually, or morally unless he be accepted in fellowship by those who have attained the higher levels; it is possible for him on Monday to send his own children to a private academy so that they need not pay the price of giving the Negro what was so readily promised on Sunday.

These significantly different levels of morality are a reality in the United States today. I see no reason to doubt that they have at all times been a fact of life among all peoples. They are not to be wished away. They are to be lived with and accommodated to. But they are not to be segregated in our thinking. Too sharply segregated, today's distant contemplation would have no ameliorating effect when immediate confrontation occurs tomorrow. Surely, the long view ought to bring lessons to the short view. But, equally, the hard look at what is at hand ought to instruct the speculative image of what might be the best achievable.

Surely, also, organization for government should in some way respond to the different levels of morality. Recent writing by political scientists makes much of the fact that this is accomplished in the government of the United States. The long-run view of the general welfare gets differing receptions in local government, at the state house, and in Washington, D.C. The American people elect their congressmen with one set of values uppermost in mind; they respond to a significantly different array of values when they choose a president.

In the national government, it is Congress that hears most about the sacrifices necessary for achievement, least about the delights of vision and the rewards of magnanimity. The political roots of the congressmen are in the soil of immediate confrontation. The congressmen may say that they traffic in ideals marked with a high price, for they suffer when they commit the people to more than their constituents will tolerate.

The congressmen may say that the Supreme Court traffics in low-priced ideals. The judges are not confronted by the people who make the sacrifices necessary for achieving ideals. Peckham was not visited by a delegation of bakers demanding relief after ten hours in front of an oven. Sutherland was not taken on a tour of the rooming houses for women in the District of Columbia. Warren and his colleagues were not given a preview by the men who rioted in Little Rock, by the women who picketed in New Orleans, or by the state officials and state police who stood off federal marshals in Oxford, Mississippi.

One reason for having an independent judiciary, no doubt, is to free one part of the great complex called government for response to ideals not always likely to be honored by officials who are more readily accountable to the population. The practice of judicial review gives the members of the United States Supreme Court unusual opportunities to impress their visions, individual and collective, on public policy. Surely, all thoughtful men who look with favor on a principle of separation of powers would wish the judges to be imaginative in conceiving ideals and courageous in expressing them.

But such a commitment does not force the thoughtful man to conclude that the nation's highest judges should feel free, or be freed, to impose their noblest visions on the life of the people. He may think that the judge should learn something from the experience of the clergyman. It is a national belief, I suppose, that the minister of the gospel typically speaks for the highest ethical conceptions of the population. It is also a national commitment that the ministers, associated in religious organizations, should have no power but that of persuasion to induce the people to live by the ethics which the ministers recommend.

The judicial branch of government is not a religious organization, and the wall that separates church from state is not matched by a wall between the judges and the elected officials. But there is a lesson in the analogy. There is a place for persuasion and there is a place for force in the progress of a people to higher ethical levels. The judicial office was constructed for the coercive act, not for argument, pleading, exhortation. The traffic of judges in ethical standards must be confined to standards that can be made effective in conduct by orders for compliance.

The norms of conduct which I have called the morality of immediate confrontation set inescapable conditions for advance to a higher morality. The realities of current conduct and the persisting expectations as to probable conduct determine what changes must come first in order that more significant changes may come later. They dictate the compensations which are exacted as the price for each crucial concession. The strategy of advance to a more praiseworthy reality must be constructed with fine appreciation of these restraining conditions.

Those conscious acts which, in the judgment of time, contribute significantly to progress are a product of statesmanship. It is a task of scholarship to assist the act of statesmanship—to identify immediate and long-range goals, to clarify the problems of choice when choice among goals must be made, to calculate feasibilities and make recommendations on means to ends. It is most improbable that scholarship will adequately prepare the way for statesmanship; indeed, it is likely that most scholarly effort will be spent on explication of what statesmen have already done.

There is a better prospect that scholarship may prepare the nation for a wise location of authority to deal with the problems that present the greatest demands for statesmanship. Scholarly writing which examines the judicial process and evaluates the practice of judicial review has made only a marginal attack on the central question of how power is most wisely distributed in a system of government. This is, indeed, the central question for the student who directs his attention to the judges and their activities, as it is for the student who starts his inquiry with the elected officials and what they do. We will appreciate what our judges have in fact been doing and we will be prepared for judgments about a proper use of judicial power in the future only when we understand how judges, elected officials, and appointed bureaucracies are knitted together in a compact governmental structure.

APPENDIX

John Marshall on Judicial Review

FROM THE OPINION OF CHIEF JUSTICE JOHN MARSHALL IN *MARBURY* V. *MADISON* (1 CRANCH 137), DECIDED IN 1803

The question, whether an act, repugnant to the constitution, can become the law of the land, is a question deeply interesting to the United States; but, happily, not of an intricacy proportioned to its interest. It seems only necessary to recognize certain principles, supposed to have been long and well established, to decide it. . . .

The constitution is either a superior paramount law, unchangeable by ordinary means, or it is on a level with ordinary legislative acts, and, like other acts, is alterable when the legislature shall please to alter it.

If the former part of the alternative be true, then a legislative act contrary to the constitution is not law: if the latter part be true, then written constitutions are absurd attempts, on the part of the people, to limit a power in its own nature illimitable.

Certainly all those who have framed written constitutions contemplate them as forming the fundamental and paramount law of the nation, and, consequently, the theory of every such government must be, that an act of the legislature, repugnant to the constitution, is void. . . .

It is emphatically the province and duty of the judicial department to say what the law is. Those who apply the rule to particular cases, must of necessity expound and interpret that rule. If two laws conflict with each other, the courts must decide on the operation of each.

So if a law be in opposition to the constitution; if both the law and the constitution apply to a particular case, so that the court must either decide that case conformably to the law, disregarding the constitution; or conformably to the constitution, disregarding the law; the court must determine which of these conflicting rules governs the case. This is of the very essence of judicial duty.

If, then, the courts are to regard the constitution, and the constitution is superior to any ordinary act of the legislature, the constitution, and not such ordinary act, must govern the case to which they both apply.

Those, then, who controvert the principle that the constitution is to be considered, in court, as a paramount law, are reduced to the necessity of maintaining that courts must close their eyes on the constitution, and see only the law.

This doctrine would subvert the very foundation of all written constitutions. It would declare that an act which, according to the principles and theory of our government, is entirely void, is yet, in practice, completely obligatory. It would declare that if the legislature shall do what is expressly forbidden, such act, notwithstanding the express prohibition, is in reality effectual. It would be giving to the legislature a practical and real omnipotence, with the same breath which professes to restrict their powers within narrow limits. It is prescribing limits, and declaring that those limits may be passed at pleasure.

That it thus reduces to nothing what we have deemed the greatest improvement on political institutions, a written constitution, would of itself be sufficient, in America, where written constitutions have been viewed with so much reverence, for rejecting the construction. But the peculiar expressions of the constitution of the United States furnish additional arguments in favor of its rejection.

The judicial power of the United States is extended to all cases arising under the constitution.

Could it be the intention of those who gave this power, to say that in using it the constitution should not be looked into? That a case arising under the constitution should be decided without examining the instrument under which it arises?

This is too extravagant to be maintained.

In some cases, then, the constitution must be looked into by the judges. And if they can open it at all, what part of it are they forbidden to read or to obey?

There are many other parts of the constitution which serve to illustrate this subject.

It is declared that "no tax or duty shall be laid on articles exported from any state." Suppose a duty on the export of cotton, of tobacco, or of flour; and a suit instituted to recover it. Ought judgment to be rendered in such a case? Ought the judges to close their eyes on the constitution, and only see the law?

The constitution declares "that no bill of attainder or ex post facto law shall be passed."

If, however, such a bill should be passed, and a person should be prosecuted under it; must the court condemn to death those victims whom the constitution endeavors to preserve?

"No person," says the constitution, "shall be convicted of treason unless on the testimony of two witnesses to the same overt act, or on confession in open court."

Here the language of the constitution is addressed especially to the courts. It prescribes, directly for them, a rule of evidence not to be departed from. If the legislature should change that rule, and declare one witness, or a confession out of court, sufficient for conviction, must the constitutional principle yield to the legislative act?

From these, and many other selections which might be made, it is apparent, that the framers of the constitution contemplated that instrument as a rule for the government of courts, as well as of the legislature. . . .

It is also not entirely unworthy of observation, that in declaring what shall be the supreme law of the land, the constitution itself is first mentioned; and not the laws of the United States generally, but those only which shall be made in pursuance of the constitution, have that rank.

Thus, the particular phraseology of the constitution of the United States confirms and strengthens the principle, supposed to be essential to all written constitutions, that a law repugnant to the constitution is void; and that courts, as well as other departments, are bound by that instrument.

BIBLIOGRAPHIC NOTES

1. RACIAL DISCRIMINATION AND CONSTITUTIONAL DOCTRINE AFFECTING RACE RELATIONS

There is considerable literature examining the status of the Negro in American life. Some of it is carefully researched, but one must not expect a well-fortified neutrality in writing on this subject. Comprehensive and thoughtful works include: Hodding Carter, *Southern Legacy* (Baton Rouge: Louisiana State University Press, 1950); W.J. Cash, *The Mind of the South* (New York: Vintage Books, 1960); John Dollard, *Caste and Class in a Southern Town* (3rd ed.; New York: Doubleday, 1957); John W. Franklin, *From Slavery to Freedom,* "A History of American Negroes" (New York: Knopf, 1956); E. Franklin Frazier, *Black Bourgeoisie* (Glencoe, Ill.: Free Press, 1957); *idem, The Negro in the United States* (New York: Macmillan, 1957); Oscar Handlin, *Race and Nationality in American Life* (Boston: Little, Brown, 1957); Gunnar Myrdal, *An American Dilemma* (2nd ed.; New York: Harper, 1962); Truman M. Pierce *et al., White and Negro Schools in the South* (Englewood Cliffs, N.J.: Prentice-Hall, 1955); Hugh D. Price, *The Negro and Southern Politics* (New York: New York University Press, 1957); George E. Simpson and J.M. Yinger, *Racial and Cultural Minorities,* "An Analysis of Prejudice and Discrimination" (New York: Harper, 1953); Edgar T. Thompson, ed., *Race Relations and the Race Problem* (Durham: Duke University Press, 1939); Comer Vann Woodward, *The Strange Career of Jim Crow* (New York: Oxford University Press, 1955).

The surest way for the nonlawyer to inform himself about recent developments in law and other governmental acts affecting the status of Negroes is to consult the *Race Relations Law Reporter*. This journal appears in six issues each year, the first issue being for February, 1956. Documents ranging widely in character and printed in full text include statutes and legislative resolutions, local government ordinances, judicial opinions and orders, and pronouncements and orders of executive and administrative officials. Summary surveys of developments in law and public policy appear from time to time, and bibliographies of current literature are provided. Editorship and publication is by Vanderbilt University School of Law, Nashville, Tennessee.

Comment, critique, and criticism of the position taken by the Supreme Court in the Segregation cases and later decisions affecting separation of the races is voluminous. No doubt every law journal in the country has carried at least one article on this subject. Articles range from the coldly objective analysis to the passionate diatribe. It would be no favor to the reader for me to select a few for mention. They are listed in *Race Relations Law Reporter, op. cit.* See also Albert P. Blaustein and Clarence C. Ferguson, *Desegregation and the Law* (New Brunswick, N. J.: Rutgers University Press, 1957); Jack Greenberg, *Race Relations and American Law* (New York: Columbia University Press, 1959); and W.E. Michael, *The Age of Error* (New York: Vantage Press, 1957).

References to literature dealing with the constitutional guarantee of equal protection of the laws will be found in Note 16.

2. RECENT AND CURRENT OPPOSITION TO THE SUPREME COURT

The "Declaration of Constitutional Principles" by ninety-six Southern congressmen is printed in *Congressional Record*, 102 (1956), 4460, 4515–4516, and reprinted in *Race Relations Law Reporter*, 1 (1956), 435–437. The eight interposition statements of Southern states are most readily available in *Race Relations Law Reporter*, 1.

For continuing coverage of response to the Supreme Court's desegregation orders, see successive issues of *Race Relations Law Reporter*. For a comprehensive and critical examination of this experience done with imagination, thoughtfulness, and restraint, see Jack W. Peltason, *58 Lonely Men*, "Southern Federal Judges and School

Desegregation" (New York: Harcourt, Brace & World, 1961). Other accounts of obstructive efforts include: Hodding Carter, *The South Strikes Back* (Garden City, N. Y.: Doubleday, 1959); John Bartlow Martin, *The Deep South Says "Never"* (New York: Ballantine Books, 1957); Benjamin Muse, *Virginia's Massive Resistance* (Bloomington: Indiana University Press, 1961); Don Shoemaker, ed., *With All Deliberate Speed* (New York: Harper, 1958); Robert Penn Warren, *Segregation* (New York: Random House, 1956; now a Modern Library paperback). The Little Rock episode is fully documented in Virgil Blossom, *It Has Happened Here* (New York: Harper, 1959), and Wilson Record and Jane C. Record, eds., *Little Rock, U.S.A.*, "Materials for Analysis" (San Francisco: Chandler Publishing Company, 1960).

The resolutions of the Conference of State Chief Justices were adopted on August 23, 1958. Full text of the resolutions and report of the conference's Committee on Federal-State Relationships as Affected by Judicial Decisions appear in *U.S. News & World Report*, 45 (Oct. 3, 1958), No. 14. Full text of the report, without the resolutions, was printed in a pamphlet for distribution free of charge by the Virginia Commission on Constitutional Government (Richmond, Va.) with the title: *Report of the Conference of Chief Justices: Pasadena, California, August, 1958.* For a reply to the chief justices and refutation of their contentions, see Eugene V. Rostow, "The Court and Its Critics," *South Texas Law Review*, 4 (1959), 160.

Senator Jenner's bill to remove certain questions from review by the Supreme Court was S. 2646 of the 85th Congress. The committee's report, both majority and minority statements, is Senate Report 1586, 85th Congress, 2nd Session. Hearings on the bill are printed in two parts under the title: *Limitation of Appellate Jurisdiction of the United States Supreme Court*, "Hearings before the Sub-Committee to Investigate the Administration of the Internal Security Act and Other Internal Security Laws of the Committee on the Judiciary, United States Senate, 85th Congress, 1st Session." Debate on the bill was intermittent during the second session of the 85th Congress, but see especially the remarks of Aug. 20, 1957, in *Congressional Record*, 104, pp. 18, 635 ff. Jenner's remarks which I quote in Chapter II are from a speech of July 26, 1957, reported *ibid.*, 103, pp. 12, 806–813, and reprinted on pp. 2–13 of Part I of the hearings cited above. Jenner's bill is printed in full in the hearings, Part I, pp. 1–2. This legislative episode, with events leading up to it and other efforts to curb the Supreme Court in the 85th and 86th Congresses, is examined in detail in C. Herman Pritchett,

Congress versus the Supreme Court (Minneapolis: University of Minnesota Press, 1961). Walter F. Murphy, in his *Congress and the Court* (Chicago: University of Chicago Press, 1962), supplies an equally careful examination of this controversy and admirably sets it in a broader context, historical and contemporary, of judicial and legislative behavior.

The authority of Congress and the president to fix the appellate jurisdiction of the United States by statute is disputed by students of constitutional law. One interested in this issue should begin his study with careful reading of Article III of the Constitution. The principal court decision indicating comprehensive legislative authority in this matter is *Ex Parte McCardle* (7 Wallace 506, 1868). This decision is printed in Part 2 of the hearings cited above, together with other leading decisions on the same subject, selected legal essays, testimony by lawyers, and letters from students and practitioners of law. The Jenner bill stimulated further analysis in law reviews, for example, Leonard G. Rathner, "Congressional Power over the Appellate Jurisdiction of the Supreme Court," *University of Pennsylvania Law Review,* 109 (1961), 157.

3. CONSTITUTIONAL CONVENTION OF 1787 AND PROBABLE INTENT OF THE FRAMERS

A meager journal of the proceedings of the Convention of 1787 was maintained, but the speeches and remarks of delegates were not officially recorded. Day-to-day accounts of what was said and what was decided were kept by several delegates. Of these, the notes of James Madison were by a wide margin the most complete. The new Constitution was ratified in conventions of delegates elected for that purpose in each of the states. Records of what was said in these state conventions vary from nothing whatever to several hundred pages. Such reports of these proceedings as he could find were brought together by Jonathan Elliot in several volumes published in successive printings that varied in content. Perhaps most likely to be available in college or public library is a five-volume set bearing the title *The Debates in the Several State Conventions on the Adoption of the Federal Constitution* (Philadelphia: J.B. Lippincott Co., 1836–1845).

Enough materials to satisfy most readers will be found in either of two collections of documents relating to the framing and ratification of the Constitution—Charles C. Tansill, ed., *Documents Illustrative of the Formation of the Union of the American States,* printed by the Government Printing Office in 1927 as House Document No. 398, 69th Congress, 1st Session; and Max Farrand, ed., *The Records of the Federal Convention of 1787* (3 vols.; New Haven: Yale University Press, 1911). I relied principally on Farrand in writing this book. Volumes I and II print the journal of the Convention and all the notes of delegates—drafts of their speeches and accounts of what others said—that Farrand could find. Volume III consists mainly of letters, pamphlets, and speeches written after the Convention by delegates and others which throw light on the questions pondered in the Convention and the probable intent of the men who drafted and ratified the Constitution.

The Federalist is no doubt the greatest classic of American political literature. It is a series of essays written by Alexander Hamilton, John Jay, and James Madison to explain the new Constitution and argue for its adoption. It is available, complete or most interesting essays only, in several low-priced editions.

Interesting accounts of the Convention—the men and how they did their work—are: Arthur T. Prescott, compiler, *Drafting the Federal Constitution* (Baton Rouge: Louisiana State University Press, 1941); Charles A. Beard, *An Economic Interpretation of the Constitution of the United States* (New York: Macmillan Co., 1913); Forrest McDonald, *We the People,* "The Economic Origins of the Constitution" (Chicago: University of Chicago Press, 1958); and Carl Van Doren, *The Great Rehearsal* (New York: Viking Press, 1948).

4. INTERPOSITION, NULLIFICATION, AND CONFLICT BETWEEN SUPREME COURT AND STATE COURTS

The one best place to go for a running account, with luxuriant verbatim quotation, of praise, criticism, and the efforts to curb the Supreme Court is Charles Warren's *The Supreme Court in United States History,* originally published in three volumes by Little, Brown, and Company (Boston: 1922), and in 1932 reissued in two volumes by the same publishers. References to volumes and pages throughout this book are to the two-volume edition. A long article in which Warren brings together his principal material relating to legislative and judicial attack on the power of the Supreme Court to review the decisions of state courts on appeal is reprinted in the Senate hearings cited in Note 2. The article originally appeared in *American Law Review,* 47 (1913), 1, 161. Bringing the account up to date, but also mentioning several earlier occurrences which Warren bypassed, is an excellent review entitled "Interposition vs. Judicial Power," *Race Relations Law Reporter,* 1 (1956), 465.

The most inclusive collection of documents recording conflict between national and state governments including efforts at nullification, is Herman V. Ames, ed., *State Documents on Federal Relations, 1789–1861* (Philadelphia: University of Pennsylvania, 1900). Several of the earlier resolutions of interposition, assembled by James Raburn, are printed in whole or in part in *Journal of Public Law,* 5 (1956), 49. Immediately preceding these documents, pp. 2–48, is a thorough, careful, and notably objective essay by A.S. Miller and R.F. Howell, "Interposition, Nullification and the Delicate Division of Power in a Federal System"; a third essay, at p. 90, by James and Marilyn Blawie, reports precedents for interposition and secession in New England. The Virginia and Kentucky resolutions, the South Carolina Nullification Ordinance of 1832, and other documents of interest are printed in Henry S. Commager, ed., *Documents of American History* (6th ed.; New York: Appleton-Century-Crofts, 1958). The Virginia and Kentucky resolutions, James Madison's report on the Virginia Resolutions of 1799, and the most interesting part of John C. Calhoun's Fort Hill address are distributed free of charge by the Virginia Commission on Constitutional Government (Richmond, Virginia). Charles Homer Hockett gives considerable, and thoughtful, attention to nullification, other evidences of strain between national and state governments, and dissatisfaction with the Supreme Court in his *The Constitutional History of the United States, 1826-1876* (New York: Macmillan, 1939), Chaps. 2 and 3. Hockett gives references to other informative and critical literature. See also Edward S. Corwin, "National Power and State Interposition, 1787–1861," *Michigan Law Review,* 10 (1912), 535, reprinted in a most valuable publication of the American Association of Law Schools, *Selected Essays on Constitutional Law,* Vol. 3, p. 1171 (4 vols.; Chicago: Foundation Press, 1938). References to recent literature on the theory and practice of interposition, evaluating the doctrine against a background of constitutional theory and development, appear from time to time in the bibliography section of *Race Relations Law Reporter.*

On clash between the United States Supreme Court and state judges, the best general treatments are in two items cited above: Warren's three volumes and the review in *Race Relations Law Reporter.* The Wisconsin rebellion centering on the Booth case is carefully examined by A.J. Beitzinger in "Federal Law Enforcement and the Booth Cases," *Marquette Law Review,* 41 (1957), 7.

5. SUPREME COURT BEFORE PRESIDENT AND CONGRESS

There is no comprehensive and incisive study of the political environment of American courts in general or the Supreme Court in particular. Charles Warren's *Supreme Court in United States History,* cited in Note 4, appears to be wholly trustworthy for identification of the main ups and downs of the Supreme Court. The extensive quotations he gives are mainly from newspapers. Warren does not tell much about what presidents and congressmen said when the Court was under attack, and he makes virtually no effort to relate the acts and statements of congressmen to attitudes prevailing among their constituents. Most of the books that deal generally with the Supreme Court or, more broadly, with American constitutional history give some information about relationships between the Supreme Court and the elected branches of the government. Among the best for matters discussed in Chapter IV are: Charles Warren, *Congress, the Constitution, and the Supreme Court* (Boston: Little, Brown & Co., 1925); Gustavus Myers, *History of the United States Supreme Court* (2 vols.; New York: Macmillan, 1949); Andrew C. McLaughlin, *A Constitutional History of the United States* (New York: D. Appleton-Century, 1935); and Albert J. Beveridge, *The Life of John Marshall* (4 vols.; Boston: Houghton Mifflin, 1916–1919). See also Note 6 on the effort to reorganize the judiciary in 1937.

Joseph P. Harris, in his *The Advice and Consent of the Senate* (Berkeley: University of California Press, 1953), devotes one chapter to the confirmation of Justice Louis D. Brandeis and a few paragraphs to each of the other cases of confirmation which encountered notable opposition during this century. See also Cortez A.M. Ewing, *The Judges of the Supreme Court, 1789–1937* (Minneapolis: University of Minnesota Press, 1938); Daniel McHargue, "President Taft's Appointments to the Supreme Court," *Journal of Politics,* 12 (1950), 478; and Walter F. Murphy, "In His Own Image; Mr. Chief Justice Taft and Supreme Court Appointments," *Supreme Court Review, 1961,* p. 159.

The best thing on efforts to limit the Supreme Court's power or to control the use of its power is Warren's *Congress, Constitution, and Supreme Court, op. cit.* Three law review articles are also helpful. The first, by Warren, is cited in Note 4. The other two are Maurice S. Culp, "A Survey of the Proposals to Limit or Deny the Power of Judicial Review by the Supreme Court of the United

States," *Indiana Law Review*, 4 (1929), 386, 474, and Katherine B. Fite and L.B. Rubinstein, "Curbing the Supreme Court—State Experiences and Federal Proposals," *Michigan Law Review*, 35 (1937), 762. See also Charles G. Haines, *The American Doctrine of Judicial Supremacy* (Berkeley: University of California Press, 1932), Chaps. 16 and 17. For references to the scope of congressional authority over the Supreme Court's appellate jurisdiction, see the final paragraph of Note 2.

6. "COURT-PACKING" PLAN OF 1937

The Roosevelt drive against the Supreme Court in 1937 is discussed in all recent studies of the Court and major biographies of the great New Dealer. Two small books recount the episode in detail—Merlo J. Pusey, *The Supreme Court Crisis* (New York: Macmillan, 1937), and Joseph Alsop and Turner Catledge, *The 168 Days* (New York: Doubleday, Doran, 1938). Robert H. Jackson's, *The Struggle for Judicial Supremacy* (New York: Knopf, 1941), tells the story from the point of view of a protagonist of the President. James M. Burns remarkably captures (or imaginatively supplies) the color and flavor of the great drama in his *Roosevelt*, "The Lion and the Fox" (New York: Harcourt, Brace, 1956). A deep interest in the episode can best be satisfied by examining the six volumes of hearings published by the Government Printing Office in 1937. This is the record of the inquiry of the Senate committee into the President's proposal and includes testimony, tabulations of data, memorandums relating to the proposal, and reprints of articles thought relevant to the issue. The full title is *Reorganization of the Federal Judiciary*, "Hearings before Committee on the Judiciary, U.S. Senate, 75th Congress, 1st Session, on S. 1392." The report of the committee which conducted the hearing is Senate Report No. 711, 75th Congress, 1st Session (Serial 10076).

7. RESPONSE OF THE SUPREME COURT TO CRITICISM

For further comment on change of position by Supreme Court judges in 1937 or thereabouts, in addition to the books cited in footnotes, see: Edward S. Corwin, *Constitutional Revolution, Ltd.* (Pomona, Calif.: Claremont Colleges, 1941); Merlo J. Pusey, *Charles Evans Hughes*, Vol. 2, Chaps. 69–71 (2 vols.; New York: Macmillan, 1951); and James W. Moore and Shirley Adelson, "The Supreme Court: 1938 Term," *Virginia Law Review*, 26 (1939), 1.

On judicial behavior in the issues involving paper money as legal tender, see: Leon Sachs, "Stare Decisis and the Legal Tender Cases," *Virginia Law Review,* 20 (1934), 856, and Charles Fairman, "Mr. Justice Bradley's Appointment to the Supreme Court and the Legal Tender Cases," *Harvard Law Review,* 54 (1941), 977, 1128.

The following are more general treatments of the response of Supreme Court judges to criticism, attack, and other evidences of public expectations, including election returns: Walter D. Coles, "Politics and the Supreme Court of the United States," *American Law Review,* 27 (1893), 182; Earl Latham, "The Supreme Court as a Political Institution," *Minnesota Law Review,* 31 (1947), 205; *idem,* "Supreme Court and the Supreme People," *Journal of Politics,* 16 (1954), 207; Murphy, *Congress and the Court,* pp. 246 ff. (cited in Note 2); and Walter F. Murphy and C. Herman Pritchett, eds., *Courts, Judges, and Politics* (New York: Random House, 1961), Chap. 15. The relationship of judges to the political branches of government and to the general public and public leaders is illuminated throughout Charles Warren's *The Supreme Court and United States History* (cited in Note 4).

8. CHARACTER OF THE UNION AND ITS CONTROLLING DOCUMENT

Americans do not argue today about whether their political system was formed by a voluntary joining of sovereign states that vested some of their authority in a central government which those states created or whether a population scattered over a part of North America declared itself a nation and created a new governmental system which allowed previously established state governments to continue with some of their former authority. Dropping this issue from its concern, the nation ceased to be interested in whether the Constitution should be viewed as a contract between states or a social compact entered into by a nation-wide citizenry. These issues were at the heart of political dispute and conceptions of statesmanship for several decades beginning with the adoption of the Articles of Confederation in 1781. For a quick résumé of the arguments, see one of these: Alan P. Grimes, *American Political Thought* (New York: Henry Holt, 1955), Chap. 12; Alpheus T. Mason and Richard H. Leach, *In Quest of Freedom* (Englewood Cliffs, N. J.: Prentice-Hall, 1959), Chaps. 7, 8, 12, and 13; Vernon L. Parrington, *Main Currents in American Thought* (3 vols.; New York: Harcourt, Brace and Company, 1930), Vol. 2, pp. 67–98. For a thorough inquiry, start with *The Federalist,* generally Nos. 40 to 46, and go from there to the documents printed in the collections by Commager (cited in Note 4) and Alpheus T. Mason, ed., *Free Government in the Making* (New York: Oxford University Press, 1956), Chap. 14. For the full-dress debate, try these: John Taylor, *Construction Construed and Constitutions Vindicated* (Richmond: Shepherd and Pollard, 1820); John Taylor, *New Views on the Constitution of the United States* (Washington: Way and Gideon, 1823); John C. Calhoun, *A Disquisition on Government and a Discourse on the Constitution and Government of the United States,* ed. Richard Cralle (New York: D. Appleton & Co., 1854); Alexander H. Stephens, *A Constitutional View of the Late War Between the States* (Philadelphia: National Publishing Co., 1868–1870); Joseph Story, *Commentaries on the Constitution of the United States* [1833], Vol. I, Book 3, Chap. 3 (4th ed.; Boston: Little, Brown, and Company, 1873); and Francis Lieber, *Civil Liberty and Self-Government* (3d ed.; Philadelphia: J. B. Lippincott & Company, 1875).

9. ESTABLISHMENT OF JUDICIAL REVIEW

Few subjects have attracted more finished scholarship by American historians, lawyers, and political scientists, and few subjects have excited more vigorous debate. Scholarship has certainly not carried the field, for contrary statements continue to appear in print about what Marshall intended to accomplish in *Marbury* v. *Madison,* about what provision the framers intended to make for authoritative interpretation of the Constitution, and about the precedents for judicial nullification of statutes available to Marshall and his colleagues. If only one man's findings are to be examined, read Edward S. Corwin's *The Doctrine of Judicial Review* (Princeton: Princeton University Press, 1914) and his *Court Over Constitution* (Princeton: Princeton University Press, 1938). The later book revises Professor Corwin's earlier conclusions, the change being toward less confidence that the Constitution's makers intended to provide for judicial review. A pioneer inquiry that still enjoys great confidence is James B. Thayer, "The Origin and Scope of the American Doctrine of Constitutional Law," *Harvard Law Review,* 7 (1893), 129. For differing conclusions reached by men who enjoy high regard, see: Charles A. Beard, *The Supreme Court and the Constitution* (New York: Macmillan, 1912); Louis B. Boudin, *Government by Judiciary* (2 vols.; New York: William Godwin, 1932); William W. Crosskey, *Politics and the Constitution in the*

History of the United States, Vol. 2, Chaps. 27–29 (2 vols.; Chicago: University of Chicago Press, 1953); Charles G. Haines, *The American Doctrine of Judicial Supremacy* (cited in Note 5); Andrew C. McLaughlin, *The Courts, Constitution, and Parties* (Chicago: University of Chicago Press, 1912), Chap. 1; and Charles Warren, *Congress, The Constitution, and the Supreme Court* (cited in Note 5).

The essay by Thayer, the part of Corwin's *Doctrine of Judicial Review* which deals with *Marbury* v. *Madison* and its precedents, and many other items of the best writing on the role of courts in constitutional interpretation are reprinted in Book I of *Selected Essays on Constitutional Law* (cited in Note 4).

10. *MARBURY V. MADISON* AS STRATEGIC ACT AND LOGICAL ESSAY

The reader having special interest in Marshall's goals and strategy and the quality of his reasoning in the Marbury case may consult, in addition to the works cited in Note 9: Beveridge's *Life of Marshall,* Vol. 3, Chap. 3 (cited in Note 5); Thomas R. Powell, *Vagaries and Varieties in Constitutional Interpretation* (New York: Columbia University Press, 1956), Chap. 1; and James A.C. Grant, "Marbury v. Madison Today," *American Political Science Review,* 23 (1929), 673.

Referring to debate going on in Congress while *Marbury* v. *Madison* was pending—debate relating to reorganization of the federal judiciary—Beveridge gives us this counsel: "All the reasons for the opinion which John Marshall, exactly one year later, pronounced in *Marbury* v. *Madison* were given during this debate. Indeed, the legislative struggle now in progress and the result of it, created conditions which forced Marshall to execute that judicial *coup d'état.* It should be repeated that an understanding of *Marbury* v. *Madison* is impossible without a thorough knowledge of the debate in Congress which preceded and largely caused that epochal decision" (*op. cit.,* Vol. 3, p. 75). Popular support—mainly in Kentucky—for the idea that the inferior federal courts should be abolished is mentioned by Warren in his *Supreme Court in United States History,* Vol. 1, pp. 218–222 (cited in Note 4).

One interested in retracing the ground covered in my critique of Marshall's reasoning might well start with Haines, *The American Doctrine of Judicial Supremacy* (cited in Note 5). His chapters 3–9 are most relevant. Haines cited the more useful books and articles which confirm or contest his analysis and conclusions, up to time of printing (1932). In the same year appeared a two-volume study by Louis B. Boudin which rejects the findings of Haines and sharply attacks the reasoning in the first edition of Haines's book (1914). Boudin's study, *Government by Judiciary* (cited in Note 9), is a tough-minded effort to convince the reader that the decision and the opinion in *Marbury* v. *Madison* "was not warranted by the Constitution, and the present exercise of power by the Judiciary is not warranted by the court's own theory of the Constitution as laid down by Marshall" (Vol. 1, p. *iv*).

Colonial charters, the early state constitutions, and subsequent constitutions of the several states up to time of printing are in Francis N. Thorpe, ed., *The Federal and State Constitutions, Colonial Charters, and Other Organic Laws* (7 vols.; Washington: Government Printing Office, 1909).

11. LEGITIMATION OF JUDICIAL REVIEW

For a careful, authoritative, but also succinct statement of the conditions governing the exercise of judicial power to nullify statutes, see Edward S. Corwin, "Judicial Review in Action," *University of Pennsylvania Law Review*, 74 (1926), 639, reprinted in *Selected Essays on Constitutional Law*, Vol. 1, p. 449 (cited in Note 4). Justice Brandeis summarized the conditions which he understood to limit the Supreme Court's inquiry into constitutionality in a concurring opinion for *Ashwander* v. *Tennessee Valley Authority* (297 U.S. 288, at 346–348, 1936).

Most American scholars who have personally investigated the origins of our constitutional system have concluded that the power of judicial review was conferred upon the judiciary by the Constitution. Among the more prominent efforts to establish the legitimate character of this practice are Beveridge, *Life of Marshall*, Vol. 3, Chap. 3 (cited in Note 5), and all the items cited in Note 9 except Boudin and Crosskey. The content of *The Federalist* is severely examined in Gottfried Dietze, *The Federalist*, "A Classic on Federalism and Free Government" (Baltimore: Johns Hopkins Press, 1960). Dietze finds strong endorsement of a power of judicial review in *The Federalist* (see mainly pp. 171–175 and 277–281).

A recent book, Charles L. Black, Jr., *The People and the Court* (New York: Macmillan, 1960), pursues a line of reasoning differing from earlier writings. Black asserts that the Constitution is obviously a legal document, that the men who drafted it intended it to be treated as other expressions of law are treated and as law supreme over all other expressions of law. Marshall, Black says, made a poor argument in support of his conclusion in *Marbury* v. *Madison* and therefore lent strength to the arguments which reject his conclusion. Black concedes that the rooting of judicial review in the Constitution itself cannot be proven by any line of reasoning that is convincing to people reluctant to be convinced. He is personally convinced that the ability of judges to void legislation which they believe to conflict with language in the Constitution is essential to any hope for continued satisfaction with our form of government, and he calls on all reasonable men to agree that there is sufficient evidence and reason for believing that the framers intended the courts to exercise this power.

12. THE ELASTIC CLAUSES

There is a brief discussion of the necessary-and-proper clause in No. 44 of *The Federalist.* Hamilton and Jefferson set forth their respective views of expressed and implied powers in opinions on the constitutionality of a United States bank in 1791. The essentials of their arguments are reprinted in Commager's *Documents,* Nos. 93 and 94 (cited in Note 4). Their debate was continued by others in Congress and is reported in *Annals of Congress,* Vol. 2, pp. 1891–1960 (1st Congress, 3rd session, 1791). Alexander Hamilton's report supporting creation of a bank is in the same volume at page 2023. A part of this debate may be more readily available in Elliot's *Debates* (cited in Note 3), Vol. 4, p. 411. The "strict–versus–loose-construction" controversy is reviewed in Hockett, *Constitutional History of the United States* (cited in Note 4), Vol. 1, Chap. 18. Justice Joseph Story, associate of Chief Justice Marshall on the Supreme Court, has an extended discussion of the general-welfare clause and of expressed and implied powers in chapters 14 and 24–27 of his *Commentaries on the Constitution* (cited in Note 8). Crosskey's views about the implications of the constitutional language are in Chapter 3 of his *Politics and the Constitution* (cited in Note 9).

Students of constitutional law tend to direct their attention to the main issues that arise in litigation; for that reason, their discussion of general welfare, necessary-and-proper, and reservation of powers to the states or to the people are in the main subordinated to a more comprehensive inquiry into power to tax or to regulate commerce. Exceptions to this rule are Charles S. Collier, Jr., "Judicial Bootstraps and the General Welfare Clause," *George Washington Law Review,* 4 (1936), 211; and Henry St. George Tucker, "The General Welfare," *Virginia Law Review,* 8 (1922), 167. Both articles are reprinted in *Selected Essays on Constitutional Laws* (cited in Note 4), Vol. 3, pp. 593, 603. Reprinted in the same volume, chapters 6 and 7, are several excellent articles on the scope of national power to raise money and spend it. Three that deal comprehensively with this problem are Robert E. Cushman, "Social and Economic Control through Federal Taxation," *Minnesota Law Review,* 18 (1934), 759; J.A.C. Grant, "Commerce, Production, and the Fiscal Powers of Congress," *Yale Law Journal,* 45 (1936), 751, 991; and Edward S. Corwin, "The Spending Power of Congress—apropos the Maternity Act," *Harvard Law Review,* 36 (1923), 548. Too late to get into the *Selected Essays* was Herman J. Herbert, Jr., "The General Welfare Clauses in the Constitution of the United States," *Fordham Law Review,* 7 (1938), 390.

13. MARSHALL'S VIEWS OF JUDICIAL POWER

McCulloch v. *Maryland* and *Gibbons* v. *Ogden* are discussed in all general works dealing with American constitutional development. An interesting recent criticism of the first case is Harold J. Plous and Gordon E. Baker, "McCulloch v. Maryland: Right Principle, Wrong Case," *Stanford Law Review,* 9 (1957), 710. Crosskey's treatment is unique, but one should not tackle him unless willing to read carefully a few hundred pages in his *Politics and the Constitution.* For other evaluations of Marshall's contributions in these cases which differ in varying ways from my own, read Beveridge, *Life of Marshall* (cited in Note 5), Vol. 3, Chaps. 6 and 8; Warren, *The Supreme Court in United States History* (cited in Note 4), Chap. 15; and Ben W. Palmer, *Marshall and Taney* (Minneapolis: University of Minnesota Press, 1939), pp. 104–141. For interpretation of Marshall's views on the proper scope of judicial power in constitutional cases, see, in addition to the foregoing, Beveridge, *op. cit.,* Vol. 3, Chap. 3; Edward S. Corwin, *John Marshall and the Constitution* (New Haven: Yale University Press, 1919); Felix Frankfurter, "John Marshall and the Judicial Function," *Harvard Law Review,* 69 (1955), 217; Max Lerner, "John Marshall and the Campaign of History," *Columbia Law Review,* 39 (1936), 396; and the symposium on Marshall in *University of Pennsylvania Law Review,* 104 (1955), 1–68.

14. JUDICIAL INTERPRETATION OF THE COMMERCE CLAUSE

All items cited in the preceding note are relevant here. For an over-all view of judicial interpretation of the commerce clause, see C. Herman Pritchett, *The American Constitution* (New York: McGraw-Hill Book Co., 1959), Chaps. 14–16. The leading decisions are cited and summarized with much additional commentary in Edward S. Corwin, ed., *The Constitution of the United States of America,* "Analysis and Interpretation," pp. 108–253 (Washington: Senate Document No. 170, 82nd Congress, 2nd Session; Government Printing Office, 1953). Much of the most searching analysis (mainly law review articles) which appeared before the shift in judicial position in 1937 is reprinted in Vol. 3, Chaps. 2, 10, and 11, of *Selected Essays on Constitutional Law* (cited in Note 4). Two articles, the first a short one and the second a long one, which survey interpretation of the commerce clause during the New Deal period and later are Vincent M. Barnette, Jr., "The Power to Regulate Commerce," *American Political Science Review,* 41 (1947), 1170, and Robert L. Stern, "The Commerce Clause and the National Economy, 1933–1946," *Harvard Law Review,* 59 (1946), 645, 883.

Discussions of a more general character, dealing with both national and state power over commerce and likely to be in any good college or public library include: Edward S. Corwin, *The Commerce Power versus States Rights* (Princeton: Princeton University Press, 1936); Felix Frankfurter, *The Commerce Clause under Marshall, Taney and Waite* (Chapel Hill: University of North Carolina Press, 1937); Joseph E. Kallenbach, *Federal Cooperation with the States under the Commerce Clause* (Ann Arbor: University of Michigan Press, 1942); Alpheus T. Mason and William M. Beaney, *The Supreme Court in a Free Society* (Englewood Cliffs, N.J.: Prentice-Hall, 1959), Chaps. 5–8; Henry Rottschaefer, *The Constitution and Socio-Economic Change* (Ann Arbor: University of Michigan, 1948), Chaps. 1–2; John R. Schmidhauser, *The Supreme Court as Final Arbiter in Federal-State Relations* (Chapel Hill: University of North Carolina Press, 1958); and Carl B. Swisher, *American Constitutional Development* (Boston: Houghton Mifflin Co., 1943), *passim.*

The reconsideration of position by Supreme Court judges which was dramatized by certain decisions in the year 1937 has been examined and re-examined. The following appear to be good items to start with: Edward S. Corwin, *Constitutional Revolution, Ltd.*

(Claremont, Calif.: Claremont Colleges, 1941); Samuel Hendel, *Charles Evans Hughes and the Supreme Court* (New York: Columbia University Press, 1951), Chaps. 16–21; Robert H. Jackson, *The Struggle for Judicial Supremacy* (cited in Note 6); Alpheus T. Mason, *Security through Freedom* (Ithaca: Cornell University Press, 1955), Chaps. 3–4; *idem, The Supreme Court from Taft to Warren* (Baton Rouge: Louisiana State University Press, 1958), Chap. 3; and Bernard Schwartz, *The Supreme Court,* "Constitutional Revolution in Retrospect" (New York: Ronald Press, 1957).

15. DUE PROCESS OF LAW

Judicial interpretation of the due-process clauses is a point of major attention in all textbooks of American constitutional law. Most recent of these is Pritchett (cited in Note 14). An earlier book which attempted to say all there was to say about due process of law and did say a great deal, indeed, is Rodney L. Mott, *Due Process of Law* (Indianapolis: Bobbs-Merrill, 1926).

More than a dozen casebooks offer easy access to some of the most interesting Supreme Court decisions. Some of them, designed for undergraduate college students, contain excellent summary notes by the editors. Very good in this respect are Robert E. Cushman and Robert F. Cushman, *Cases in Constitutional Law* (New York: Appleton-Century-Crofts, 1958); Wallace Mendelson, *The Constitution and the Supreme Court* (New York: Dodd, Mead and Co., 1959); Glendon A. Schubert, *Constitutional Politics* (New York: Holt, Rinehart and Winston, 1960); and Rocco J. Tresoloni, *American Constitutional Law* (New York: Macmillan Co., 1959).

Many of the best law review articles which appeared before 1938 are in *Selected Essays on Constitutional Law* (cited in Note 4), Book 2, Chaps. 1–2. Two that are of special value to the beginner are Robert E. Cushman, "The Social and Economic Interpretation of the Fourteenth Amendment," *Michigan Law Review,* 20 (1922), 737, and Ray A. Brown, "Due Process of Law, Police Power, and the Supreme Court," *Harvard Law Review,* 40 (1927), 943. Sanford H. Kadish makes an effort to determine to what extent the due-process requirement has been reduced to rule in a most interesting article, "Methodology and Criteria in Due Process Adjudication—A Survey and Criticism," *Yale Law Journal,* 66 (1957), 319. Other recent examinations of the due-process requirement are Morris D. Forkosch, "American Democracy and Procedural Due Process," *Brooklyn Law Review,* 24 (1958), 173; Howard J. Graham, "Our

'Declaratory' Fourteenth Amendment," *Stanford Law Review,* 7 (1954), 3; Monrad G. Paulsen, "The Persistence of Substantive Due Process in the States," *Minnesota Law Review,* 34 (1950), 91; Robert E. Rodes, Jr., "Due Process and Social Legislation in the Supreme Court—A Post Mortem," *Notre Dame Lawyer,* 33 (1957), 5.

One interested in the application of the due-process requirement to freedom of expression and other personal freedoms may properly start his reading with Pritchett and one of the casebooks cited above. Alexander Meiklejohn's *Political Freedom,* originally published as *Free Speech and its Relation to Self-Government,* is a famous argument; both editions were published by Harper and Brothers, in 1948 and in 1960.

16. EQUAL PROTECTION OF THE LAWS

The newcomer to the study of constitutional law who wants a short excursion into the equal-protection guarantee might start with any of the following items: "Separate-but-Equal: A Study of the Career of a Constitutional Concept,"*Race Relations Law Reporter,* 1 (1956), 283; Alfred H. Kelley, "The Fourteenth Amendment Reconsidered: the Segregation Question," *Michigan Law Review,* 54 (1956), 1049; and either of two documents of the United States Civil Rights Commission—the Commission's *Report* of 1959 or its *Equal Protection of the Laws in Public Higher Education* (1960).

I noted, in Chapter XV, the high acclaim accorded Bickel's study of the understandings surrounding the insertion of the equal-protection guarantee into the Constitution. Other persons have examined the same evidence and reached different conclusions—John P. Frank and Robert F. Munro, "The Original Understanding of 'Equal Protection of the Laws,'" *Columbia Law Review,* 50 (1950), 131, and Robert J. Harris, *The Quest for Equality* (Baton Rouge: Louisiana State University Press, 1960), Chap. 2. Dealing generally with the Fourteenth Amendment or parts other than the equal-protection clause are Horace E. Flack, *Adoption of the Fourteenth Amendment* (Urbana: University of Illinois Press, 1908); Joseph B. James, *The Framing of the Fourteenth Amendment* (Urbana: University of Illinois Press, 1956); Jacobus tenBroek, *The Anti-Slavery Origins of the Fourteenth Amendment* (Berkeley: University of California Press, 1951); Howard J. Graham, "Our 'Declaratory' Fourteenth Amendment," *Stanford Law Review,* 7 (1954), 3; Howard J. Graham, "The 'Conspiracy Theory' of the Fourteenth Amendment," *Yale Law Journal,* 47–48 (1938), 371, 171; and Charles

Fairman, "Does the Fourteenth Amendment Incorporate the Bill of Rights?" *Stanford Law Review,* 2 (1949), 5.

On the question, when is a discriminatory act an act of the state, see Glenn Abernathy, "Expansion of the State Action Concept under the Fourteenth Amendment," *Cornell Law Quarterly,* 43 (1958), 375; Thomas P. Lewis, "The Meaning of State Action," *Columbia Law Review,* 60 (1960), 1083; and Theodore J. St. Antoine, "Color Blindness but not Myopia," *Michigan Law Review,* 59 (1961), 993.

17. JUDICIAL METHOD

There is a substantial literature on constitutional construction—the rules that judges are supposed to follow in fixing meaning for constitutional language—and criticism of what the judges have done in this respect. The article by tenBroek cited in Chapter XVI is one of the best short treatments. If one wants to go further into the subject, these may be the most helpful items: Story, *Commentaries on the Constitution* (cited in Note 8), Vol. I, Book 3, Chap. 5; Westell W. Willoughby, *The Constitutional Law of the United States* (3 vols.; New York: Baker, Vorhis & Co., 1929), Vol. 1, Chap. 2; Edmond Cahn, ed., *Supreme Court and Supreme Law* (Bloomington: Indiana University Press, 1954), pp. 55 ff. The two volumes by Crosskey (cited in Note 9) are a majestic attempt to find the original, correct meaning of the Constitution by ascertaining the meaning which its vocabulary and idiom generally carried at the time the Constitution was written.

It would require a small book to list the writings that describe, explain, and criticize judicial method. Most highly praised is a little book by a distinguished American judge, later a member of the Supreme Court—Benjamin N. Cardozo, *The Nature of the Judicial Process* (New Haven: Yale University Press, 1921). Edward H. Levi, *An Introduction to Legal Reasoning* (Chicago: University of Chicago Press, 1949), is a pamphlet-sized volume frequently assigned to students. Other items of value, because informative and thoughtful, are Fred V. Cahill, *Judicial Legislation* (New York: Ronald Press, 1952); Jerome Frank, *Courts on Trial* (Princeton: Princeton University Press, 1949); James W. Hurst, *The Growth of American Law,* "The Law Makers" (Boston: Little, Brown & Co., 1950), Part 3; Claud Mullins, *In Quest of Justice* (London: V. Murray, 1931); and William Zelermyer, *Legal Reasoning* (Englewood Cliffs, N.J.: Prentice-Hall, 1960). Useful items are reprinted in several collections, including Carl A. Auerbach *et al., The Legal Process* (San Francisco: Chandler Publishing Co., 1961); Murphy and Pritchett, *Courts, Judges, and Politics* (cited in Note 7); and Robert Scigliano, *The Courts,* "A Reader in the Judicial Process" (Boston: Little, Brown & Co., 1962). A small book, available in paperback, is John R. Schmidhauser, *The Supreme Court,* "Its Politics, Personalities and Procedures" (New York: Holt, Rinehart & Winston, 1960).

Especially good on the concept of judicial self-restraint is George D. Braden, "The Search for Objectivity in Constitutional Law," *Yale Law Journal,* 57 (1948), 571. See also John P. Roche, "Judicial Self-Restraint," *American Political Science Review,* 49 (1955), 762.

My effort to explain the character of the two opinions in the Brown and Bolling cases and the failure of the Supreme Court to give opinions in later cases involving segregation will be disputed by many thoughtful students of constitutional law. Criticism of the Court's method is often veiled, accomplished more by a raising of eyebrows than by outspoken complaint; defense of the Court is usually stated in firm language. For raising of eyebrows, see Alexander M. Bickel, "Legislative Purpose and the Judicial Process: the Lincoln Mills Case," *Harvard Law Review,* 71 (1957), 1; Ray Forrester, "The Supreme Court and the Rule of Law," *South Texas Law Journal,* 4 (1959), 107; Herbert Wechsler, "Towards Neutral Principles of Constitutional Law," *Harvard Law Review,* 73 (1959), 1; and Paul G. Kauper, "The Supreme Court and the Rule of Law," *Michigan Law Review,* 59 (1961), 531. Wechsler's article is reprinted in his *Principles, Politics and Fundamental Law,* "Selected Essays" (Cambridge: Harvard University Press, 1961). The following articles defend the Court: Louis H. Pollak, "Racial Discrimination and Judicial Integrity: A Reply to Professor Wechsler," *University of Pennsylvania Law Review,* 108 (1959), 1; Addison Mueller and Murray L. Schwartz, "The Principle of Neutral Principles," *U.C.L.A. Law Review,* 7 (1960), 571; Arthur S. Miller and Ronald F. Howell, "The Myth of Neutrality in Constitutional Adjudication," *University of Chicago Law Review,* 27 (1960), 666.

When the Supreme Court judges put their heads together to agree on decisions and discuss the reasoning that should go into opinions, they do it in secret. Moreover, they think this a subject not to talk about on other occasions. Some reviewers of his book thought Alpheus T. Mason disclosed too much about relationships among judges in his biography, *Harlan Fiske Stone,* "Pillar of the Law"

(New York: Viking Press, 1956). Several other biographies of Supreme Court justices supply some knowledge of the judicial conference. See also these: Felix Frankfurter, *Of Law and Men,* ed. Philip Elman (New York: Harcourt, Brace, 1956); Charles E. Hughes, *The Supreme Court of the United States* (New York: Columbia University Press, 1928), Chap. 2; and John P. Frank, *Marble Palace,* "The Supreme Court in American Life" (New York: Knopf, 1958), Chaps. 2–6. Some information can also be found in speeches and other comments by men who have served on the Supreme Court in recent years, reprinted in Alan F. Westin, ed., *The Supreme Court,* "Views from the Inside" (New York: W.W. Norton, 1961).

18. POLITICIAL ROLE OF THE SUPREME COURT

All histories of the Supreme Court and all general treatises on American constitutional law attempt to show how the Supreme Court helped build our main political institutions and made an impress on major public policies. The same can be said of many of the biographies of individual Supreme Court judges. The beginner is likely to find the great work of Charles Warren (cited in Note 4) especially good. Crosskey's thesis (cited in Note 9) is that the Supreme Court was the main offender in a political revolution that abandoned the original Constitution and substituted a drastically different one.

The histories, treatises, and biographies do not bring together in one or two chapters a summary description and evaluation of the Court's contributions to broad issues of policy. Among the illuminating efforts to appraise the work of the Supreme Court in this respect are Alpheus T. Mason, *Security through Freedom* (Ithaca: Cornell University Press, 1955); C. Herman Pritchett, *Civil Liberties and the Vinson Court* (Chicago: University of Chicago Press, 1950), Chaps. 9–11; Earl Latham, "The Supreme Court as a Political Institution," *Minnesota Law Review,* 31 (1947), 205; a symposium on "Policy-Making in a Democracy; the Role of the United States Supreme Court," *Journal of Public Law,* 6 (1957), 275; and a symposium on "The Supreme Court in the American Constitutional System," *Notre Dame Lawyer,* 32 (1958), 521.

Differences in the way thoughful men interpret and evaluate the contributions of the Supreme Court come out in a report of a conference edited by Edmond Cahn and entitled *Supreme Court and Supreme Law* (Bloomington: Indiana University Press, 1954).

The school of thought that has been labeled "judicial activism" is perhaps sufficiently represented in items cited in Chapter XVII. One of the nation's truly great judges in some recent lectures took issue with the activists and stimulated some counterattack—Learned Hand, *The Bill of Rights* (Cambridge: Harvard University Press, 1958; also available in the Vintage paperback series).

19. RELATION OF JUDICIAL REVIEW TO POLITICS AND DEMOCRATIC GOVERNMENT

Books that describe the political process and praise or deplore particular political institutions and practices fill many shelves in any good college library. Perhaps the best way to introduce oneself to printed materials dealing with politics in this country is to examine one of a dozen textbooks for the introductory college course in American government and politics. Ask, in any good library, for one that supplies best references in footnotes or bibliographies.

The same method will turn up some of the literature that attempts to specify the character of democratic government and to differentiate government of democratic character from government that is not democratic. Statements of personal preference tend to subdue development of theory in most writing on this subject. Four recent additions seem to me to be among the best we have on the distinguishing characteristics of democratic government. They might be read in this order: Austin Ranney and Willmoore Kendall, *Democracy and the American Party System* (New York: Harcourt Brace, 1956), Chaps. 1–4; Henry B. Mayo, *An Introduction to Democratic Theory* (New York: Oxford University Press, 1960); Robert A. Dahl, *A Preface to Democratic Theory* (Chicago: University of Chicago Press, 1956); and Thomas L. Thorson, *The Logic of Democracy* (New York: Holt, Rinehart & Winston, 1962). A thing never to be forgotten is Alexis de Tocqueville, *Democracy in America;* a good paperback edition is in the Vintage series (2 vols.; New York: Knopf, 1956).

Writings that discuss the democratic character of judicial review are limited in number. Most attempt to convince the reader that the power which our courts have exercised is or is not compatible with the national ideal of democratic government. With one exception, they throw little light on the correspondence of the Supreme Court's decision in a given case and the public expectations and preferences that can be related to the issue before the court. The exception is an article by Prof. Robert Dahl in the symposium on "Policy-Making in a Democracy" cited in Note 18. An article by Eugene V. Rostow was cited in Chapter XX. Other items worth reading include Henry S. Commager, *Majority Rule and Minority Rights* (New York: Oxford University Press, 1944); Wallace Mendelson, *Justices Black and Frankfurter,* "Conflict in the Court" (Chicago: University of Chicago Press, 1961), Chap. 5; Chap. 13 of the book by Pritchett cited in Note 18; and an article by Eugene V. Rostow in the symposium in *Notre Dame Lawyer* cited in Note 18. On the relationship of levels of morality to election of congressmen and election of the president, see Willmoore Kendall, "The Two Majorities," *Midwest Journal of Politics,* 4 (1960), 317.

For Chief Justice Stone's views about a special obligation of the Supreme Court to police the democratic process, see Louis Lusky, "Minority Rights and Public Interest," *Yale Law Journal,* 52 (1942), 1, and Chap. 31 of Mason's biography of Stone cited in Note 17.

Writing about the relation of the judiciary to legislative apportioning is only now beginning to appear. Useful first items include Malcolm E. Jewell, ed., *The Politics of Reapportionment* (New York: Atherton Press, 1962); Robert G. Dixon, "Legislative Apportionment and the Federal Constitution," *Law and Contemporary Problems,* 27 (1962), 329; Gus Tyler, "Courts versus Legislature," *ibid.,* p. 390; and a symposium, "The Problems of Malapportionment," *Yale Law Journal,* 72 (1962), 7.

INDEX